ESSENTIALS
of Supply Chain Management

Third Edition

Essentials Series

The Essentials Series was created for busy business advisory and corporate professionals. The books in this series were designed so that these busy professionals can quickly acquire knowledge and skills in core business areas.

Each book provides need-to-have fundamentals for those professionals who must:

- Get up to speed quickly, because they have been promoted to a new position or have broadened their responsibility scope
- Manage a new functional area
- Brush up on new developments in their area of responsibility
- Add more value to their company or clients

Books in this series include:

For more information on any of the above titles, visit www.wiley.com.

ESSENTIALS
of Supply Chain Management
Third Edition

Michael Hugos

WILEY

John Wiley & Sons, Inc.

For general information on our other products and services or for technical support, please contact our Customer Care Department within the United States at (800) 762-2974, outside the United States at (317) 572-3993, or fax (317) 572-4002.

Wiley also publishes its books in a variety of electronic formats. Some content that appears in print may not be available in electronic books. For more information about Wiley products, visit our web site at www.wiley.com.

Library of Congress Cataloging-in-Publication Data:

Hugos, Michael H.
    Essentials of supply chain management / Michael Hugos. -- 3rd ed.
       p. cm. -- (Essentials series)
    Includes index.
     ISBN 978-0-470-94218-5 (paperback); ISBN 978-1-118-10060-8 (ebk);
     ISBN 978-1-118-10061-5 (ebk); ISBN 978-1-118-10062-2 (ebk)
  1. Business logistics. I. Title.
   HD38.5.H845 2011
   658.7--dc22

                             2011008883

10 9 8 7 6 5 4 3 2

To my wife,
Venetia

Contents

Book Manifesto

This book is dedicated to the idea that there is a set of highly effective concepts and practices that supply chain professionals can use to significantly increase the competitiveness and profitability of their companies. Even though supply chains and the technology they employ are changing rapidly, these concepts and practices remain highly relevant over time—they are the essentials of supply chain management.

From decades of personal experience in the field and from many conversations and reading the works of other supply chain professionals and researchers, I have distilled out these supply chain essentials. I know you are busy and your time is valuable so I make every attempt to get to the point quickly and explain things clearly and concisely. This book provides a framework to understand the structure and operation of any supply chain. It also provides guidance in how to make effective use of the flood of new supply chain technologies, and how to operate the constantly changing real-time supply chains that support our global economy.

Supply Chains as Massively Multi-Player Online Role Playing Games

One of the most promising new technologies for designing and coordinating the operation of supply chains comes from the world of online gaming. I'm referring to a type of game called a "massively multi-player online role playing game" (MMORPG). In these online games, players from all over the globe log into virtual worlds via the Internet; they learn different roles and skill sets, and come together in self-selecting teams to carry out missions in pursuit of common goals. Question: How is this any different than the challenges that await us in the global real-time economy we now inhabit?

If you're part of the generation just starting out in business, answers to this question probably seem pretty obvious. If you're part of a generation that's already been in business for a while, answers might not seem so obvious (at first). Unfortunately, the word "game" is associated with activities that seem frivolous or unimportant. That is not what I mean here; please hold your judgement while I explain. Popular MMORPGs such as EVE-Online and World of Warcraft bring together hundreds of thousands of simultaneous online players from countries around the globe to interact in complex, realistic three dimensional worlds. What if we did the same to design, monitor and operate the global supply chains that support our real-time economy?

As a companion to this book I have collaborated with a group of people to create a massively multi-player online role playing game to use for gaining a better understanding of the dynamics that underlie supply chains and their operations. This game allows people from all over the world to collaborate in the design and operation of supply chains. In effect, the game creates one big "sandbox" where people can experiment with the effects of different supply chain designs. It can be used to model real or imaginary supply chains and simulate their operations. It will show the performance characteristics and operating costs of these supply chains under different circumstances. The purpose of this game is to engage people in an interactive experience that accelerates their learning and increases their mastery of the skills involved in supply chain management.

The ideas behind this game and its operation are explored in more detail in Chapter 7—Supply Chain Innovation for the Real-Time Economy. The game is titled "SCM Globe" and it can be accessed through my web site at www.MichaelHugos.com.

A Real-Time Supply Chain Simulation System

SCM Globe is a simulation game that provides a map of the world and on that map, people working together in supply chains can draw in their factories, warehouses, retail stores, and the transportation routes such as roads, railways, and harbors that connect those locations. Then people can define the production volumes of the factories, storage capacity of the warehouses, and movement capacity of the different modes of transportation. And finally, they can associate operating costs with each facility and each mode of transportation.

This supply chain game has some pretty challenging dynamics. Players need to figure out how to deliver products where and when they are needed to meet demand while at the same time minimizing inventory levels and holding down transportation and manufacturing costs. If you succeed in keeping down inventory levels and costs but fail to meet product demand, you lose. And if you always deliver the products but fail to keep the other factors under control, then your costs get out of hand and you don't make any money.

If supply chain professionals and researchers can literally draw supply chain designs on an electronic map display and simulate the operations of those supply chains over some time period, they will quickly learn what designs produce the best results. And in the process, they will become immersed and involved in exploring supply chain dynamics. How long would it be before the people playing such a game developed high levels of skill in designing and operating high performance supply chains that responded effectively to changing market conditions? I invite you to try this game and see for yourself. This game is an evolving work in progress and I invite your feedback. Your feedback on what you like and what additional features you would like to see will guide the enhancement of this system.

To explore this real-time supply chain simulation system (or supply chain MMO depending on how you look at it) please visit my website, www.MichaelHugos.com, and click on the link to "SCM Global."

MICHAEL HUGOS
Chicago, IL USA
www.MichaelHugos.com
Email: mhugos@yahoo.com

Preface

In this book my intention is to provide a clear framework for understanding the essential concepts of supply chain management. Then build on that understanding and show how to develop and deploy supply chains to achieve success in the fast-paced, global economy we all live in. Chapters 1, 2, and 3 provide an introduction to the basic principles and business activities that drive supply chain operations. Chapters 4, 5, and 6 discuss techniques, technologies, and metrics for use in managing a company's internal supply chain operations and coordinating them with those of its supply chain partners.

Chapter 7 is an exploration of the ways that new technologies and new operating procedures can be used to significantly impact and improve the way supply chains are monitored and managed. Specific examples for this kind of innovation are provided.

Chapters 8 and 9 provide a pragmatic approach based on personal experience for defining supply chain opportunities and designing and building systems to effectively respond to those opportunities. I present two business case studies and show how a company in those situations could develop supply chain capabilities to best support its strategic goals. I am glad to answer your questions and discuss the merits of other ideas in addition to the ones I have presented. I can be contacted at my website, www.MichaelHugos.com.

The last chapter, Chapter 10, outlines the opportunities available to companies and alliances of companies that learn to work together to harness the power and potential of real-time supply chains. Real-time supply chains are the next step in the evolution of supply chains; they deliver a new level of operating efficiency and responsiveness to markets and customers. Real-time supply chains will support much of the world's economic activity in the years to come.

MICHAEL HUGOS
Center for Systems Innovation
Chicago, Illinois USA
June 2011

ESSENTIALS
of Supply Chain
Management

Third Edition

CHAPTER 1

Key Concepts of Supply Chain Management

After reading this chapter you will be able to

- Appreciate what a supply chain is and what it does
- Understand where your company fits in the supply chains it participates in and the role it plays in those supply chains
- Discuss ways to align your supply chain with your business strategy
- Start an intelligent conversation about the supply chain management issues in your company

This book is organized to give you a solid grounding in the "nuts and bolts" of supply chain management. The book explains the essential concepts and practices and then shows examples of how to put them to use. When you finish you will have a solid foundation in supply chain management to work from.

The first three chapters give you a working understanding of the key principles and business operations that drive any supply chain. The next four chapters present the techniques, technologies, and metrics to use to improve your internal operations and coordinate more effectively with your customers and suppliers in the supply chains your company is a part of. Chapter 7 presents specific ideas for using technologies such as social media and real-time simulation gaming to promote supply chain collaboration.

The last three chapters show you how to find supply chain opportunities and respond effectively to best capitalize on these opportunities. Case studies are used to illustrate supply chain challenges and to present solutions for those challenges. These case studies and their solutions bring together the material presented in the rest of the book and show how it applies to real-world business situations.

Supply chains encompass the companies and the business activities needed to design, make, deliver, and use a product or service. Businesses depend on their supply chains to provide them with what they need to survive and thrive. Every business fits into one or more supply chains and has a role to play in each of them.

The pace of change and the uncertainty about how markets will evolve has made it increasingly important for companies to be aware of the supply chains they participate in and to understand the roles that they play. Those companies that learn how to build and participate in strong supply chains will have a substantial competitive advantage in their markets.

Nothing Entirely New...Just a Significant Evolution

The practice of supply chain management is guided by some basic underlying concepts that have not changed much over the centuries. Several hundred years ago, Napoleon made the remark, "An army marches on its stomach." Napoleon was a master strategist and a skillful general and this remark shows that he clearly understood the importance of what we would now call an efficient supply chain. Unless the soldiers are fed, the army cannot move.

Along these same lines, there is another saying that goes, "Amateurs talk strategy and professionals talk logistics." People can discuss all sorts of grand strategies and dashing maneuvers but none of that will be possible without first figuring out how to meet the day-to-day demands of providing an army with fuel, spare parts, food, shelter, and ammunition.

It is the seemingly mundane activities of the quartermaster and the supply sergeants that often determine an army's success. This has many analogies in business.

The term "supply chain management" arose in the late 1980s and came into widespread use in the 1990s. Prior to that time, businesses used terms such as "logistics" and "operations management" instead. Here are some definitions of a supply chain:

- "A supply chain is the alignment of firms that bring products or services to market."—from Lambert, Stock, and Ellram. (Lambert, Douglas M., James R. Stock, and Lisa M. Ellram, 1998, *Fundamentals of Logistics Management,* Boston, MA: Irwin/ McGraw-Hill, Chapter 14).

- "A supply chain consists of all stages involved, directly or indirectly, in fulfilling a customer request. The supply chain not only includes the manufacturer and suppliers, but also transporters, warehouses, retailers, and customers themselves."—from Chopra and Meindl (Chopra, Sunil, and Peter Meindl, 2003, *Supply Chain, Second Edition,* Upper Saddle River, NJ: Prentice-Hall, Inc., Chapter 1).

- "A supply chain is a network of facilities and distribution options that performs the functions of procurement of materials, transformation of these materials into intermediate and finished products, and the distribution of these finished products to customers."—from Ganeshan and Harrison (Ganeshan, Ram, and Terry P. Harrison, 1995, "An Introduction to Supply Chain Management," Department of Management Sciences and Information Systems, 303 Beam Business Building, Penn State University, University Park, Pennsylvania).

If this is what a supply chain is then we can define supply chain management as the things we do to influence the behavior of the supply chain and get the results we want. Some definitions of supply chain management are:

- "The systemic, strategic coordination of the traditional business functions and the tactics across these business functions within a particular company and across businesses within the supply chain, for the purposes of improving the long-term performance of the individual companies and the supply chain as a whole."—from Mentzer, DeWitt, Keebler, Min, Nix, Smith, and Zacharia (Mentzer, John T., William DeWitt, James S. Keebler, Soonhong Min, Nancy W. Nix, Carlo D. Smith, and Zach G. Zacharia, 2001, "Defining Supply Chain Management," *Journal of Business Logistics*, Vol. 22, No. 2, p. 18).
- "Supply chain management is the coordination of production, inventory, location, and transportation among the participants in a supply chain to achieve the best mix of responsiveness and efficiency for the market being served."—my own words.

There is a difference between the concept of supply chain management and the traditional concept of logistics. Logistics typically refers to activities that occur within the boundaries of a single organization and supply chains refer to networks of companies that work together and coordinate their actions to deliver a product to market. Also, traditional logistics focuses its attention on activities such as procurement, distribution, maintenance, and inventory management. Supply chain management acknowledges all of traditional logistics and also includes activities such as marketing, new product development, finance, and customer service.

In the wider view of supply chain thinking, these additional activities are now seen as part of the work needed to fulfill customer requests. Supply chain management views the supply chain and the organizations in it as a single entity. It brings a systems approach to understanding and managing the different activities needed to coordinate the flow of products and services to best serve the ultimate customer. This systems approach provides the framework in which to best respond to business requirements that otherwise would seem to be in conflict with each other.

Taken individually, different supply chain requirements often have conflicting needs. For instance, the requirement of maintaining high levels of customer service calls for maintaining high levels of inventory, but then the requirement to operate efficiently calls for reducing inventory levels. It is only when these requirements are seen together as parts of a larger picture that ways can be found to effectively balance their different demands.

Effective supply chain management requires simultaneous improvements in both customer service levels and the internal operating efficiencies of the companies in the supply chain. Customer service at its most basic level means consistently high order-fill rates, high on-time delivery rates, and a very low rate of products returned by customers for whatever reason. Internal efficiency for organizations in a supply chain means that these organizations get an attractive rate of return on their investments in inventory and other assets and that they find ways to lower their operating and sales expenses.

There is a basic pattern to the practice of supply chain management. Each supply chain has its own unique set of market demands and operating challenges and yet the issues remain essentially the same in every case. Companies in any supply chain must make decisions individually and collectively regarding their actions in five areas:

1. *Production*—What products does the market want? How much of which products should be produced and by when? This activity includes the creation of master production schedules that take into account plant capacities, workload balancing, quality control, and equipment maintenance.

2. *Inventory*—What inventory should be stocked at each stage in a supply chain? How much inventory should be held as raw materials, semifinished, or finished goods? The primary purpose of inventory is to act as a buffer against uncertainty in the supply chain. However, holding inventory can be expensive, so what are the optimal inventory levels and reorder points?

3. *Location*—Where should facilities for production and inventory storage be located? Where are the most cost efficient locations for production and for storage of inventory? Should existing facilities be used or new ones built? Once these decisions are made they determine the possible paths available for product to flow through for delivery to the final consumer.

4. *Transportation*—How should inventory be moved from one supply chain location to another? Air-freight and truck delivery are generally fast and reliable but they are expensive. Shipping by sea or rail is much less expensive but usually involves longer transit times and more uncertainty. This uncertainty must be compensated for by stocking higher levels of inventory. When is it better to use which mode of transportation?

5. *Information*—How much data should be collected and how much information should be shared? Timely and accurate information holds the promise of better coordination and better decision making. With good information, people can make effective decisions about what to produce and how much, about where to locate inventory, and how best to transport it.

The sum of these decisions will define the capabilities and effectiveness of a company's supply chain. The things a company can do and the ways that it can compete in its markets are all very much dependent on the effectiveness of its supply chain. If a company's strategy is to serve a mass market and compete on the basis of price, it had better have a supply chain that is optimized for low cost. If a company's strategy is to serve a market segment and compete on the basis of customer service and convenience, it had better have a supply chain optimized for responsiveness. Who a company is and what it can do is shaped by its supply chain and by the markets it serves.

How the Supply Chain Works

Two influential source books that define principles and practices of supply chain management are *The Goal* (Goldratt, Eliyahu M., 1984, *The Goal*, Great Barrington, MA: The North River Press Publishing Corporation); and *Supply Chain Management, Fourth Edition* by Sunil Chopra and Peter Meindl. *The Goal* explores the issues and provides answers to the problem of optimizing operations in any business system, whether it be manufacturing, mortgage loan processing, or supply chain management. *Supply Chain Management, Fourth Edition* is an in-depth presentation of the concepts and techniques of the profession. Much of the material presented in this chapter and in the next two chapters can be found in greater detail in these two books.

IN THE REAL WORLD

Alexander the Great based his strategies and campaigns on his army's unique capabilities and these were made possible by effective supply chain management.

In the spirit of the saying, "Amateurs talk strategy and professionals talk logistics," let's look at the campaigns of Alexander the Great. For those who think that his greatness was only due to his ability to dream up bold moves and cut a dashing figure in the saddle, think again. Alexander was a master of supply chain management and he could not have succeeded otherwise. The authors from Greek and Roman times who recorded his deeds had little to say about something so apparently unglamorous as how he secured supplies

(Continued)

for his army. Yet, from these same sources, many small details can be pieced together to show the overall supply chain picture and how Alexander managed it. A modern historian, Donald Engels, has investigated this topic in his book *Alexander the Great and the Logistics of the Macedonian Army* (Engles, Donald W., 1978, *Alexander the Great and the Logistics of the Macedonian Army*, Los Angeles, CA: University of California Press).

He begins by pointing out that given the conditions and the technology that existed in Alexander's time, his strategy and tactics had to be very closely tied to his ability to get supplies and to run a lean, efficient organization. The only way to transport large amounts of material over long distances was by oceangoing ships or by barges on rivers and canals. Once away from rivers and seacoasts, an army had to be able to live off the land over which it traveled. Diminishing returns set in quickly when using pack animals and carts to haul supplies, because the animals themselves had to eat and would soon consume all the food and water they were hauling unless they could graze along the way.

Alexander's army was able to achieve its brilliant successes because it managed its supply chain so well. The army had a logistics structure that was fundamentally different from other armies of the time. In other armies the number of support people and camp followers was often as large as the number of actual fighting soldiers, because armies traveled with huge numbers of carts and pack animals to carry their equipment and provisions, as well as the people needed to tend them. In the Macedonian army the use of carts was severely restricted. Soldiers were trained to carry their own equipment and provisions. Other contemporary armies did not require their soldiers to carry such heavy burdens but they paid for this because the resulting baggage trains reduced their speed and mobility. The result of the Macedonian army's logistics structure was that it became the fastest, lightest, and most mobile army of its time. It was capable of making lightning strikes against an opponent, often before they were even aware of what was happening. Because the army was able to move quickly and suddenly, Alexander could use this capability to devise strategies and employ tactics that allowed him to surprise and overwhelm enemies that were numerically much larger.

The picture that emerges of how Alexander managed his supply chain is an interesting one. For instance, time and again the historical sources mention that before he entered a new territory, he would receive the surrender of its ruler and arrange in advance with local officials for the supplies his army would need. If a region did not surrender to him in advance, Alexander would not commit his entire army to a campaign in that land. He would not risk putting his army in a situation where it could be crippled or destroyed by a lack of provisions. Instead, he would gather intelligence about the routes, the resources, and the climate of the region and then set off with a small, light force to surprise his opponent. The main army would remain behind at a well-stocked base until Alexander secured adequate supplies for it to follow.

Whenever the army set up a new base it looked for an area that provided easy access to a navigable river or a seaport. Then ships would arrive from other parts of Alexander's empire, bringing in large amounts of supplies. The army always stayed in its winter camp until the first spring harvest of the new year so that food supplies would be available. When it marched, it avoided dry or uninhabited areas and moved through river valleys and populated regions whenever possible so the horses could graze and the army could requisition supplies along the route.

Alexander had a deep understanding of the capabilities and limitations of his supply chain. He learned well how to formulate strategies and use tactics that built upon the unique strengths that his logistics and supply chain capabilities gave him, and he wisely took measures to compensate for the limitations of his supply chain. His opponents often outnumbered him and were usually fighting on their own home territory. Yet their advantages were undermined by clumsy and inefficient supply chains that restricted their ability to act and limited their options for opposing Alexander's moves.

The goal or mission of supply chain management can be defined using Eli Goldratt's words as "Increase throughput while simultaneously reducing both inventory and operating expense." In this definition, throughput refers to the rate at which sales to the end customer occur. Depending on the market being served, sales or throughput occur for different reasons. In some markets, customers value and will pay for high levels of service. In other markets customers seek simply the lowest price for an item.

As we saw in the previous section, there are five areas where companies can make decisions that will define their supply chain capabilities: production; inventory; location; transportation; and information. Chopra and Meindl define the first four and I add the fifth as performance drivers that can be managed to produce the capabilities needed for a given supply chain.

Effective supply chain management calls first for an understanding of each driver and how it operates. Each driver has the ability to directly affect the supply chain and enable certain capabilities. The next step is to develop an appreciation for the results that can be obtained by mixing different combinations of these drivers. Let's start by looking at the drivers individually.

Production

Production refers to the capacity of a supply chain to make and store products. The facilities of production are factories and warehouses. The fundamental decision that managers face when making production decisions is how to resolve the trade-off between responsiveness and efficiency. If factories and warehouses are built with a lot of excess capacity, they can be very flexible and respond quickly to wide swings in product demand. Facilities where all or almost all capacity is being used are not capable of responding easily to fluctuations in demand. On the other hand, capacity costs money and excess capacity is idle capacity not in use and not generating revenue. So the more excess capacity that exists, the less efficient the operation becomes.

Factories can be built to accommodate one of two approaches to manufacturing:

1. *Product Focus*—A factory that takes a product focus performs the range of different operations required to make a given product line from fabrication of different product parts to assembly of these parts.

2. *Functional Focus*—A functional approach concentrates on performing just a few operations such as only making a select group of parts or only doing assembly. These functions can be applied to making many different kinds of products.

A product approach tends to result in developing expertise about a given set of products at the expense of expertise about any particular function. A functional approach results in expertise about particular functions instead of expertise in a given product. Companies need to decide which approach or what mix of these two approaches will give them the capability and expertise they need to best respond to customer demands.

As with factories, warehouses too can be built to accommodate different approaches. There are three main approaches to use in warehousing:

1. *Stock Keeping Unit (SKU) Storage*—In this traditional approach, all of a given type of product is stored together. This is an efficient and easy to understand way to store products.

2. *Job Lot Storage*—In this approach, all the different products related to the needs of a certain type of customer or related to the needs of a particular job are stored together. This allows for

an efficient picking and packing operation but usually requires more storage space than the traditional SKU storage approach.

3. *Crossdocking*—An approach that was pioneered by Wal-Mart in its drive to increase efficiencies in its supply chain. In this approach, product is not actually warehoused in the facility. Instead the facility is used to house a process where trucks from suppliers arrive and unload large quantities of different products. These large lots are then broken down into smaller lots. Smaller lots of different products are recombined according to the needs of the day and quickly loaded onto outbound trucks that deliver the products to their final destinations.

Inventory

Inventory is spread throughout the supply chain and includes everything from raw material to work in process to finished goods that are held by the manufacturers, distributors, and retailers in a supply chain. Again, managers must decide where they want to position themselves in the trade-off between responsiveness and efficiency. Holding large amounts of inventory allows a company or an entire supply chain to be very responsive to fluctuations in customer demand. However, the creation and storage of inventory is a cost and to achieve high levels of efficiency, the cost of inventory should be kept as low as possible.

There are three basic decisions to make regarding the creation and holding of inventory:

1. *Cycle Inventory*—This is the amount of inventory needed to satisfy demand for the product in the period between purchases of the product. Companies tend to produce and to purchase in large lots in order to gain the advantages that economies of

scale can bring. However, with large lots also come increased carrying costs. Carrying costs come from the cost to store, handle, and insure the inventory. Managers face the tradeoff between the reduced cost of ordering and better prices offered by purchasing product in large lots and the increased carrying cost of the cycle inventory that comes with purchasing in large lots.

2. *Safety Inventory*—Inventory that is held as a buffer against uncertainty. If demand forecasting could be done with perfect accuracy, then the only inventory that would be needed would be cycle inventory. But since every forecast has some degree of uncertainty in it, we cover that uncertainty to a greater or lesser degree by holding additional inventory in case demand is suddenly greater than anticipated. The tradeoff here is to weigh the costs of carrying extra inventory against the costs of losing sales due to insufficient inventory.

3. *Seasonal Inventory*—This is inventory that is built up in anticipation of predictable increases in demand that occur at certain times of the year. For example, it is predictable that demand for antifreeze will increase in the winter. If a company that makes antifreeze has a fixed production rate that is expensive to change, then it will try to manufacture product at a steady rate all year long and build up inventory during periods of low demand to cover for periods of high demand that will exceed its production rate. The alternative to building up seasonal inventory is to invest in flexible manufacturing facilities that can quickly change their rates of production of different products to respond to increases in demand. In this case, the tradeoff is between the cost of carrying seasonal inventory and the cost of having more flexible production capabilities.

Location

Location refers to the geographical site of supply chain facilities. It also includes the decisions related to which activities should be performed in each facility. The responsiveness versus efficiency tradeoff here is the decision whether to centralize activities in fewer locations to gain economies of scale and efficiency, or to decentralize activities in many locations close to customers and suppliers in order for operations to be more responsive.

When making location decisions, managers need to consider a range of factors that relate to a given location including the cost of facilities, the cost of labor, skills available in the workforce, infrastructure conditions, taxes and tariffs, and proximity to suppliers and customers. Location decisions tend to be very strategic decisions because they commit large amounts of money to long-term plans.

Location decisions have strong impacts on the cost and performance characteristics of a supply chain. Once the size, number, and location of facilities are determined, that also defines the number of possible paths through which products can flow on the way to the final customer. Location decisions reflect a company's basic strategy for building and delivering its products to market.

Transportation

This refers to the movement of everything from raw material to finished goods between different facilities in a supply chain. In transportation the tradeoff between responsiveness and efficiency is manifested in the choice of transport mode. Fast modes of transport such as airplanes are very responsive but also more costly. Slower modes such as ship and rail are very cost efficient but not as responsive. Since transportation costs can be as much as a third of the operating cost of a supply chain, decisions made here are very important.

There are six basic modes of transport that a company can choose from:

1. *Ship*—which is very cost efficient but also the slowest mode of transport. It is limited to use between locations that are situated next to navigable waterways and facilities such as harbors and canals.

2. *Rail*—which is also very cost efficient but can be slow. This mode is also restricted to use between locations that are served by rail lines.

3. *Pipelines*—which can be very efficient but are restricted to commodities that are liquids or gases such as water, oil, and natural gas.

4. *Trucks*—which are a relatively quick and very flexible mode of transport. Trucks can go almost anywhere. The cost of this mode is prone to fluctuations though, as the cost of fuel fluctuates and the condition of roads varies.

5. *Airplanes*—which are a very fast mode of transport and are very responsive. This is also the most expensive mode, and it is somewhat limited by the availability of appropriate airport facilities.

6. *Electronic Transport*—which is the fastest mode of transport and is very flexible and cost efficient. However, it can only be used for movement of certain types of products such as electric energy, data, and products composed of data such as music, pictures, and text. Someday technology that allows us to convert matter to energy and back to matter again may completely rewrite the theory and practice of supply chain management ("beam me up, Scotty...").

Given these different modes of transportation and the location of the facilities in a supply chain, managers need to design routes and networks for moving products. A route is the path through which products move, and networks are composed of the collection of the paths and facilities connected by those paths. As a general rule, the higher the value of a product (such as electronic components or pharmaceuticals), the more its transport network should emphasize responsiveness, and the lower the value of a product (such as bulk commodities like grain or lumber), the more its network should emphasize efficiency.

Information

Information is the basis upon which to make decisions regarding the other four supply chain drivers. It is the connection between all of the activities and operations in a supply chain. To the extent that this connection is a strong one (i.e., the data is accurate, timely, and complete), the companies in a supply chain will each be able to make good decisions for their own operations. This will also tend to maximize the profitability of the supply chain as a whole. That is the way that stock markets or other free markets work and supply chains have many of the same dynamics as markets.

Information is used for two purposes in any supply chain:

1. *Coordinating daily activities* related to the functioning of the other four supply chain drivers: production; inventory; location; and transportation. The companies in a supply chain use available data on product supply and demand to decide on weekly production schedules, inventory levels, transportation routes, and stocking locations.

2. *Forecasting and planning* to anticipate and meet future demands. Available information is used to make tactical forecasts to guide the setting of monthly and quarterly production schedules and timetables. Information is also used

for strategic forecasts to guide decisions about whether to build new facilities, enter a new market, or exit an existing market.

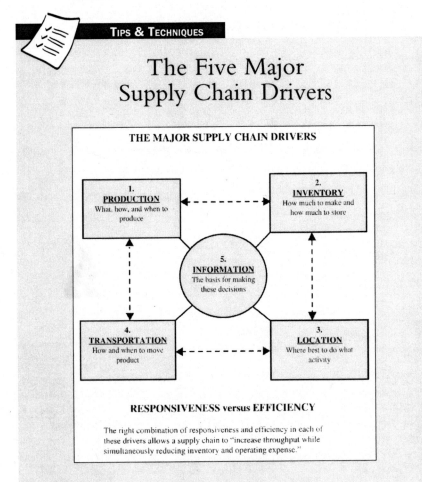

TIPS & TECHNIQUES

The Five Major Supply Chain Drivers

THE MAJOR SUPPLY CHAIN DRIVERS

1. PRODUCTION
What, how, and when to produce

2. INVENTORY
How much to make and how much to store

5. INFORMATION
The basis for making these decisions

4. TRANSPORTATION
How and when to move product

3. LOCATION
Where best to do what activity

RESPONSIVENESS versus EFFICIENCY

The right combination of responsiveness and efficiency in each of these drivers allows a supply chain to "increase throughput while simultaneously reducing inventory and operating expense."

Each market or group of customers has a specific set of needs. The supply chains that serve different markets need to respond effectively to these needs. Some markets demand and will pay for high levels of responsiveness. Other markets require their supply chains to focus more on efficiency. The overall effect of the decisions made concerning each driver will determine how well the supply chain serves its market and how profitable it is for the participants in that supply chain.

Within an individual company the tradeoff between responsiveness and efficiency involves weighing the benefits that good information can provide against the cost of acquiring that information. Abundant, accurate information can enable very efficient operating decisions and better forecasts but the cost of building and installing systems to deliver this information can be very high.

Within the supply chain as a whole, the responsiveness versus efficiency tradeoff that companies make is one of deciding how much information to share with the other companies and how much information to keep private. The more information about product supply, customer demand, market forecasts, and production schedules that companies share with each other, the more responsive everyone can be. Balancing this openness however, are the concerns that each company has about revealing information that could be used against it by a competitor. The potential costs associated with increased competition can hurt the profitability of a company.

EXECUTIVE INSIGHT

Wal-Mart is a company shaped by its supply chain and the efficiency of its supply chain has made it a leader in the markets it serves.

Sam Walton decided to build a company that would serve a mass market and compete on the basis of price. He did this by creating one of the world's most efficient supply chains. The structure and operations of this company have been defined by the need to lower its costs and increase its productivity so that it could pass these savings on to its customers in the form of lower prices. The techniques that Wal-Mart pioneered are now being widely adopted by its competitors and by other companies serving entirely different markets.

Wal-Mart introduced concepts that are now industry standards. Many of these concepts come directly from the way the company builds and operates its supply chain. Let's look at four such concepts:

1. The strategy of expanding around distribution centers (DCs)

2. Using electronic data interchange (EDI) with suppliers

3. The "big box" store format

4. "Everyday low prices"

The strategy of expanding around DCs is central to the way Wal-Mart enters a new geographical market. The company looks for areas that can support a group of new stores, not just a single new store. It then builds a new DC at a central location in the area and opens its first store at the same time. The DC is the supply chain bridgehead into the new territory. It supports the opening of more new stores in the area at a very low additional cost. Those savings are passed along to the customers.

The use of EDI with suppliers provides the company two substantial benefits. First of all this cuts the transaction costs associated with the ordering of products and the paying of invoices. Ordering products and paying invoices are, for the most part, well-defined and routine processes that can be made very productive and efficient through EDI. The second benefit is that these electronic links with suppliers allow Wal-Mart a high degree of control and coordination in the scheduling and receiving of product deliveries. This helps to ensure a steady flow of the right products at the right time, delivered to the right DCs, by all Wal-Mart suppliers.

EDI

The "big box" store format allows Wal-Mart to, in effect, combine a store and a warehouse in a single facility and get great operating efficiencies from doing so. The big box is big enough to hold large amounts of inventory like a warehouse. And since this inventory is being held at the same location where the customer buys it, there is no delay or cost that would otherwise be associated with moving products from warehouse to store. Again, these savings are passed along to the customer.

(Continued)

"Everyday low prices" are a way of doing two things. The first thing is to tell its price-conscious customers that they will always get the best price. They need not look elsewhere or wait for special sales. The effect of this message to customers helps Wal-Mart do the second thing, which is to accurately forecast product sales. By eliminating special sales and assuring customers of low prices, it smoothes out demand swings, making demand more steady and predictable. This way stores are more likely to have what customers want when they want it.

Taken individually, these four concepts are each useful but their real power comes from being used in connection with each other. They combine to form a supply chain that drives a self-reinforcing business process. Each concept builds on the strengths of the others to create a powerful business model for a company that has grown to become a dominant player in its markets.

There seem to be some similarities between Wal-Mart and Alexander the Great. Both developed very effective supply chains that were central to their success.

The Evolving Structure of Supply Chains

The participants in a supply chain are continuously making decisions that affect how they manage the five supply chain drivers. Each organization tries to maximize its performance in dealing with these drivers through a combination of outsourcing, partnering, and in-house expertise. In the fast-moving markets of our present economy, a company usually will focus on what it considers to be its core competencies in supply chain management and outsource the rest.

This was not always the case though. In the slower-moving mass markets of the industrial age it was common for successful companies to attempt to own much of their supply chain. That was known as vertical integration. The aim of vertical integration was to gain maximum efficiency through economies of scale (see Exhibit 1.1).

EXHIBIT 1.1

Old Supply Chains Versus New

Vertically integrated companies serving slow-moving mass markets once attempted to own much of their supply chains. Today's fast-moving markets require more flexible and responsive supply chains.

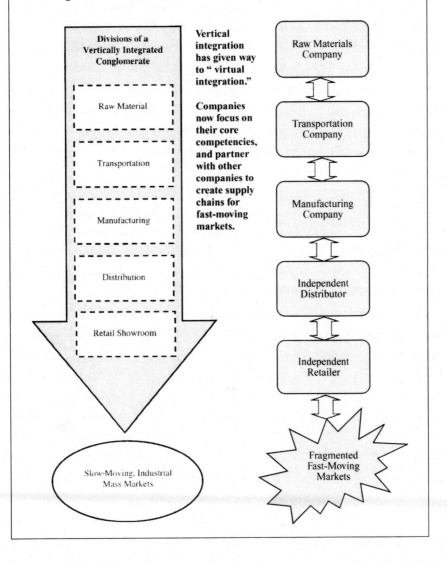

In the first half of the 1900s, Ford Motor Company owned much of what it needed to feed its car factories. It owned and operated iron mines that extracted iron ore, steel mills that turned the ore into steel products, plants that made component car parts, and assembly plants that turned out finished cars. In addition, they owned farms where they grew flax to make into linen car tops and forests that they logged and sawmills where they cut the timber into lumber for making wooden car parts. Ford's famous River Rouge Plant was a monument to vertical integration—iron ore went in at one end and cars came out at the other end. Henry Ford in his 1926 autobiography, *Today and Tomorrow*, boasted that his company could take in iron ore from the mine and put out a car 81 hours later (Ford, Henry, 1926, *Today and Tomorrow*, Portland, Oregon: Productivity Press, Inc.).

This was a profitable way of doing business in the more predictable, one-size-fits-all industrial economy that existed in the early 1900s. Ford and other businesses churned out mass amounts of basic products. But as the markets grew and customers became more particular about the kind of products they wanted, this model began to break down. It could not be responsive enough or produce the variety of products that were being demanded. For instance, when Henry Ford was asked about the number of different colors a customer could request, he said, "They can have any color they want as long as it's black." In the 1920s Ford's market share was more than 50 percent, but by the 1940s it had fallen to below 20 percent. Focusing on efficiency at the expense of being responsive to customer desires was no longer a successful business model.

Globalization, highly competitive markets, and the rapid pace of technological change are now driving the development of supply chains where multiple companies work together, each company focusing on the activities that it does best. Mining companies focus on mining, timber companies focus on logging and making lumber, and manufacturing companies focus on different types of manufacturing from making component parts to doing final assembly. This way people in each company can keep up with rapid rates of change and keep learning the new skills needed to compete in their particular businesses.

Where companies once routinely ran their own warehouses or operated their own fleets of trucks, they now have to consider whether those operations are really a core competency or whether it is more cost effective to outsource those operations to other companies that make logistics the center of their business. To achieve high levels of operating efficiency and to keep up with continuing changes in technology, companies need to focus on their core competencies. It requires this kind of focus to stay competitive.

Instead of vertical integration, companies now practice "virtual integration." Companies find other companies whom they can work with to perform the activities called for in their supply chains. How a company defines its core competencies and how it positions itself in the supply chains it serves is one of the most important decisions it can make.

Participants in the Supply Chain

In its simplest form, a supply chain is composed of a company and the suppliers and customers of that company. This is the basic group of participants who create a simple supply chain. Extended supply chains contain three additional types of participants. First there is the supplier's supplier or the ultimate supplier at the beginning of an extended supply chain. Then there is the customer's customer or ultimate customer at the end of an extended supply chain. Finally there is a whole category of companies who are service providers to other companies in the supply chain. These are companies who supply services in logistics, finance, marketing, and information technology.

In any given supply chain there is some combination of companies who perform different functions. There are companies who are producers, distributors or wholesalers, retailers, and companies or individuals who are the customers, the final consumers of a product. Supporting these companies there will be other companies that are service providers that provide a range of needed services.

Producers

Producers or manufacturers are organizations that make a product. This includes companies that are producers of raw materials and companies that are producers of finished goods. Producers of raw materials are organizations that mine for minerals, drill for oil and gas, and cut timber. It also includes organizations that farm the land, raise animals, or catch seafood. Producers of finished goods use the raw materials and sub-assemblies made by other producers to create their products.

Producers can create products that are intangible items such as music, entertainment, software, or designs. A product can also be a service such as mowing a lawn, cleaning an office, performing surgery, or teaching a skill. In many instances the producers of tangible, industrial products are moving to areas of the world where labor is less costly. Producers in the developed world of North America, Europe, and parts of Asia are increasingly producers of intangible items and services.

Distributors

Distributors are companies that take inventory in bulk from producers and deliver a bundle of related product lines to customers. Distributors are also known as wholesalers. They typically sell to other businesses and they sell products in larger quantities than an individual consumer would usually buy. Distributors buffer the producers from fluctuations in product demand by stocking inventory and doing much of the sales work to find and service customers. For the customer, distributors fulfill the "Time and Place" function—they deliver products when and where the customer wants them.

A distributor is typically an organization that takes ownership of significant inventories of products that they buy from producers and sell to consumers. In addition to product promotion and sales, other functions the distributor performs are inventory management, warehouse operations, and product transportation, as well as customer support and post-sales service. A distributor can also be an organization that only brokers a product between the producer and the customer, and never takes ownership of that product. This kind of distributor performs mainly the functions of product promotion and sales. In both of these cases, as the needs of customers evolve and the range of available products changes, the distributor is the agent that continually tracks customer needs and matches them with products available.

Retailers

Retailers stock inventory and sell in smaller quantities to the general public. This organization also closely tracks the preferences and demands of the customers that it sells to. It advertises to its customers and often uses some combination of price, product selection, service, and convenience as the primary draw to attract customers for the products it sells. Discount department stores attract customers using price and wide product selection. Upscale specialty stores offer a unique line of products and high levels of service. Fast food restaurants use convenience and low prices as their draw.

Customers

Customers or consumers are any organization that purchases and uses a product. A customer organization may purchase a product in order to incorporate it into another product that they in turn sell to other customers. Or a customer may be the final end user of a product who buys the product in order to consume it.

Service Providers

These are organizations that provide services to producers, distributors, retailers, and customers. Service providers have developed special expertise and skills that focus on a particular activity needed by a supply chain. Because of this, they are able to perform these services more effectively and at a better price than producers, distributors, retailers, or consumers could do on their own.

Some common service providers in any supply chain are providers of transportation services and warehousing services. These are trucking companies and public warehouse companies and they are known as logistics providers. Financial service providers deliver services such as making loans, doing credit analysis, and collecting on past due invoices. These are banks, credit rating companies, and collection agencies. Some service providers deliver market research and advertising, while others provide product design, engineering services, legal services, and management advice. Still other service providers offer information technology and data collection services. All of these service providers are integrated to a greater or lesser degree into the ongoing operations of the producers, distributors, retailers, and consumers in the supply chain.

Supply chains are composed of repeating sets of participants that fall into one or more of these categories. Over time the needs of the supply chain as a whole remain fairly stable. What changes is the mix of participants in the supply chain and the roles that each participant plays. In some supply chains, there are few service providers because the other participants perform these services on their own. In other supply chains very efficient providers of specialized services have evolved and the other participants outsource work to these service providers instead of doing it themselves. Examples of supply chain structure are shown in Exhibit 1.2.

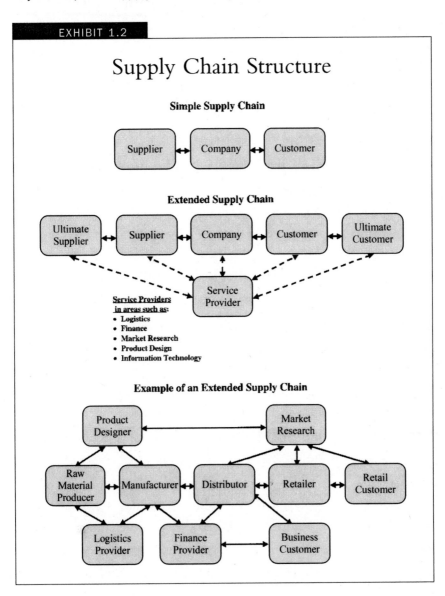

EXHIBIT 1.2

Supply Chain Structure

Simple Supply Chain

Supplier ↔ Company ↔ Customer

Extended Supply Chain

Ultimate Supplier ↔ Supplier ↔ Company ↔ Customer ↔ Ultimate Customer

Service Provider

Service Providers in areas such as:
- Logistics
- Finance
- Market Research
- Product Design
- Information Technology

Example of an Extended Supply Chain

Product Designer ↔ Market Research

Raw Material Producer ↔ Manufacturer ↔ Distributor ↔ Retailer ↔ Retail Customer

Logistics Provider   Finance Provider   Business Customer

Aligning the Supply Chain with Business Strategy

A company's supply chain is an integral part of its approach to the markets it serves. The supply chain needs to respond to market requirements and do so in a way that supports the company's business strategy. The business strategy a company employs starts with the needs of the customers that the company serves or will serve. Depending on the needs of its customers, a company's supply chain must deliver the appropriate mix of responsiveness and efficiency. A company whose supply chain allows it to more efficiently meet the needs of its customers will gain market share at the expense of other companies in that market and also will be more profitable.

For example, let's consider two companies and the needs that their supply chains must respond to. The two companies are 7-Eleven and Sam's Club, which is a part of Wal-Mart. The customers who shop at convenience stores like 7-Eleven have a different set of needs and preferences from those who shop at a discount warehouse like Sam's Club. The 7-Eleven customer is looking for convenience and not the lowest price. That customer is often in a hurry, and prefers that the store be nearby and have enough variety of products so that they can pick up small amounts of common household or food items that they need immediately. Sam's Club customers are looking for the lowest price. They are not in a hurry and are willing to drive some distance and buy large quantities of limited numbers of items in order to get the lowest price possible.

Clearly the supply chain for 7-Eleven needs to emphasize responsiveness. That group of customers expects convenience and will pay for it. On the other hand, the Sam's Club supply chain needs to focus tightly on efficiency. The Sam's Club customer is very price conscious and the supply chain needs to find every opportunity to reduce costs so that these savings can be passed on to the customers. Both of these companies' supply chains are well aligned with their business strategies and because of this they are each successful in their markets.

There are three steps to use in aligning your supply chain with your business strategy. The first step is to understand the markets that your company serves. The second step is to define the strengths or core competencies of your company and the role the company can or could play in serving its markets. The last step is to develop the needed supply chain capabilities to support the roles your company has chosen.

Understand the Markets Your Company Serves

Begin by asking questions about your customers. What kind of customer does your company serve? What kind of customer does your customer sell to? What kind of supply chain is your company a part of? The answers to these questions will tell you what supply chains your company serves and whether your supply chain needs to emphasize responsiveness or efficiency. Chopra and Meindl have defined the following attributes that help to clarify requirements for the customers you serve. These attributes are:

- *The quantity of the product needed in each lot*—Do your customers want small amounts of products or will they buy large quantities? A customer at a convenience store or a drug store buys in small quantities. A customer of a discount warehouse club, such as Sam's Club, buys in large quantities.

- *The response time that customers are willing to tolerate*—Do your customers buy on short notice and expect quick service or is a longer lead time acceptable? Customers of a fast food restaurant certainly buy on short notice and expect quick service. Customers buying custom machinery would plan the purchase in advance and expect some lead time before the product could be delivered.

- *The variety of products needed*—Are customers looking for a narrow and well-defined bundle of products or are they looking for a wide selection of different kinds of products? Customers of a fashion boutique expect a narrowly defined group of products. Customers of a "big box" discount store like Wal-Mart expect a wide variety of products to be available.

- *The service level required*—Do customers expect all products to be available for immediate delivery or will they accept partial deliveries of products and longer lead times? Customers of a music store expect to get the CD they are looking for immediately or they will go elsewhere. Customers who order a custom-built new machine tool expect to wait a while before delivery.

- *The price of the product*—How much are customers willing to pay? Some customers will pay more for convenience or high levels of service and other customers look to buy based on the lowest price they can get.

- *The desired rate of innovation in the product*—How fast are new products introduced and how long before existing products become obsolete? In products such as electronics and computers, customers expect a high rate of innovation. In other products, such as house paint, customers do not desire such a high rate of innovation.

Define Core Competencies of Your Company

The next step is to define the role that your company plays or wants to play in these supply chains. What kind of supply chain participant is your company? Is your company a producer, a distributor, a retailer, or a service provider? What does your company do to enable the supply chains that it is part of? What are the core competencies of your company? How does your company make money? The answers to these questions tell you what roles in a supply chain will be the best fit for your company.

Be aware that your company can serve multiple markets and participate in multiple supply chains. A company like W. W. Grainger serves several different markets. It sells maintenance, repair, and operating (MRO)
supplies to large national account customers such as Ford and Boeing
and it also sells these supplies to small businesses and building contractors. These two different markets have different requirements as measured by the above customer attributes.

When you are serving multiple market segments, your company will
need to look for ways to leverage its core competencies. Parts of these
supply chains may be unique to the market segment they serve, while
other parts can be combined to achieve economies of scale. For example,
if manufacturing is a core competency for a company, it can build a
range of different products in common production facilities. Then different inventory and transportation options can be used to deliver the
products to customers in different market segments.

Develop Needed Supply Chain Capabilities

Once you know what kind of markets your company serves and the role
your company does or will play in the supply chains of these markets,
then you can take this last step, which is to develop the supply chain
capabilities needed to support the roles your company plays. This development is guided by the decisions made about the five supply chain
drivers. Each of these drivers can be developed and managed to emphasize responsiveness or efficiency depending on the business requirements.

1. *Production*—This driver can be made very responsive by building factories that have a lot of excess capacity and that use
   flexible manufacturing techniques to produce a wide range
   of items. To be even more responsive, a company could do
   their production in many smaller plants that are close to major

groups of customers so that delivery times would be shorter. If efficiency is desirable, then a company can build factories with very little excess capacity and have the factories optimized for producing a limited range of items. Further efficiency could be gained by centralizing production in large central plants to get better economies of scale.

2. *Inventory*—Responsiveness here can be had by stocking high levels of inventory for a wide range of products. Additional responsiveness can be gained by stocking products at many locations so as to have the inventory close to customers and available to them immediately. Efficiency in inventory management would call for reducing inventory levels of all items and especially of items that do not sell as frequently. Also, economies of scale and cost savings could be obtained by stocking inventory in only a few central locations.

3. *Location*—A location approach that emphasizes responsiveness would be one where a company opens up many locations to be physically close to its customer base. For example, McDonald's has used location to be very responsive to its customers by opening up lots of stores in its high-volume markets. Efficiency can be achieved by operating from only a few locations and centralizing activities in common locations. An example of this is the way Dell Computers serves large geographical markets from only a few central locations that perform a wide range of activities.

4. *Transportation*—Responsiveness can be achieved by a transportation mode that is fast and flexible. Many companies that sell products through catalogs or over the Internet are able to provide high levels of responsiveness by using transportation to deliver their products, often within 24 hours. FedEx and UPS are two companies that can provide very responsive

transportation services. Efficiency can be emphasized by trans-porting products in larger batches and doing it less often. The use of transportation modes such as ship, rail, and pipelines can be very efficient. Transportation can be made more efficient if it is originated out of a central hub facility instead of from many branch locations.

5. *Information*—The power of this driver grows stronger each year as the technology for collecting and sharing information becomes more widespread, easier to use, and less expensive. Information, much like money, is a very useful commodity because it can be applied directly to enhance the perfor-mance of the other four supply chain drivers. High levels of responsiveness can be achieved when companies collect and share accurate and timely data generated by the operations of the other four drivers. The supply chains that serve the elec-tronics markets are some of the most responsive in the world. Companies in these supply chains, from manufacturers to distributors to the big retail stores collect and share data about customer demand, production schedules, and inven-tory levels.

Where efficiency is more the focus, less information about fewer activities can be collected. Companies may also elect to share less infor-mation among themselves so as not to risk having that information used against them. Please note, however, that these information efficiencies are only efficiencies in the short term and they become less efficient over time because the cost of information continues to drop and the cost of the other four drivers usually continues to rise. Over the longer term, those companies and supply chains that learn how to maximize the use of information to get optimal performance from the other drivers will gain the most market share and be the most profitable.

Three Steps to Align
Supply Chain and Business Strategy

1. Understand the requirements of your customers.

2. Define core competencies and the roles your company will play to serve your customers.

3. Develop supply chain capabilities to support the roles your company has chosen.

	Responsiveness	Efficiency
1. Production	• Excess capacity • Flexible manufacturing • Many smaller factories	• Little excess capacity • Narrow focus • Few central plants
2. Inventory	• High inventory levels • Wide range of items	• Low inventory levels • Fewer items
3. Location	• Many locations close to customers	• Few central locations serve wide areas
4. Transportation	• Frequent shipments • Fast and flexible mode	• Shipments few, large • Slow, cheaper modes
5. Information	• Collect & share timely, accurate data	• Cost of information drops while other costs rise

Supply chain capabilities of responsiveness and efficiency come from decisions made about the five supply chain drivers.

Professor Sunil Chopra is a keen observer of the ways that supply chains respond over time to changes in their economic and regulatory environments and to shifts in technology and customer demands. In an interview, Professor Chopra shared some of his observations.

"Look at a company's products and how they're being changed by advances in technology," he said. "For instance, Dell's build-to-order business model and its practice of selling directly to customers are not so valuable anymore because people don't customize their computer purchases very much anymore."

People used to buy mostly desktop PCs, but now sales of laptops surpass PCs, and people don't feel the need to customize their laptops the way they did with their PCs. "So Dell now is saying they will ship from stock instead of their traditional model, which was to build-to-order-and-ship customized PCs."

And Professor Chopra points out that Dell is also restructuring its retail channels. Dell not only sells direct, but also sells through retailers such as Wal-Mart for standard low-end PCs. On a $500 machine the shipping expense is a significant part of the total cost, so it's better to sell low-end PCs through a local retailer like Wal-Mart

Apple, on the other hand, has a different strategy, according to Professor Chopra. "They make the user interface the customized part of their product while their hardware is a commodity. Their hardware is standard and it's the apps that run on the hardware that customize the product."

Unlike Dell, Apple has only about 15 basic product models, and this enables them to have a simple hardware supply chain. Apple adds value to the hardware it sells by designing a user interface (UI) that customers find very attractive. So they are willing to pay premium prices for what would otherwise be commodity hardware because they want the UI that Apple puts on its hardware.

(Continued)

However, one of the challenges that this business model creates for Apple is that they need to have a big hit product every few years in order to keep ahead of their competitors who come out with close copies of the Apple products and offer them for sale at lower prices. For instance, just as Google's Android is starting to cut into sales of Apple's iPhone, Apple comes out with a compelling new product in the iPad. "iPad is doing well now," said Chopra, "but they have to come up with another big hit product in another couple of years as competitors learn to copy the iPad."

He also pointed out how regulations such as the current tax structure on Internet sales channels like the one Dell uses can influence and even distort supply chain structures. Dell is not taxed on out-of-state sales. So that causes them to remain centralized and keep using an Internet direct-sales channel when, if they had to pay out-of-state sales taxes, they would otherwise move to a decentralized model. If the regulations and tax structures related to Internet sales change, then Dell's supply chain structure will also change.

Supply chains are becoming so efficient and customer preferences change so quickly that profit margins are relentlessly squeezed. Companies need to find ways to cut their fixed costs of producing products. And they cannot risk getting too invested in a business model that emphasizes either low-cost efficiency or high-cost responsiveness. Efficiency and responsiveness are two ends of a continuum, and companies need to be flexible enough to reposition themselves on that continuum quickly when markets shift.

Professor Chopra observes that the question of efficiency versus responsiveness can be addressed like an investment portfolio question. If you are concentrated at either end of the spectrum you are in a risky position because the world will probably change suddenly and your company might not be able to adjust fast enough to keep pace.

How do you position your company or your portfolio of business to best fit the markets you serve? Some portion of your business

must be responsive, so you move that part ___
ers, and another part of your business mu___
position it offshore in low-cost-labor count___
server market is still a market that values ___
so that is the part they make responsive ___
assembly onshore near its customers. But customers no ~~~
value customization in PCs and laptops so they have outsourced
that part of their business to emphasize efficiency and that work
is now done offshore.

And this leads to another issue that Professor Chopra pointed out.
As markets and the supply chains that serve them get more and
more efficient and fluid, the middle class in developed countries
tends to get hollowed out. "If you are a highly skilled worker in a
developed nation, then your services are sought after and you can
leverage the low-cost labor of workers in developing nations to build
products you design," said Chopra. But this also displaces large
numbers of low- and medium-skilled workers in developed countries, as jobs once performed by them are sent offshore to be done
by low-cost workers in developing nations.

From the 1990s through the first decade of this century, wages in
developed countries have polarized. There are some who have seen
their incomes increase dramatically as they leveraged the low-cost
labor available in developing nations. And a lot of middle class workers in developed nations have seen their wages drop significantly
because their work is now being done elsewhere. "This produces
greater value for the world as a whole, but now the question is how
are we going to distribute that value in order to maintain a broad
middle class in the developed countries?"

Professor Sunil Chopra is the IBM Distinguished Professor of
Operations Management at Northwestern University's Kellogg
School of Management. He has co-authored the books *Managing
Business Process Flows* and *Supply Chain Management: Strategy,
Planning, and Operation,* 4th Edition.

er Summary

upply chain is composed of all the companies involved in the design, production, and delivery of a product to market. Supply chain management is the coordination of production, inventory, location, and transportation among the participants in a supply chain to achieve the best mix of responsiveness and efficiency for the market being served. The goal of supply chain management is to increase sales of goods and services to the final, end-use customer while at the same time reducing both inventory and operating expenses.

The business model of vertical integration that came out of the industrial economy has given way to "virtual integration" of companies in a supply chain. Each company now focuses on its core competencies and partners with other companies that have complementary capabilities for the design and delivery of products to market. Companies must focus on improvements in their core competencies in order to keep up with the fast pace of market and technological change in today's economy.

To succeed in the competitive markets that make up today's economy, companies must learn to align their supply chains with the demands of the markets they serve. Supply chain performance is now a distinct competitive advantage for companies who excel in this area. One of the largest companies in North America is a testament to the power of effective supply chain management. Wal-Mart has grown steadily over the last several decades and much, if not most, of its success is directly related to its evolving capabilities to continually improve its supply chain.

CHAPTER 2

Supply Chain Operations

Planning and Sourcing

After reading this chapter you will be able to

- Gain a conceptual appreciation of the business operations in any supply chain
- Exercise an executive-level understanding of operations involved in supply chain planning and sourcing
- Start to assess how well these operations are working within your own company

As the saying goes, "It's not what you know, but what you can remember when you need it." Since there is an infinite amount of detail in any situation, the trick is to find useful models that capture the salient facts and provide a framework to organize the rest of the relevant details. The purpose of this chapter is to provide some useful models of the business operations that make up the supply chain.

A Useful Model of Supply Chain Operations

In the first chapter we saw that there are five drivers of supply chain performance. These drivers can be thought of as the design parameters or policy decisions that define the shape and capabilities of any supply chain. Within the context created by these policy decisions, a supply chain goes about doing its job by performing regular, ongoing operations. These are the "nuts and bolts" operations at the core of every supply chain.

As a way to get a high-level understanding of these operations and how they relate to each other, we use a simplified version of the supply chain operations reference (SCOR) model developed by the Supply Chain Council (Supply Chain Council Inc., 12320 Barker Cypress Rd, Suite 600, PMB 321, Cypress, TX 77429, *www.supply-chain.org*). Readers can get information on the full model at their web site. Our simplified model identifies four categories of operations:

1. Plan
2. Source
3. Make
4. Deliver

Plan

This refers to all the operations needed to plan and organize the operations in the other three categories. We will investigate three operations in this category in some detail: demand forecasting, product pricing, and inventory management.

Source

Operations in this category include the activities necessary to acquire the inputs to create products or services. We look at two operations here. The first, procurement, is the acquisition of materials and services. The second operation, credit and collections, is not traditionally seen as a sourcing activity but it can be thought of as, literally, the acquisition of cash. Both these operations have a big impact on the efficiency of a supply chain.

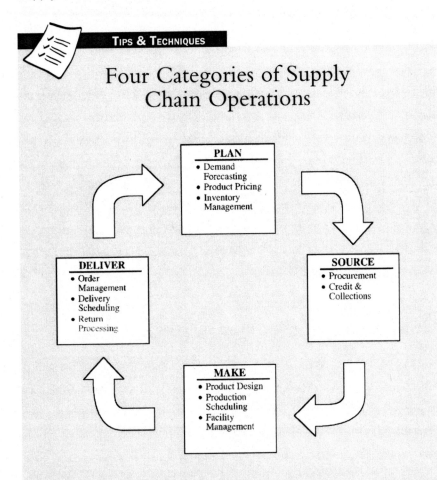

Four Categories of Supply Chain Operations

PLAN
- Demand Forecasting
- Product Pricing
- Inventory Management

SOURCE
- Procurement
- Credit & Collections

DELIVER
- Order Management
- Delivery Scheduling
- Return Processing

MAKE
- Product Design
- Production Scheduling
- Facility Management

Within the constraints set by decisions about the four supply chain drivers, these business operations do the work that makes the supply chain a reality.

Make

This category includes the operations required to develop and build the products and services that a supply chain provides. Operations that we discuss in this category are product design, production management, and facility and management. The SCOR model does not specifically include the product design and development process, but it is included here because it is integral to the production process.

Deliver

These operations encompass the activities that are part of receiving customer orders and delivering products to customers. The three operations we review are management, product delivery, and return processing. These are the operations that constitute the core connections between companies in a supply chain.

The rest of this chapter presents further detail in the categories of Plan and Source. There is an executive-level overview of the three main operations that constitute the planning process and two operations that comprise the sourcing process. Chapter 3 presents an executive overview of the key operations in making and delivering.

Demand Forecasting and Planning (Plan)

Supply chain management decisions are based on forecasts that define which products will be required, what amount of these products will be called for, and when they will be needed. The demand forecast becomes the basis for companies to plan their internal operations and to cooperate among each other to meet market demand.

All forecasts deal with four major variables that combine to determine what market conditions will be like. Those variables are:

1. Supply
2. Demand
3. Product Characteristics
4. Competitive Environment

Supply is determined by the number of producers of a product and by the lead times that are associated with a product. The more producers there are of a product and the shorter the lead times, the more predictable this variable is. When there are only a few suppliers or when lead times are longer, then there is more potential uncertainty in a market. Like variability in demand, uncertainty in supply makes forecasting more difficult. Also, longer lead times associated with a product require a longer time horizon over which forecasts must be made. Supply chain forecasts must cover a time period that encompasses the combined lead times of all the components that go into the creation of a final product.

Demand refers to the overall market demand for a group of related products or services. Is the market growing or declining? If so, what is the yearly or quarterly rate of growth or decline? Or maybe the market is relatively mature and demand is steady at a level that has been predictable for some period of years. Also, many products have a seasonal demand pattern. For example, snow skis and heating oil are more in demand in the winter, and tennis rackets and sun screen are more in demand in the summer. Perhaps the market is a developing market—the products or services are new and there is not much historical data on demand or the demand varies widely because new customers are just being introduced to the products. Markets where there is little historical data and lots of variability are the most difficult when it comes to demand forecasting.

Product characteristics include the features of a product that influence customer demand for the product. Is the product new and developing quickly like many electronic products or is the product mature and changing slowly or not at all, as is the case with many commodity products? Forecasts for mature products can cover longer timeframes than forecasts for products that are developing quickly. It is also important to know whether a product will steal demand away from another product. Can it be substituted for another product? Or will the use of one product drive the complementary use of a related product? Products that either compete with or complement each other should be forecasted together.

Competitive environment refers to the actions of a company and its competitors. What is the market share of a company? Regardless of whether the total size of a market is growing or shrinking, what is the trend in an individual company's market share? Is it growing or declining? What is the market share trend of competitors? Market share trends can be influenced by product promotions and price wars, so forecasts should take into account such events that are planned for the upcoming period. Forecasts should also account for anticipated promotions and price wars that will be initiated by competitors.

Forecasting Methods

There are four basic methods to use when doing forecasts. Most forecasts are done using various combinations of these four methods. Chopra and Meindl define these methods as:

1. Qualitative
2. Causal
3. Time Series
4. Simulation

Qualitative methods rely upon a person's intuition or subjective opinions about a market. These methods are most appropriate when there is little historical data to work with. When a new line of products is introduced, people can make forecasts based on comparisons with other products or situations that they consider similar. People can forecast using production adoption curves that they feel reflect what will happen in the market.

Causal methods of forecasting assume that demand is strongly related to particular environmental or market factors. For instance, demand for commercial loans is often closely correlated to interest rates. So if interest rate cuts are expected in the next period of time, then loan forecasts can be derived using a causal relationship with interest rates. Another strong causal relationship exists between price and demand. If prices are lowered, demand can be expected to increase and if prices are raised, demand can be expected to fall.

Time series methods are the most common form of forecasting. They are based on the assumption that historical patterns of demand are a good indicator of future demand. These methods are best when there is a reliable body of historical data and the markets being forecast are stable and have demand patterns that do not vary much from one year to the next. Mathematical techniques such as moving averages and exponential smoothing are used to create forecasts based on time series data. These techniques are employed by most forecasting software packages.

Simulation methods use combinations of causal and time series methods to imitate the behavior of consumers under different circumstances. This method can be used to answer questions such as what will happen to revenue if prices on a line of products are lowered or what will happen to market share if a competitor introduces a competing product or opens a store nearby.

Few companies use only one of these methods to produce forecasts. Most companies do several forecasts using several methods and then combine the results of these different forecasts into the actual forecast that they use to plan their businesses. Studies have shown that this process of creating forecasts using different methods and then combining the results into a final forecast usually produces better accuracy than the output of any one method alone.

Regardless of the forecasting methods used, when doing forecasts and evaluating their results it is important to keep several things in mind. First of all, short-term forecasts are inherently more accurate than long-term forecasts. The effect of business trends and conditions can be much more accurately calculated over short periods than over longer periods. When Wal-Mart began restocking its stores twice a week instead of twice a month, the store managers were able to significantly increase the accuracy of their forecasts because the time periods involved dropped from two or three weeks to three or four days. Most long range, multi-year forecasts are highly speculative.

Aggregate forecasts are more accurate than forecasts for individual products or for small market segments. For example, annual forecasts for soft drink sales in a given metropolitan area are fairly accurate but when these forecasts are broken down to sales by districts within the metropolitan area, they become less accurate. Aggregate forecasts are made using a broad base of data that provides good forecasting accuracy. As a rule, the more narrowly focused or specific a forecast is, the less data is available and the more variability there is in the data, so the accuracy is diminished.

Finally, forecasts are always wrong to a greater or lesser degree. There are no perfect forecasts and businesses need to assign some expected degree of error to every forecast. An accurate forecast may have a degree of error that is plus or minus 5 percent. A more speculative forecast may have a plus or minus 20 percent degree of error. It is important to know the degree of error because a business must have contingency plans to cover those outcomes. What would a company do if raw material prices were 5 percent higher than expected? What would it do if demand was 20 percent higher than expected?

Aggregate Planning

Once demand forecasts have been created, the next step is to create a plan for the company to meet the expected demand. This is called aggregate planning, and its purpose is to satisfy demand in a way that maximizes profit for the company. The planning is done at the aggregate level and not at the level of individual stock keeping units (SKUs). It sets the optimum levels of production and inventory that will be followed over the next 3 to 18 months.

The aggregate plan becomes the framework within which short-term decisions are made about production, inventory, and distribution. Production decisions involve setting parameters such as the rate of production and the amount of production capacity to use, the size of the workforce, and how much overtime and subcontracting to use.

The Four Forecasting Variables and the Four Forecasting Methods

Forecasting VARIABLES		
1.	Supply	Amount of product available
2.	Demand	Overall market demand for product
3.	Product Characteristics	Product features that influence demand
4.	Competitive Environment	Actions of product suppliers in the market

Forecasting METHODS		
1.	Qualitative	Relies on a person's intuition or opinions
2.	Causal	Assumes that demand is strongly related to certain factors
3.	Time Series	Based on historical demand patterns
4.	Simulation	Combines causal and time series methods

Inventory decisions include how much demand will be met immediately by inventory on hand and how much demand can be satisfied later and turned into backlogged orders. Distribution decisions define how and when product will be moved from the place of production to the place where it will be used or purchased by customers.

There are three basic approaches to take in creating the aggregate plan. They involve trade-offs among three variables. Those variables are: (1) amount of production capacity; (2) the level of utilization of the production capacity; and (3) the amount of inventory to carry. We look briefly at each of these three approaches. In actual practice, most companies create aggregate plans that are a combination of these three approaches.

1. *Use Production Capacity to Match Demand.* In this approach the total amount of production capacity is matched to the level of demand. The objective here is to use 100 percent of capacity at all times. This is achieved by adding or eliminating plant capacity as needed and hiring and laying off employees as needed. This approach results in low levels of inventory but it can be very expensive to implement if the cost of adding or reducing plant capacity is high. It is also often disruptive and demoralizing to the workforce if people are constantly being hired or fired as demand rises and falls. This approach works best when the cost of carrying inventory is high and the cost of changing capacity plant and workforce—is low.

2. *Utilize Varying Levels of Total Capacity to Match Demand.* This approach can be used if there is excess production capacity available. If existing plants are not used 24 hours a day and 7 days a week then there is an opportunity to meet changing demand by increasing or decreasing utilization of production capacity. The size of the workforce can be maintained at a steady rate and overtime and flexible work scheduling used to match production rates. The result is low levels of inventory and also lower average levels of capacity utilization. The approach makes sense when the cost of carrying inventory is high and the cost of excess capacity is relatively low.

3. *Use Inventory and Backlogs to Match Demand.* Using this approach provides for stability in the plant capacity and workforce and enables a constant rate of output. Production is not matched with demand. Instead inventory is either built up

during periods of low demand in anticipation of future demand or inventory is allowed to run low and backlogs are built up in one period to be filled in a following period. This approach results in higher capacity utilization and lower costs of changing capacity but it does generate large inventories and backlogs over time as demand fluctuates. It should be used when the cost of capacity and changing capacity is high and the cost of carrying inventory and backlogs is relatively low.

Product Pricing (Plan)

Companies and entire supply chains can influence demand over time by using price. Depending how price is used, it will tend to maximize either revenue or gross profit. Typically marketing and salespeople want to make pricing decisions that will stimulate demand during peak seasons. The aim here is to maximize total revenue. Often financial or production people want to make pricing decisions that stimulate demand during low periods. Their aim is to maximize gross profit in peak demand periods and generate revenue to cover costs during low demand periods.

Relationship of Cost Structure to Pricing

The question for each company to ask is, "Is it better to do price promotion during peak periods to increase revenue or during low periods to cover costs?" The answer depends on the company's cost structure. If a company has flexibility to vary the size of its workforce and productive capacity and the cost of carrying inventory is high, then it is best to create more demand in peak seasons. If there is less flexibility to vary workforce and capacity and if cost to carry inventory is low, it is best to create demand in low periods.

An example of a company that can quickly ramp up production would be an electronics component manufacturer. Such companies have invested in plant and equipment that can be quickly reconfigured to produce different final products from an inventory of standard component parts. The finished goods inventory is expensive to carry because it soon becomes obsolete and must be written off.

These companies are generally motivated to run promotions in peak periods to stimulate demand even further. Since they can quickly increase production levels, a reduction in the profit margin can be made up for by an increase in total sales if they are able to sell all the product that they manufacture.

A company that cannot quickly ramp up production levels is a paper mill. The plant and equipment involved in making paper is very expensive and requires a long lead time to build. Once in place, a paper mill operates most efficiently if it is able to run at a steady rate all year long. The cost of carrying an inventory of paper products is less expensive than carrying an inventory of electronic components because paper products are commodity items that will not become obsolete. These products also can be stored in less expensive warehouse facilities and are less likely to be stolen.

A paper mill is motivated to do price promotions in periods of low demand. In periods of high demand the focus is on maintaining a good profit margin. Since production levels cannot be increased anyway, there is no way to respond to or profit from an increase in demand. In periods where demand is below the available production level, then there is value in increased demand. The fixed cost of the plant and equipment is constant so it is best to try to balance demand with available production capacity. This way the plant can be run steadily at full capacity.

Inventory Management (Plan)

Inventory management is a set of techniques that are used to manage the inventory levels within different companies in a supply chain. The aim

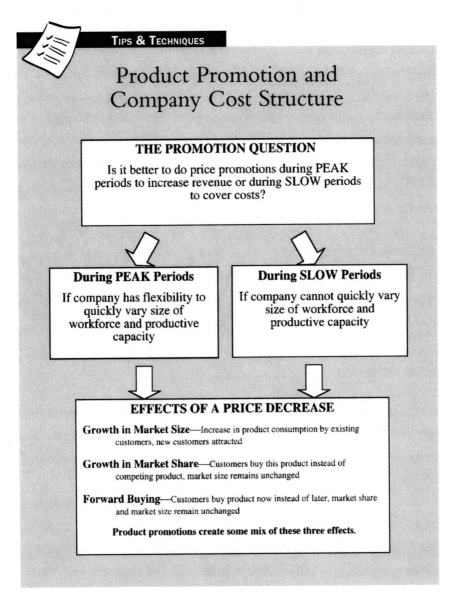

TIPS & TECHNIQUES

Product Promotion and Company Cost Structure

THE PROMOTION QUESTION

Is it better to do price promotions during PEAK periods to increase revenue or during SLOW periods to cover costs?

During PEAK Periods

If company has flexibility to quickly vary size of workforce and productive capacity

During SLOW Periods

If company cannot quickly vary size of workforce and productive capacity

EFFECTS OF A PRICE DECREASE

Growth in Market Size—Increase in product consumption by existing customers, new customers attracted

Growth in Market Share—Customers buy this product instead of competing product, market size remains unchanged

Forward Buying—Customers buy product now instead of later, market share and market size remain unchanged

Product promotions create some mix of these three effects.

is to reduce the cost of inventory as much as possible while still maintaining the service levels that customers require. Inventory management takes its major inputs from the demand forecasts for products and the prices of products. With these two inputs, inventory management is an ongoing process of balancing product inventory levels to meet demand and exploiting economies of scale to get the best product prices.

As we discussed in Chapter 1, there are three kinds of inventory: (1) cycle inventory; (2) seasonal inventory; and (3) safety inventory. Cycle inventory and seasonal inventory are both influenced by economy of scale considerations. The cost structure of the companies in any supply chain will suggest certain levels of inventory based on production costs and inventory carrying cost. Safety inventory is influenced by the predictability of product demand. The less predictable product demand is, the higher the level of safety inventory is required to cover unexpected swings in demand.

The inventory management operation in a company or an entire supply chain is composed of a blend of activities related to managing the three different types of inventory. Each type of inventory has its own specific challenges and the mix of these challenges will vary from one company to another and from one supply chain to another.

Cycle Inventory

Cycle inventory is the inventory required to meet product demand over the time period between placing orders for the product. Cycle inventory exists because economies of scale make it desirable to make fewer orders of large quantities of a product rather than continuous orders of small product quantity. The end-use customer of a product may actually use a product in continuous small amounts throughout the year. But the distributor and the manufacturer of that product may find it more cost efficient to produce and stock the product in large batches that do not match the usage pattern.

Cycle inventory is the buildup of inventory in the supply chain due to the fact that production and stocking of inventory is done in lot sizes that are larger than the ongoing demand for the product. For example, a distributor may experience an ongoing demand for Item A that is 100 units per week. The distributor finds, however, that it is most cost effective to order in batches of 650 units. Every six weeks or so the distributor places an order causing cycle inventory to build up in the distributor's warehouse at the beginning of the ordering period. The manufacturer of Item A that all the distributors order from may find that it is most efficient for them to manufacture in batches of 14,000 units at a time. This also results in the buildup of cycle inventory at the manufacturer's location.

Economic Order Quantity

Given the cost structure of a company, there is an order quantity that is the most cost-effective amount to purchase at a time. This is called the economic order quantity (EOQ) and it is calculated as:

$$EOQ = \sqrt{\frac{2UO}{hC}}$$

where:

U = annual usage rate

O = ordering cost

C = cost per unit

h = holding cost per year as a percentage of unit cost

For instance, let's say that Item Z has an annual usage rate (U) of 240, a fixed cost per order (O) of $5.00, a unit cost (C) of $7.00, and an annual holding cost (h) of 30 percent per unit. If we do the math, it works out as:

$$EOQ = \sqrt{\frac{2 \times 240 \times 5.00}{.30 \times 7.00}}$$

$$EOQ = \sqrt{\frac{2400}{2.1}}$$

$$EOQ = \sqrt{1142.86}$$

EOQ = 33.81 and rounded to the nearest whole unit, it is 34

If the annual usage rate for Item Z is 240, then the monthly usage rate is 20. An EOQ of 34 represents about seven weeks' supply. This may not be a convenient order size. Small changes in the EOQ do not have a big impact on total ordering and holding costs so it is best to round off the EOQ quantity to the nearest standard ordering size. In the case of Item Z, there may be 30 units in a case. So it would make sense to adjust the EOQ for Item Z to 30.

The EOQ formula works to calculate an order quantity that results in the most efficient investment of money in inventory. Efficiency here is defined as the lowest total unit cost for each inventory item. If a certain inventory item has a high usage rate and is expensive, the EOQ formula recommends a low order quantity which results in more orders per year but less money invested in each order. If another inventory item has a low usage rate and is inexpensive, the EOQ formula recommends a high order quantity. This means fewer orders per year but since the unit cost is low, it still results in the most efficient amount of money to invest in that item.

Seasonal Inventory

Seasonal inventory happens when a company or a supply chain with a fixed amount of productive capacity decides to produce and stockpile products in anticipation of future demand. If future demand is going to exceed productive capacity, then the answer is to produce product in times of low demand that can be put into inventory to meet the high demand in the future.

Decisions about seasonal inventory are driven by a desire to get the best economies of scale given the capacity and cost structure of each company in the supply chain. If it is expensive for a manufacturer to increase productive capacity, then capacity can be considered as fixed. Once the annual demand for the manufacturer's products is determined, the most efficient schedule to utilize that fixed capacity can be calculated.

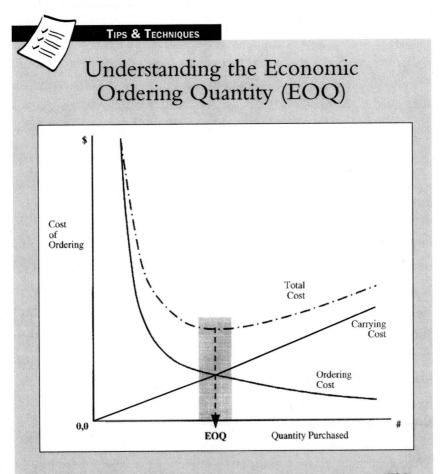

Understanding the Economic Ordering Quantity (EOQ)

Good inventory management requires a company to know the EOQ for all the products it buys. The EOQ for different products changes over time so a company needs an ongoing measurement process to keep the numbers accurate and up to date.

This schedule will call for seasonal inventory. Managing seasonal inventory calls for demand forecasts to be accurate since large amounts of inventory can be built up this way and it can become obsolete, or holding costs can mount if the inventory is not sold off as anticipated. Managing seasonal inventory also calls for manufacturers to offer price incentives to persuade distributors to purchase the product and put it in their warehouses well before demand for it occurs.

Safety Inventory

Safety inventory is necessary to compensate for the uncertainty that exists in a supply chain. Retailers and distributors do not want to run out of inventory in the face of unexpected customer demand or unexpected delay in receiving replenishment orders, so they keep safety stock on hand. As a rule, the higher the level of uncertainty, the higher the level of safety stock that is required.

Safety inventory for an item can be defined as the amount of inventory on hand for an item when the next replenishment EOQ lot arrives. This means that the safety stock is inventory that does not turn over. In effect, it becomes a fixed asset and it drives up the cost of carrying inventory. Companies need to find a balance between their desire to carry a wide range of products and offer high availability on all of them, and their conflicting desire to keep the cost of inventory as low as possible. That balance is reflected quite literally in the amount of safety stock that a company carries.

Procurement (Source)

Traditionally, the main activities of a purchasing manager were to beat up potential suppliers on price and then buy products from the lowest-cost supplier that could be found. That is still an important activity, but there are other activities that are becoming equally important. Because of this, the purchasing activity is now seen as part of a broader function called procurement. The procurement function can be broken into five main activity categories:

1. Purchasing
2. Consumption Management
3. Vendor Selection
4. Contract Negotiation
5. Contract Management

TIPS & TECHNIQUES

Key Points to Remember about Inventory Management

Economic Order Quantity (EOQ)

The ordering quantity of a product that minimizes both the ordering cost and the carrying cost

---

THREE KINDS OF INVENTORY

1. **Cycle Inventory**—Needed to meet product demand between normally scheduled orders

2. **Seasonal Inventory**—Produced and stockpiled in anticipation of future demand

3. **Safety Inventory**—Necessary to compensate for demand uncertainty and order lead times

---

FOUR WAYS TO REDUCE SAFETY INVENTORY

1. **Reduce Demand Uncertainty**—Learn to do better product demand forecasts

2. **Reduce Order Lead Times**—Shorter lead times mean less safety inventory needed for coverage

3. **Reduce Lead Time Variability**—Further reduces need for safety inventory

4. **Reduce Availability Uncertainty**—Ensure product availability when demand occurs

With the spread of our global, interconnected economy, there also comes the need to understand cultural and behavioral drivers that influence the procurement process. Huseyin Eskici is the head of the Procurement Department of the Istanbul Stock Exchange and he negotiates contracts with suppliers from all over the world. In an interview I posed three questions and asked him to share his insights on this topic.

1 In your experience negotiating purchasing contracts with suppliers from different countries, what differences do you see in the negotiating process? For instance what are the negotiating differences you see between a British company or a Turkish company or a Chinese or an American company?

In my experience, negotiating purchasing contracts with suppliers from different countries has to do with their cultures. When negotiating purchasing contracts with suppliers from different countries, world-class purchasing specialists should know that they have different cultural backgrounds. What I mean by culture is *"the system of values and norms that are shared among a group of people and taken togather constitute a design for living and negotiating"*.

When I compare and contrast the Western or English negotiation culture with Turkish negotiation culture it is possible to list several differences. To begin with, Turkish suppliers generally give more importance and allocate more time to personal relations before and during the process of contract negotiation, whereas English suppliers prefer to start contract negotiations after completing generally accepted business protocols, such as meeting, exchanging business cards, and drinking traditional Turkish black tea or Turkish coffee. For example, when you are negotiating a contract with a Turkish supplier you may find yourself chatting about economic and political problems of the country or complaining about your organizational problems. You may even be talking about which soccer team is going to be champion this year. Almost 80 percent of the time is allocated to establishing trust and a good personal relationship and 20 percent is allocated to contract negotiation.

Turkish negotiation culture is based on verbal communication rather than on numbers, financial information, and analysis relating to the contract and the companies involved, whereas Western or English negotiation culture is mainly based on numerical communication such as facts, figures, numbers, and process analysis relating to the supply contract and the supplier firm.

Turkish culture is collectivist in nature, that is, individuals rarely prefer to take personal initiative or responsibility in making a final decision unless his or her authority is clearly defined. They prefer collective decision making when faced with critical and risky cases, whereas Western culture is individualistic in nature, that is, individuals are prone to make final decisions within their jurisdiction since they regard the success or failure as their personal responsibility. In critical cases, Turkish suppliers and negotiators like the boss or general manager to make final decisions because of our risk- averse culture.

English or U.S. suppliers do not hesitate to make decisions and conclude contracts because their limits of authority are usually clearly defined by their organizations. This relates to their individualistic cultural background. But, I have to admit, there are now many younger well-educated and trained business professionals in Turkey, and they know how to start, manage, and close a contract-negotiation process based on the Western model.

2 You observe that negotiating behaviors are based on the culture and social structure of the country where a company is based. Can you describe some common patterns that you see when negotiating with companies from different countries.

(Continued)

I have observed that the socio-economic structure and economic and political power of countries where companies are based shape both organizational and personal negotiation styles. If we keep aside global and multi-national companies, I can describe some common patterns regarding negotiating behaviors that I have seen when negotiating a purchasing contract with companies from the United States:

Negotiators of the U.S. companies are self confident in general because their country is almost as large as a continent and they believe that their country is the most powerful one in the world. Their body language reflects that they are free and self-confident. They ideologically believe strongly in individual rights and freedoms and the superiority of private business. They are prone to use personal initiative and take risk, if necessary, to conclude a purchasing contract because their common national ideology is based on the virtues of individualism and capitalism. They generally act aggressively in the process of negotiations, since capitalist ideology supports and reproduces the belief that "Competition is good and the best one will be the winner." If a Turkish negotiator is not aware of fundamentals of American culture, she or he may interpret their negotiating style as rude, arrogant, opportunistic, and unethical.

Americans, when they like and respect the people they meet, call them by first names. This represents their sincerity and real friendship. In contrast, a real Londoner usually prefers to call people by their surnames. In Turkish business etiquette, when you call someone by first name immediately after you meet, if she or he does not know much about American culture, may interpret this behavior as impolite and disrespectful. In the Turkish business culture during negotiations, it is better and safer for foreigners to use formal surnames. My name is Huseyin Eskici so it is best to start by addressing me as "Mr. Eskici". Later on, if things go well then one could shift and call me "Mr. Huseyin". If a Turk has academic or professional titles such as "Doctor" or "Professor" it is usually best to say "Mr. Doctor" or "Mr. Professor" instead of using their first names or surnames.

Americans value time and like to start negotiation as soon as possible. They express themselves frankly and use a straight-forward get-to-the-point business style. This manner may be interpreted as arrogant or disrespectful in Asiatic cultures or collectivist cultures like the Chinese and the Turks. Americans prefer to know and follow laws, rules, and regulations when they are negotiating purchasing contracts, because they are living in a strictly regulated society and they are well aware of the cost of breaching laws and regulations. Whereas tax evasion is a big crime for American citizens, in developing countries like Turkey, it may be tolerated and regarded as normal or ordinary.

3 Describe an experience in your career that has taught you an important lesson in purchasing and describe the lesson you learned and how you have used that lesson since then.

In 2007, I negotiated a supplier contract with a marketing manager who represents one of the prominent computer system companies in the world. I had to purchase additional servers and software for the system used by the Istanbul Stock Exchange to run its stock-trading operations. We had to purchase the servers from this particular company because we already were using their hardware and software to run our trading operations. They quoted us an initial purchase price of almost a million U.S. dollars.

Before the negotiation, I read all their technical documents about the system and asked our IT specialists about technical matters that I could not understand. I also asked why we had to buy the system and what were the components (hardware, software, UPS, etc.). Moreover, I learned that the marketing manager from England would personally come and negotiate the contract. After that, I did research about negotiating culture

(Continued)

and business etiquette in England. Also, I read all the purchasing and other contracts that were signed between that company and the Istanbul Stock Exchange in order to estimate my desired target price and estimate his desired target price. From this I discovered that the discount rate from initially quoted prices with this company was typically 45 percent and the ratio of maintenance costs to purchase price was around 20 percent.

When the English marketing manager and the Turkish partner came to my office, I was ready to negotiate based on my research. After a short initial meeting, as we were drinking Turkish coffee, I told the marketing manager that I knew exactly what we needed to buy, and that I never engaged in "horse-trading" but instead worked from principles based on signed contracts already in place with his company. I told him they had to give us a larger discount on the purchase price than they had before because we would be working with them for at least 10 years, and his firm would be making more profit from the maintenance service than on the one-time sale of the system.

He told me that in order to receive a higher discount than before, his company wanted prepayment of 80 percent of the contract. I told him that we had to follow strict rules and regulations, so if they could give us a guarantee letter from an English bank, our financial department would allow us to make that prepayment. He told me that his firm could get the guarantee letter and on this basis we could negotiate the price. He told me there was no need for him to refer this issue to headquarters, because he was sure about the guarantee letter and had the authority to make a final price offer for the contract. At the end of the day we concluded the contract at a discount of slightly more than 60 percent off their initially quoted price and the ratio of maintenance service costs to the purchase price was about 24 percent.

The contract was officially ratified by the supplier and the Stock Exchange and we sent the purchase order to their sales office in England and awaited the delivery of a bank guarantee letter in order to make our prepayment. Two weeks later the marketing manager wrote me a letter stating their finance department could not get a guarantee letter from their bank and even though they could not collect 80 percent of the total contracted price before delivery of the hardware and software, they would still keep their promises about the price, discount rates, and delivery terms. They said they did not want to lose a prominent customer in Turkey and in the Mediterranean and Eurasian Zones.

What I have learned from this experience is that, if you study and prepare your negotiation strategy by taking into account a supplier's business etiquette and negotiating culture, you can make effective and efficient purchasing contracts even if the supplier has a monopoly in the business and is the exclusive seller of the product. Since then, I have continued to learn more about intercultural negotiation strategies. I am now writing a book in English for executive MBA students in my country. I would like to name the book *Negotiation Strategies for Purchasing Specialists*.

Huseyin Eskici is the Director of Administrative Affairs at the Istanbul Stock Exchange (ISE). He had served as Inspector and later as Chief Inspector in the Auditing and Inspection Board of the ISE from 1991 to 1998. He has been actively working as the Head of the Procurement Department in the ISE since 1998. He is a CPA and has an MBA degree in Contemporary Management Studies.

Purchasing

These activities are the routine activities related to issuing purchase orders for needed products. There are two types of products that a company buys: (1) direct or strategic materials that are needed to produce the products that the company sells to its customers; and (2) indirect or maintenance, repair, and operations (MRO) products that a company consumes as part of daily operations.

The mechanics of purchasing both types of products are largely the same. Purchasing decisions are made, purchase orders are issued, vendors are contacted, and orders are placed. There is a lot of data communicated in this process between the buyer and the supplier—items and quantities ordered, prices, delivery dates, delivery addresses, billing addresses, and payment terms. One of the greatest challenges of the purchasing activity is to see to it that this data communication happens in a timely manner and without error. Much of this activity is very predictable and follows well-defined routines.

Consumption Management

Effective procurement begins with an understanding of how much of what categories of products are being bought across the entire company as well as by each operating unit. There must be an understanding of how much of what kinds of products are bought from whom and at what prices.

Expected levels of consumption for different products at the various locations of a company should be set and then compared against actual consumption on a regular basis. When consumption is significantly above or below expectations, this should be brought to the attention of the appropriate parties so possible causes can be investigated and appropriate actions taken. Consumption above expectations is either a problem to be corrected or it reflects inaccurate expectations that need to be reset. Consumption below expectations may point to an opportunity that should be exploited or it also may simply reflect inaccurate expectations to begin with.

Vendor Selection

There must be an ongoing process to define the procurement capabilities needed to support the company's business plan and its operating model. This definition will provide insight into the relative importance of vendor capabilities. The value of these capabilities has to be considered in addition to simply the price of a vendor's product. The value of product quality, service levels, just-in-time delivery, and technical support can only be estimated in light of what is called for by the business plan and the company's operating model.

Once there is an understanding of the current purchasing situation and an appreciation of what a company needs to support its business plan and operating model, a search can be made for suppliers who have both the products and the service capabilities needed. As a general rule, a company seeks to narrow down the number of suppliers it does business with. This way it can leverage its purchasing power with a few suppliers and get better prices in return for purchasing higher volumes of product.

Contract Negotiation

As particular business needs arise, contracts must be negotiated with individual vendors on the preferred vendor list. This is where the specific items, prices, and service levels are worked out. The simplest negotiations are for contracts to purchase indirect products where suppliers are selected on the basis of lowest price. The most complex negotiations are for contracts to purchase direct materials that must meet exacting quality requirements and where high service levels and technical support are needed.

Increasingly, though, even negotiations for the purchase of indirect items such as office supplies and janitorial products are becoming more complicated because they fall within a company's overall business plan to gain greater efficiencies in purchasing and inventory management. Suppliers of both direct and indirect products need a common set of capabilities. Gaining greater purchasing efficiencies requires that suppliers of these products have the capabilities to set up electronic connections for purposes of receiving orders, sending delivery notifications, sending invoices, and receiving payments. Better inventory management requires that inventory levels be reduced, which often means suppliers need to make more frequent and smaller deliveries and orders must be filled accurately and completely.

All these requirements need to be negotiated in addition to the basic issues of products and prices. The negotiations must make trade-offs between the unit price of a product and all the other value-added services that are required. These other services can either be paid for by a higher margin in the unit price, by separate payments, or by some combination of the two. Performance targets must be specified and penalties and other fees defined when performance targets are not met.

Contract Management

Once contracts are in place, vendor performance against these contracts must be measured and managed. Because companies are narrowing their base of suppliers, the performance of each supplier that is chosen becomes more important. A particular supplier may be the only source of a whole category of products that a company needs, and if it is not meeting its contractual obligations, the activities that depend on those products will suffer.

A company needs the ability to track the performance of its suppliers and hold them accountable to meet the service levels they agreed to in their contracts. Just as with consumption management, people in a company need to routinely collect data about the performance of suppliers. Any supplier that consistently falls below requirements should be made aware of its shortcomings and asked to correct them.

Often the suppliers themselves should be given responsibility for tracking their own performance. They should be able to proactively take action to keep their performance up to contracted levels. An example of this is the concept of vendor-managed inventory (VMI). VMI calls for the vendor to monitor the inventory levels of its product within a customer's business. The vendor is responsible for watching usage rates and calculating EOQs. The vendor proactively ships products to the customer locations that need them and invoices the customer for those shipments under terms defined in the contract.

Credit and Collections (Source)

Procurement is the sourcing process a company uses to get the goods and services it needs. Credit and collections is the sourcing process that a company uses to get its money. The credit operation screens potential customers to make sure the company only does business with customers who will be able to pay their bills. The collections operation is what actually brings in the money that the company has earned.

Approving a sale is like making a loan for the sale amount for a length of time defined by the payment terms. Good credit management tries to fulfill customer demand for products and also minimize the amount of money tied up in receivables. This is analogous to the way good inventory management strives to meet customer demand and also minimize the amount of money tied up in inventory.

The supply chains that a company participates in are often selected on the basis of credit decisions. Much of the trust and cooperation that is possible between companies who do business together is based upon good credit ratings and timely payments of invoices. Credit decisions affect who a company will sell to and also the terms of the sale. The credit and collections function can be broken into three main categories of activity:

1. Set Credit Policy
2. Implement Credit and Collections Practices
3. Manage Credit Risk

Set Credit Policy

Credit policy is set by senior managers in a company such as the controller, chief financial officer, treasurer, and chief executive officer. The first step in this process is to review the performance of the company's receivables. Every company has defined a set of measurements that they use to analyze their receivables, such as: days sales outstanding (DSO); percent of receivables past customer payment terms; and bad debt write-off amount as percent of sales. What are the trends? Where are there problems?

Once management has an understanding of the company's receivables situation and the trends affecting that situation, they can take the next step which is to set or change risk-acceptance criteria to respond to the state of the company's receivables. These criteria should change over time as economic and market conditions evolve. These criteria define the kinds of credit risks that the company will take with different kinds of customers and the payment terms that will be offered.

Implement Credit and Collections Practices

These activities involve putting in place and operating the procedures that will carry out and enforce the credit policies of the company. The first major activity in this category is to work with the company salespeople to approve sales to specific customers. As noted earlier, making a sale is like making a loan for the amount of the sale. Customers often buy from a company because that company extends them larger lines of credit and longer payment terms than its competitors. Credit analysis goes a long way to assure that this loan is only made to customers who will pay it off promptly as called for by the terms of the sale.

After a sale is made, people in the credit area work with customers to provide various kinds of service. They work with customers to process product returns and issue credit memos for returned products. They work with customers to resolve disputes and clear up questions by providing copies of contracts, purchase orders, and invoices.

The third major activity that is performed is collections. This is a process that starts with the ongoing maintenance of each customer's accounts payable status. Customers that have past-due accounts are contacted and payments are requested. Sometimes new payment terms and schedules are negotiated.

The collections activity also includes the work necessary to receive and process customer payments that can come in a variety of different forms. Some customers will wish to pay by electronic funds transfer (EFT). Others will use bank drafts and revolving lines of credit or purchasing cards. If customers are in other countries there are still other ways that payment can be made, such as international letters of credit.

Manage Credit Risk

The credit function works to help the company take intelligent risks that support its business plan. What may be a bad credit decision from one perspective may be a good business decision from another perspective. If a company wants to gain market share in a certain area it may make credit decisions that help it to do so. Credit people work with other people in the business to find innovative ways to lower the risk of selling to new kinds of customers.

Managing risk can be accomplished by creating credit programs that are tailored to the needs of customers in certain market segments such as high technology companies, start-up companies, construction contractors, or customers in foreign countries. Payment terms that are attractive to customers in these market segments can be devised. Credit risks can be lowered by the use of credit insurance, liens on customer assets, and government loan guarantees for exports.

For important customers and particularly large individual sales, people in the credit area work with others in the company to structure special deals just for a single customer. This increases the value that the company can provide to such a customer and can be a significant part of securing important new business.

Increasing emphasis on total cost of ownership (TCO) is bringing higher cost suppliers back to the request-for-proposal (RFP) table once again. Suppliers in the United States and other developed nations have lost business over the last two decades to lower-cost suppliers in the developing world, but now factors other than price alone are important, as companies reconsider what support they need from their supply chains. Sean Correll, a director at the strategic sourcing firm Emptoris (www.Emptoris. com), explores the trend in this executive insight.

It's no secret that the desire to acquire goods and services cheaply has led U.S. companies to begin sourcing products from countries that are considered "low cost." Traditionally, such decisions have been made based on the monetary cost of an item or service. Not surprisingly, this left suppliers in North America, Western Europe, and other developed nations at a disadvantage, as labor costs of domestically produced goods and services could be undercut by those coming from low-cost markets.

However, during the past decade companies have begun to take advantage of the ability to make much more sophisticated decisions when it comes to sourcing the items and services they require. Strategic sourcing technology now makes it possible to analyze numerous factors simultaneously (this analysis is difficult to perform using traditional sourcing technology). This has led to a fundamental shift in the "analyzed cost" of contracting suppliers, from that of *monetary cost* to *total cost of ownership (TCO)*.

TCO takes into account numerous factors beyond pure price in analyzing the cost associated with engaging a given supplier. Often these factors are qualitative as well as quantitative, and they measure factors that are critical to the bottom-line cost of doing business.

For example, in addition to price, companies may be concerned with lead or delivery times. Additionally, companies are concerned with quality, which can be measured in units such as defects per million. In fact, a recent survey sponsored by Emptoris and CFO Research Services ("Supplier Side Economics: Making Vendor Relationships an Enduring Source of Competitive Advantage," *CFO Research Services*, September 2010 http://www.cfo.com/white-papers/) found that companies are now more concerned with timeliness and quality than pure price. According to the survey, senior financial executives at Fortune 1000 companies rated the two top factors with the greatest impact on their companies' business performance as the ability of suppliers to meet commitments (58 percent) and the quality of products from suppliers (54 percent). Price of products was the third factor (51 percent).

Additionally, companies tend to value the ease of doing business with a given supplier, which can be measured in factors such as the number of rejected purchase orders. All of this represents a shift in supply chain thinking with special significance for companies in the developed world that can now compete using these additional criteria.

The following example illustrates how qualitative factors are now weighed along with price in supply chain decision making:

In this sourcing event, in addition to using the monetary cost (product cost plus all logistics cost) in the analysis, we used scores based on answers to qualitative questions. One such question on a sourcing analysis performed for a Global 1000 Pharmaceutical customer was, "What percent of your warehouse facilities have been validated as being monitored for proper temperature and humidity?"

The answer could be given as any whole number from 0 to 100 (i.e., 0 percent garnered a score of 0, 1 percent garnered a score of 1, etc.)

The following formula was used to convert the score to a quantitative dollar amount:

Total Unit Cost = Price Weight × Unit Bid Cost + RFP Question Scores Weight × Unit Bid Cost × (100-RFP Question Scores Rating)/100

(*Continued*)

For our example, assume the following for a U.S. supplier:

- Total Dollar Cost of the Item = $10

- Score for question = 50

- For the analysis, 75 percent of the "analyzed cost" is obtained using the Total Dollar Cost and 25 percent is obtained using the score converted to a quantitative dollar amount using the formula above (this can be modified to any 100 percent mix, for example 80/20 or 90/10 depending on how much importance is to be placed on the Total Dollar Cost and how much importance is placed on the question score). For this item:

Total Cost = 75% × $10 + 25% × $10 × (100–50) /100 = $8.75

In theory, because of process controls (temperature and humidity) on 50 percent of the warehouse facilities, you are saving $1.25 per item ($10-8.75).

While U.S. manufacturers may not be able to compete on "unit bid cost," oftentimes they can provide other qualitative advantages that make them more competitive.

By contrast, let's assume that a supplier from a low-cost country was able to deliver a unit price of $9, yet a Question score of 10 (i.e., 10 percent of the supplier's warehouse facilities have the required temperature and humidity controls). Using the same formula for comparison:

Total Cost = 75% x $9 + 25% x $9 x (100-10)/100 = $8.78

As you can see, in this case, the U.S. supplier is able to provide a lower cost by offering a superior "qualitative" score, despite a unit bid cost that is 10 percent higher.

Because the "Price Weight/RFP Question Scores Weight" ratio will be determined at the discretion of the commodity purchasing expert or other decision-maker based on the importance they place on it, the impact of a qualitative criterion can be diminished or expanded depending on the needs of individual purchasing companies. In this example, a 70/30 split would have yielded an even more favorable total cost for the U.S. supplier—likewise, an 80/20 split would have tipped the scales in favor of the low-cost country supplier.

Similarly, just as temperature and humidity controls were a factor in this example, companies may take into account factors such as percentage of on-time deliveries, number of defects per million, and number of rejected purchase orders.

The answer to the question of whether or not to use a higher-cost supplier or a supplier in a low-cost country will vary from case to case—there is no standard answer to such a question. However, manufacturers in developed countries can, in many cases, offer such advantages as a more optimized supply chain (which means shorter transit time and smaller warehouse space), low political and operational risk, and the ability to quickly innovate. This means that in instances where the decision maker is using advanced strategic sourcing technology, manufacturers in first-world developed nations are being considered for bids where they might not otherwise have been considered.

Sean Correll, Director of Consulting Services for Emptoris (www.emptoris.com), has worked directly with hundreds of clients to deliver solutions to their supply management organizations. He provides guidance during all phases of the sourcing lifecycle, and manages the strategic direction of projects.

Chapter Summary

The business operations that drive the supply chain can be grouped into four major categories: (1) plan; (2) source; (3) make; and (4) deliver. The business operations that comprise these categories are the day-to-day operations that determine how well the supply chain works. Companies must continually make improvements in these areas.

Planning refers to all the operations needed to plan and organize the operations in the other three categories. This includes operations such as demand forecasting, product pricing, and inventory management. Increasingly, it is these planning operations that determine the potential efficiency of the supply chain.

Sourcing includes the activities necessary to acquire the inputs to create products or services. This includes operations such as procurement and credit and collections. Both these operations have a big impact on the efficiency of a supply chain.

CHAPTER 3

Supply Chain Operations

Making and Delivering

After reading this chapter you will be able to

- Exercise an executive level understanding of operations involved in the categories of making products and delivering products
- Assess supply operations in your company that may be candidates for outsourcing

Many companies and the supply chains they participate in serve customers who are growing more sophisticated every year and demanding higher levels of service. Continuous improvements to the operations described in this chapter are needed to deliver the efficiency and responsiveness that evolving supply chains require.

Product Design (Make)

Product designs and selections of the components needed to build these products are based on the technology available and product performance requirements. Until recently, little thought was given to how the design of a product and the selection of its components affect the supply chain required to make the product. Yet these costs can become 50 percent or more of the product's cost.

When considering product design from a supply chain perspective the aim is to design products with fewer parts, simple designs, and modular construction from generic sub-assemblies. This way the parts can be obtained from a small group of preferred suppliers. Inventory can be kept in the form of generic sub-assemblies at appropriate locations in the supply chain. There will not be the need to hold large finished-goods inventories because customer demand can be met quickly by assembling final products from generic sub-assemblies as customer orders arrive.

The supply chain required to support a product is molded by the product's design. The more flexible, responsive, and cost efficient the supply chain is, the more likely the product will succeed in its market. To illustrate this point, consider the following scenario.

Fantastic Company designs a fantastic new home entertainment system with wide screen TV and surround sound. It performs to demanding specifications and delivers impressive results. But the electronics that power the entertainment center are built with components from 12 different suppliers.

Demand takes off and the company ramps up production. Managing quality control and delivery schedules for 12 suppliers is a challenge. More procurement managers and staff are hired. Assembly of the components is complex and delays in the delivery of components from any of the suppliers can slow down production rates. So buffer stocks of finished goods are kept to compensate for this.

Several new suppliers were required to provide the specified product components. One of them has quality control problems and has to be replaced and another supplier decides after several months to cease production of the component it supplies to Fantastic Company. They bring out a new component with similar features but not an exact replacement.

Fantastic Company has to suspend production of the home entertainment system while a team of engineers redesigns the part of the system that used the discontinued component so that it can use the new component. During this time, buffer stocks run out in some locations and sales are lost when customers go elsewhere.

A competitor called Nimble Company is attracted by the success of Fantastic Company and comes out with a competing product. Nimble Company designed a product with fewer parts and uses components from only four suppliers. The cost of procurement is much lower since they only have to coordinate four suppliers instead of 12. There are no production delays due to lack of component parts and product assembly is easier.

While Fantastic Company, who pioneered the market, struggles with a balky supply chain, Nimble Company provides the market with lower cost and a more reliable supply of the product. Nimble Company with its responsive and less-costly supply chain takes market share away from Fantastic Company.

What can be learned here? Product design defines the shape of the supply chain and this has a great impact on the cost and availability of the product. If product design, procurement, and manufacturing people can work together in the design of a product, there is a tremendous opportunity to create products that will be successful and profitable.

There is a natural tendency for design, procurement, and manufacturing people to have different agendas unless their actions are coordinated. Design people are concerned with meeting the customer requirements. Procurement people are interested in getting the best prices from a group of pre-screened preferred suppliers. Folks in manufacturing are looking for simple fabrication and assembly methods and long production runs.

Cross-functional product design teams with representatives from these three groups have the opportunity to blend the best insights from each group. Cross-functional teams can review the new product design and discuss the relevant issues. Can existing preferred suppliers provide the components needed? How many new suppliers are

needed? What opportunities are there to simplify the design and reduce the number of suppliers? What happens if a supplier stops producing a certain component? How can the assembly of the product
be made easier?

At the same time they are reviewing product designs, a cross-
functional team can evaluate existing preferred suppliers and manufacturing facilities. What components can existing suppliers provide?
What are their service levels and technical support capabilities? How
large a workforce and what kind of skills are needed to make the
product? How much capacity is needed and which facilities should be
used?

A product design that does a good job of coordinating the three
perspectives—design, procurement, and manufacturing—will result in a
product that can be supported by an efficient supply chain. This will give
the product a fast time to market and a competitive cost.

Production Scheduling (Make)

Production scheduling allocates available capacity (equipment, labor, and
facilities) to the work that needs to be done. The goal is to use available
capacity in the most efficient and profitable manner. The production
scheduling operation is a process of finding the right balance between
several competing objectives:

- *High Utilization Rates*—This often means long production runs
  and centralized manufacturing and distribution centers. The
  idea is to generate and benefit from economies of scale.

- *Low Inventory Levels*—This usually means short production runs
  and just-in-time delivery of raw materials. The idea is to minimize the assets and cash tied up in inventory.

- *High Levels of Customer Service*—Often requires high levels of
  inventory or many short production runs. The aim is to provide

the customer with quick delivery of products and not to run out of stock in any product.

When a single product is to be made in a dedicated facility, scheduling means organizing operations as efficiently as possible and running the facility at the level required to meet demand for the product. When several different products are to be made in a single facility or on a single assembly line, this is more complex. Each product will need to be produced for some period of time and then time will be needed to switch over to production of the next product.

The first step in scheduling a multi-product production facility is to determine the economic lot size for the production runs of each product. This is a calculation much like the economic order quantity (EOQ) calculation used in the inventory control process. The calculation of economic lot size involves balancing the production set-up costs for a product with the cost of carrying that product in inventory. If set ups are done frequently and production runs are done in small batches, the result will be low levels of inventory but the production costs will be higher due to increased set-up activity. If production costs are minimized by doing long production runs, then inventory levels will be higher and product inventory carrying costs will be higher.

Once production quantities have been determined, the second step is to set the right sequence of production runs for each product. The basic rule is that if inventory for a certain product is low relative to its expected demand, then production of this product should be scheduled ahead of other products that have higher levels of inventory relative to their expected demand. A common technique is to schedule production runs based on the concept of a product's "run-out time." The run-out time is the number of days or weeks it would take to deplete the product inventory on hand given its expected demand. The run-out time calculation for a product is expressed as

$R = P / D$

where:

R = run-out time

P = number of units of product on hand

D = product demand in units for a day or week

The scheduling process is a repetitive process that begins with a calculation of the run-out times for all products—their R-values. The first production run is then scheduled for the product with the lowest

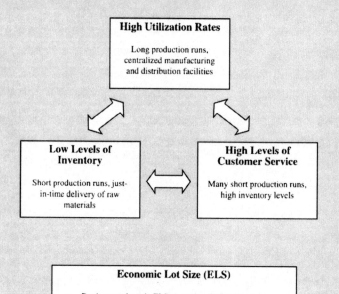

TIPS & TECHNIQUES

Production Scheduling

Production scheduling is a constant balancing act between utilization rates, inventory levels, and customer service levels.

High Utilization Rates

Long production runs, centralized manufacturing and distribution facilities

Low Levels of Inventory

Short production runs, just-in-time delivery of raw materials

High Levels of Customer Service

Many short production runs, high inventory levels

Economic Lot Size (ELS)

- Produce products in ELS quantities. ELS balances production set up costs against inventory carrying costs.

- Schedule production so that products with the shortest run out times are made first.

R-value. Assume that the economic lot size for that product has been produced, and then recalculate all product R-values. Again, select the product with the lowest R-value, and schedule its production run next. Assume the economic lot size is produced for this product and again recalculate all product R-values. This scheduling process can be repeated as often as necessary to create a production schedule going as far into the future as needed.

After scheduling is done, the resulting inventory should be continuously checked against actual demand. Is inventory building up too fast? Should the demand number be changed in the calculation of run-out time? Reality rarely happens as planned, so production schedules need to be constantly adjusted.

Facility Management (Make)

All facility-management decisions happen within the constraints set by decisions about facility locations. Location is one of the five supply chain drivers discussed in Chapter 1. It is usually quite expensive to shut down a facility or to build a new one, so companies live with the consequences of decisions they make about where to locate their facilities. Ongoing facility management takes location as a given and focuses on how best to use the capacity available. This involves making decisions in three areas:

1. The Role Each Facility Will Play
2. How Capacity Is Allocated in Each Facility
3. The Allocation of Suppliers and Markets to Each Facility

The role each facility will play involves decisions that determine what activities will be performed in which facilities. These decisions have a big impact on the flexibility of the supply chain. They largely define the ways that the supply chain can change its operations to meet changing market demand. If a facility is designated to perform only a single function or serve only a single market, it usually cannot easily be shifted to perform a different function or serve a different market if supply chain needs change.

How capacity is allocated in each facility is dictated by the role that the facility plays. Capacity allocation decisions result in the equipment and labor that is employed at the facility. It is easier to change capacity allocation decisions than to change location decisions, but still it is not cost effective to make frequent changes in allocation. So, once decided, capacity allocation strongly influences supply chain performance and profitability. Allocating too little capacity to a facility creates inability to meet demand and loss of sales. Too much capacity in a facility results in low utilization rates and higher supply chain costs.

The allocation of suppliers and markets to each facility is influenced by the first two decisions. Depending on the role that a facility plays and the capacity allocated to it, the facility will require certain kinds of suppliers and the products and volumes that it can handle mean that it can support certain types of markets. Decisions about the suppliers and markets to allocate to a facility will affect the costs for transporting supplies to the facility and transporting finished products from the facility to customers. These decisions also affect the overall supply chain's ability to meet market demands.

Order Management (Deliver)

Order management is the process of passing order information from customers back through the supply chain from retailers to distributors to service providers and producers. This process also includes passing information about order delivery dates, product substitutions, and back orders forward through the supply chain to customers. This process has long relied on the use of the telephone and paper documents such as purchase orders, sales orders, change orders, pick tickets, packing lists, and invoices.

A company generates a purchase order and calls a supplier to fill the order. The supplier who gets the call either fills the order from its own inventory or sources required products from other suppliers. If the supplier fills the order from its inventory, it turns the customer purchase order into a pick ticket, a packing list, and an invoice. If products are sourced from other suppliers, the original customer purchase order is turned into a purchase order from the first supplier to the next supplier. That supplier in turn will either fill the order from its inventory or source products from other suppliers. The purchase order it receives is again turned into documents such as pick tickets, packing lists, and invoices. This process is repeated through the length of the supply chain.

IN THE REAL WORLD

OfficeMax (www.OfficeMax.com) sells office supplies, office furniture, and office technology through a network of more than 800 stores. In the face of a tough economy and the need to improve supply chain operations, OfficeMax found that increased collaboration between different internal groups delivered significant benefits. Reuben Slone, Executive Vice President of Supply Chain, and Nikhil Sagar, Vice President of Inventory Management, describe how these improvements were achieved.

While OfficeMax was in the midst of executing a major turnaround plan, the onset of the "Great Recession" set a much greater hurdle, calling for it to overcome the effects of rapidly shrinking sales and volatile fuel costs. More than ever, OfficeMax had to deliver greatly improved working capital productivity and cost productivity levels while maintaining the customer experience through strong product availability. The case for internal collaboration was never stronger.

This was also the time that an economic value added (EVA) mindset was being developed within the company. EVA training was widely rolled out with the help of the University of Notre Dame,

(Continued)

and caused a much greater focus on asset and working capital management.

Reuben Slone, Executive Vice President of Supply Chain, called his team together and communicated his vision for the transformation needed to overcome the new economic challenge. The Supply Chain team had already established a powerful track record of delivering strong results against the turnaround plan, but the challenge at hand now called for the team to reach new and higher levels of performance, and develop and implement strategies that made conscious trade offs between supply chain operational costs and working capital productivity. The Supply Chain Operations and Inventory Management groups were asked to challenge each other's assumptions. This was not going to be easy—there was a lot of high performing talent in both groups. These were people that now had to work together on the same team.

Guidelines for the internal collaboration were established. All parties on the project were declared equal, no existing practices were considered sacred, and all parties were encouraged to question everything. The project group would make fact-based decisions, not emotional reactions, and the EVA model would be used as an empirical framework for decision making. The team was given a clear set of priorities—product availability, working capital productivity, and cost productivity. And finally, business goals were revised to reflect a broad set of shared supply chain outcomes.

Interpersonal relationships were focused on open discussions between the Supply Chain Operations and Inventory Management teams to discuss past problems (perceived or real) and close collaboration was strongly encouraged between the two teams. For example, a territorial mindset would no longer be tolerated, and a good idea would be a good idea, regardless of which team it came from. A low-cost team-building event was held to help lay the foundation for this new collaborative working model.

These guidelines and the resulting collaboration delivered a highly effective solution to the challenge. The team improved the use of delivery truck storage volume (known as cube utilization) through modification of limitations on stops per truck. They established the optimal number of deliveries for all stores based on the EVA model. By comparing delivery costs with working capital, the EVA model offers a very relevant framework for making supply chain trade-offs between operating cost and working capital.

The model's strength lies in its ability to compare the impact of decisions on post-tax net operating profit with the opportunity cost of working capital invested to implement that decision. In the delivery example, the team estimated the working capital impact of progressively increasing delivery frequencies to a store. This was done across clusters of stores grouped together based on similar sales-velocity levels. The EVA model was then used to identify the inflection point for each store velocity group—essentially the point at which the trade off was EVA positive—and this was used as the ideal delivery investment for that store group.

Clearly, higher-velocity stores deserved higher delivery frequencies, because they had the potential to sell more inventory. This model, however, allowed people to make the intuitive decision more of an exact science, allowing them to save valuable delivery-cost dollars without hurting service levels and minimizing the working capital impact. The functional teams worked together to allocate delivery frequencies down to the individual store level. In addition to looking at quarterly store rankings based on sales, they also incorporated unique location level constraints (such as isolated, single-store deliveries with higher cost per delivery) through collaborative review with the Transportation team.

The team modified delivery spacing to maximize productivity of deliveries through more even balancing of the point of sale (POS) capture between multiple deliveries. This ensured that for a two-delivery-per-week store, each replenishment run should target three or four days of sales. For a three-delivery-per-week store, each replenishment run should have two or three days of sales.

(*Continued*)

They next moved the creation of replenishment delivery schedules from evening to morning. When the deliveries were being created in the evenings, the POS capture for the current day were not completed yet, so the delivery plan was based on the POS movement up to the previous day only. By moving the delivery-creation process to the following morning, an additional day's worth of POS movement was captured, reducing the latency of the plan, without increasing the overall lead time, since the execution against the delivery plan was still allowed to commence at its normal time every morning.

The team also created Opportunistic Delivery Skipping—by introducing a check into the delivery schedule-creation process to eliminate extremely low cube loads. The inventory management group developed and executed the criteria for this check. They used criteria such as store-in-stocks measured as a percent of SKUs within a store that had one or more units on hand, ensuring at least one delivery a week and avoiding two consecutive skips.

The team then implemented palletization of loads—enabling easier loading and offloading, and allowing for reduced handling costs at distribution center (DC) and store level. The quicker receipt process at store level also enabled greater store flexibility around receipt planning; weekend deliveries and a broader receipt window being a couple of the favorable outcomes.

Next the group worked with OfficeMax's third-party transportation carrier, Werner, to migrate from a graduated stop charge to a flat stop charge. And finally, they shifted the delivery-truck trailer-storage capacity target from 1800 cubic feet to 2500 cubic feet.

All of this work resulted in breakthrough results. The total number of miles driven to retail stores was reduced by 24 percent, or 6.9 million miles, from 2007 to 2009. Store inventory shrunk by 16 percent year-over-year, while maintaining a record low number of stock outs per store. OfficeMax proved that internal collaboration enabled unprecedented supply chain improvements despite the extraordinary challenges of the Great Recession.

Reuben Slone is Executive Vice President, Supply Chain for OfficeMax. *Harvard Business Review* published two of his articles: "Leading a Supply Chain Turnaround" October 2004; and "Are You the Weakest Link in your Supply Chain?" September 2007. In May 2010, Harvard Business Press published his book, *The New Supply Chain Agenda: The 5 Steps that Drive Real Value.*

Nikhil Sagar is Vice President, Inventory Management for OfficeMax. He is the author of the article "CPFR At Whirlpool Corporation: Two Heads and An Exception Engine" *Journal of Business Forecasting,* Winter 2003–2004 and one of the authors of the article "Forecasting and Risk Analysis in Supply Chain Management – GARCH Proof of Concept" published in the book *Managing Supply Chain Risk and Vulnerability.*

In the last 20 years or so, supply chains have become noticeably more complex than they previously were. Companies now deal with multiple tiers of suppliers, outsourced service providers, and distribution-channel partners. This complexity has evolved in response to changes in the way products are sold, increased customer service expectations, and the need to respond quickly to new market demands.

The traditional order-management process has longer lead and lag times built into it due to the slow movement of data back and forth in the supply chain. This slow movement of data works well enough in some simple supply chains, but in complex supply chains faster and more accurate movement of data is necessary to achieve the responsiveness and efficiency that is needed. Modern order management focuses on techniques to enable faster and more accurate movement of order-related data.

In addition, the order-management process needs to do exception handling and provide people with ways to quickly spot problems and give them the information they need to take corrective action. This means the processing of routine orders should be automated and orders that require special handling because of issues such as insuf-ficient inventory, missed delivery dates, or customer change requests need to be brought to the attention of people who can handle these issues. Because of these requirements, order management is beginning to overlap and merge with a function called customer relationship management (CRM) that is often thought of as a marketing and sales function.

Because of supply chain complexity and changing market demands, order management is a process that is evolving rapidly. However, a handful of basic principles can be listed that guide this operation:

- *Enter the Order Data Once and Only Once*—Capture the data elec-tronically as close to its original source as possible and do not manually reenter the data as it moves through the supply chain. It is usually best if the customers themselves enter their orders into an order-entry system. This system should then transfer the relevant order data to other systems and supply chain partici-pants as needed for creation of purchase orders, pick tickets, in-voices, and so on.

- *Automate the Order Handling*—Manual intervention should be minimized for the routing and filling of routine orders. Com-puter systems should send needed data to the appropriate lo-cations to fulfill routine orders. Exception handling should identify orders with problems that require people to get in-volved to fix them.

- *Make Order Status Visible to Customers and Service Agents*—Let cus-tomers track their orders through all the stages, from entry of the order to delivery of the products. Customers should be able to see order status on demand without having to enlist the assistance of other people. When an order runs into problems, bring the order to the attention of service agents who can resolve the problems.

- *Integrate Order Management Systems with Other Related Systems to Maintain Data Integrity*—Order-entry systems need product descriptive data and product prices to guide the customer in making their choices. The systems that maintain this product data should communicate with order-management systems. Order data is needed by other systems to update inventory status, calculate delivery schedules, and generate invoices. Order data should automatically flow into these systems in an accurate and timely manner.

TIPS & TECHNIQUES

Four Rules for Efficient Order Management

1. Enter the Order Once and Only Once

Capture the order electronically as close to the original source as possible. Do not manually reenter the order.

2. Automate Order Routing

Automatically send orders to appropriate fulfillment locations. People do only exception handling.

3. Make Order Status Visible

Let customers and service agents see order status information automatically whenever they want.

4. Use Integrated Order Management Systems

Electronically connect order management systems with other related systems to maintain data integrity.

Delivery Scheduling (Deliver)

The delivery scheduling operation is of course strongly affected by the decisions made concerning the modes of transportation that will be used. The delivery-scheduling process works within the constraints set by transportation decisions. For most modes of transportation there are two types of delivery methods: direct deliveries and milk run deliveries.

Direct Deliveries

Direct deliveries are deliveries made from one originating location to one receiving location. With this method of delivery the routing is simply a matter of selecting the shortest path between the two locations. Scheduling this type of delivery involves decisions about the quantity to deliver and the frequency of deliveries to each location. The advantages of this delivery method are found in the simplicity of operations and delivery coordination. Since this method moves products directly from the location where they are made or stored in inventory to a location where the products will be used, it eliminates any intermediate operations that combine different smaller shipments into a single, combined larger shipment.

Direct deliveries are efficient if the receiving location generates economic order quantities (EOQs) that are the same size as the shipment quantities needed to make best use of the transportation mode being used. For instance, if a receiving location gets deliveries by truck and its EOQ is the same size as a truck load (TL), then the direct-delivery method makes sense. If the EOQ does not equal TL quantities, then this delivery method becomes less efficient. Receiving expenses incurred at the receiving location are high because this location must handle separate deliveries from the different suppliers of all the products it needs.

Milk Run Deliveries

Milk run deliveries are deliveries that are routed to either bring products from a single originating location to multiple receiving locations or deliveries that bring products from multiple originating locations to a single receiving location. Scheduling milk run deliveries is a much more complex task than scheduling direct deliveries. Decisions must be made about delivery quantities of different products, about the frequency of deliveries, and most importantly about the routing and sequencing of pickups and deliveries.

The advantages of this method of delivery are in the fact that more efficient use can be made of the mode of transportation used and the cost of receiving deliveries is lower because receiving locations get fewer and larger deliveries. If the EOQs of different products needed by a receiving location are less than truck load (LTL) amounts, milk run deliveries allow orders for different products to be combined until the resulting quantity equals a TL amount. If there are many receiving locations that each need smaller amounts of products, they can all be served by a single truck that starts its delivery route with a TL amount of products.

There are two main techniques for routing milk run deliveries. Each routing technique has its strengths and weaknesses, and each technique is more or less effective depending on the situation in which it is used and the accuracy of the data that is available. Both of these techniques are supported by software packages. The two techniques are:

1. The Savings Matrix Technique

2. The Generalized Assignment Technique

The savings matrix technique is the simpler of the two techniques and can be used to assign customers to vehicles and to design routes where there are delivery-time windows at receiving locations and other constraints. The technique is robust and can be modified to take into account many different constraints. It provides a reasonably good routing solution that can be put to practical use. Its weakness lies in the fact that it is often possible to find more cost-effective solutions using the generalized assignment technique. This technique is best used when there are many different constraints that need to be satisfied by the delivery schedule.

The generalized assignment technique is more sophisticated and usually gives a better solution than the savings matrix technique when there are no constraints on the delivery schedule other than the carrying capacity of the delivery vehicle. The disadvantage of this technique is that it has a harder time generating good delivery schedules as more and more constraints are included. This technique is best used when the delivery constraints are limited to vehicle capacity or to total travel time.

Delivery Sources

Deliveries can be made to customers from two sources:

1. Single-Product Locations
2. Distribution Centers

Single-product locations are facilities such as factories or warehouses where a single product or a narrow range of related items are available for shipment. These facilities are appropriate when there is a predictable and high level of demand for the products they offer and where shipments will be made only to customer locations that can receive the products in large, bulk amounts. They offer great economies of scale when used effectively.

Distribution centers are facilities where bulk shipments of products arrive from single-product locations. When suppliers are located a long distance away from customers, the use of a distribution center provides for economies of scale in long-distance transportation to bring large amounts of products to a location close to the final customers.

The distribution center may warehouse inventory for future shipment or it may be used primarily for crossdocking. Crossdocking is a technique pioneered by Wal-Mart where truckload shipments of single products arrive and are unloaded. At the same time these trucks are being unloaded, their bulk shipments are being broken down into smaller lots and combined with small lots of other products and loaded right back onto other trucks. These trucks then deliver the products to their final locations.

Distribution centers that use crossdocking provide several benefits. The first is that product flows faster in the supply chain since little inventory is held in storage. The second is that there is less handling expense since product does not have to be put away and then retrieved later from storage. The benefits of crossdocking can be realized when there are large predictable product volumes and when economies of scale can be had on both the inbound and outbound transportation. However, crossdocking is a demanding technique and it requires a considerable degree of coordination between inbound and outbound shipments.

Transporting and delivering goods is expensive so capabilities in this area are closely aligned with the actual needs of the market that the supply chain serves. Highly responsive supply chains usually have high transport and delivery costs because their customers expect quick delivery. This results in many small shipments of product. Less-responsive supply chains can aggregate orders over a period of time and make fewer and larger shipments. This results in more economies of scale and lower transport costs.

Return Processing (Deliver)

This process is also known as "reverse logistics." All supply chains have to deal with returns. This is often a difficult and inefficient process and in the Supply-Chain Council's supply chain operations reference (SCOR) model a whole category of activities has been devoted to this process. End customers, retailers, distributors, and manufacturers all return products under certain circumstances. The most common circumstances are: the wrong products were delivered; the products that were delivered were damaged in transit or were defective from the factory; and more product was delivered than was needed by the customer. All of these circumstances arise from supply chain inefficiencies that created the need to return products.

Companies and supply chains as a whole need to keep track of the kinds of returns that happen, their frequency, and if the return rates are rising or falling. Return processing should be efficient, yet at the same time remember that if other supply chain activities are managed effectively there will not be the need for a lot of return processing. Optimizing the return process can become an exercise in improving the efficiency of a process that should not be happening in the first place. If return rates are increasing it is far more effective to find and fix the sources of the problems that make returns necessary.

One area where returns are a value-added activity for the entire supply chain is where product recycling comes into play. In this area returns happen at the end of the product life cycle as the end user sends the product back to the manufacturer or some other organization that will either reuse or safely dispose of the product. As environmental awareness spreads and companies and governments adopt green policies and regulations, there will be a steadily growing volume of recycling activity. And recycling companies will emerge to handle this activity not as return processing but instead as a sourcing activity. This will be the way they acquire their raw materials.

IN THE REAL WORLD

Transforming public health supply chains in developing countries calls for collaboration between all parties in the supply chain, and Partnership for Supply Chain Management is a leader in this effort. Jay Heavner, director of communications, and David Jamieson, deputy director for project planning describe the work their organization is doing in this area.

The Partnership for Supply Chain Management (PFSCM) is a nonprofit organization established to manage the Supply Chain Management System (SCMS), a project of the United States' President's Emergency Plan for AIDS Relief (PEPFAR).

When PEPFAR began, HIV/AIDS was devastating many countries in sub-Saharan Africa and elsewhere. The disease was destroying communities and leaving an entire generation of orphans. Those living with HIV/AIDS had little or no hope of receiving treatment. In 2005, PEPFAR established SCMS to provide a reliable, cost-effective, and secure supply of products for HIV/AIDS programs focused on 15 countries. According to Richard Owens, SCMS Project Director, "PEPFAR and other international prevention, care, and treatment efforts could not begin to meet the need without national and regional supply chains that could operate at a scale and level of reliability never before seen in the developing world."

At the time, many doubted that HIV/AIDS commodities could be reliably delivered to the hardest-to-reach areas of the developing world. "But we knew they could," said Owens.

PFSCM partnered with some of the best-known companies in international public health and supply chain management, leveraging the expertise of each. As the project has developed, JSI Research and Training Institute (U.S.), Management Sciences for Health (U.S.), and Crown Agents (U.S., UK) operate field offices in 16 countries to manage technical assistance, client relations, and procurement. I+solutions (Netherlands) procures pharmaceuticals, and Crown Agents procures laboratory supplies and test kits.

(Continued)

Booz & Company monitors supply chain performance to identify areas for improvement. UPS (U.S.) manages international freight and logistics. 3i Infotech and Northrop Grumman provide world-class supply chain, Information Technology (IT), and enterprise management software and services. Additional team members provide specialty supply chain services.

When the project began, SCMS gathered staff from these companies at their offices to map out process flow on a wall measuring 8 feet high by 50 feet long. Using sticky notes and fueled by coffee and commitment, people clarified roles and responsibilities for each supply chain function and identified how they would measure supply chain performance. The scale of the health emergency meant that failure was not an option for PEPFAR or SCMS.

A key mandate of the project was to contribute to bringing down the cost of antiretroviral drugs (ARVs), which at the time was prohibitively expensive—about $1,500 per patient per year. Leveraging their purchasing power and international expertise, SCMS negotiated contracts with suppliers that over time lowered the average cost of ARVs to an affordable $100 to $200 per year. More than 90 percent of ARVs procured by SCMS are from generic suppliers approved by the U.S. Food and Drug Administration. Once SCMS was confident of the quantities required, they further reduced costs by shipping about 65 percent of commodities by sea and land versus costly airfreight, saving the U.S. government up to 80 percent on shipping costs—more than $36 million by September of 2010.

SCMS quickly built a global supply chain that began delivering large volumes of ARVs to regional distribution centers (RDCs) located in Ghana, Kenya, and South Africa, close to points of intended use. These RDCs were established by PHD (South Africa), one of their partners, and operate on a commercial basis, providing services to SCMS and other clients. This strategy meant that SCMS could reliably deliver the required amounts of ARVs to the hardest-hit countries even though the drugs were arriving in areas characterized by weak supply chain infrastructures.

The next step was to provide technical assistance to strengthen local supply chain operations. Lack of demand forecasting and supply planning was a key challenge: SCMS rejected one of the first orders they received for ARVs because they knew the recipient country already had an over-supply of stock that was likely to expire. The country had no visibility into what they had in stock or what they would need in the future.

In many countries, warehouses lacked basic equipment. Boxes were stacked on the ground, and inventory was tracked manually, if at all. Loss of stock through expiry and damage was common. And cold chain capabilities where pharmaceuticals and other perishable goods were kept at cool or frozen temperatures was rarely an option. Through a range of short- and long-term technical assistance—warehousing and distribution, logistics management information systems, and more—SCMS is helping transform the public health supply chains in many of the countries where it operates.

The project was designed to procure ARVs and test kits, and a relatively limited number of other products. But it soon became apparent that laboratory equipment, reagents, and other supplies were equally essential. Lists of these commodities can include thousands of items, many of which are practically identical. This represented a very different procurement and supply challenge. Even agreeing on product specifications was a major hurdle. The SCMS team has supported regional and national harmonization efforts to reduce the range of products being procured, and published a catalog of products available through the project to help clients with product specification.

Developing countries face a major challenge from poor-quality and counterfeit products. So the U.S. Government rightly demanded that SCMS establish a world-class quality assurance program. Partnering with North-West University in South Africa to sample and test ARVs and other pharmaceuticals, "SCMS has prevented any sub-standard medicines from reaching patients through our supply chain," said Owens.

(*Continued*)

When asked how these activities might be different in a not-for-profit world as opposed to a for-profit business, Owens observed that the technical approach is the same. SCMS brings industry best practices to their supply chain operations and to the developing countries where they work. Their supply chain includes many private sector companies, and their regional distribution centers now serve a number of public and private sector clients. "What's different," said Owens, "is the U.S. Government funds the products while local government entities like ministries of health define their needs. Interestingly, our performance is as good as, or usually better than, the private sector in Africa and elsewhere. The only real difference is that we're not motivated by profit. Our mission is to help save lives."

Jay Heavner is Communications Director for SCMS. He is the author of various publications for the project, including "From Emergency Relief to Sustained Response: long-term success of HIV/AIDS programs depends on integrated national and global supply chains", and "Three years of saving lives through stronger HIV/AIDS supply chains: A report on the global impact of SCMS."

David Jamieson is Deputy Director for Project Planning and Global Partnerships for SCMS. He is a co-author of "Improving the Economic Efficiency of PEPFAR Treatment Programs Through Increased Use of Generic Antiretroviral Drugs," *Journal of the American Medical Association* published in June 2010. He also contributed to procurement guides for condoms published by World Health Organization (WHO), and for essential drugs for WHO and the World Bank.

Supply Chain Operations Can Be Outsourced

After reading about the 11 basic supply chain operations in this chapter and the previous one, which of these operations are done by in-house staff in your company? How many of these operations are core competencies? How many of these operations bring money into your company and how many of them consume money?

The relentless pressure on profit margins that free markets create is a driving force behind the growth of outsourcing. What may be considered as overhead for Company A may be a service that Company B can offer and make a profit doing so. Company B may be able to offer this service for a price lower than it costs Company A to do it in house. Company A is going to consider outsourcing.

The traditional participants in supply chains are producers, logistics providers, distributors, and retailers. How many of the 10 supply chain operations can be called core competencies of any of these organizations? There are some operations such as credit and collections, product design, and order management that may not be a core competency of any of the traditional participants. This creates opportunities for new service providers to take on these operations and offer them to the other supply chain participants. All 10 of these operations need to be done for the supply chain as a whole, but they do not all need to be done by any single company and indeed they cannot all be done well by any single company.

The other force that drives outsourcing is the growing sophistication of the markets that supply chains serve. Gone are the days when Ford Motor Company could run a vertically integrated company that did everything from mine iron ore to produce steel to design and build automobiles. That structure was only possible because the markets it served were content to buy mass quantities of standard products. As Henry Ford said when asked about what colors his customers could choose from, "They can have any color they want as long as it's black." Markets today demand and pay for all sorts of innovations, customized features, and services. This creates complexity in the supply chain, and participants who specialize in certain areas bring the expertise and efficiencies that are required to manage this complexity.

A collaborative supply chain can enable a group of smaller companies to better compete with their larger industry rivals. There are tangible benefits generated by collaboration and also obstacles to overcome before the benefits can be achieved. Joel Sutherland, managing director at the Center for Value Chain Research at Leigh University (http://www.lehigh.edu/cvcr), describes a supply chain collaboration project called "The Confection Connection" and the results they achieved.

Candy maker Just Born Inc. may not be a household name but their products are known around the world. Located in Bethlehem, Pennsylvania, USA, Just Born was founded in 1923 and is now the eighth-largest confectioner in the United States. The company's most famous brands include marshmallow Peeps, Mike and Ike, Hot Tamales, and Peanut Chews.

The candy is manufactured in Bethlehem, and then is shipped from there to a nearby distribution center (DC) run by OHL, a global 3PL services provider. From the DC, product ships out to customers nationwide, in either less-than-truckload (LTL) or truck-load (TL) shipments. Just Born serves LTL customers via distribution centers known as "pool points." There, third-party logistics (3PL) providers break down truckloads into smaller shipments for delivery. Full truckloads, meanwhile, move directly from the DC to customers' facilities.

In 2007, Just Born began a major re-engineering of its supply chain network. To design the optimal network Just Born decided to seek help from outside the company, and they opted to work with researchers at the Center for Value Chain Research (CVCR) at Lehigh University, also located in Bethlehem. The researchers at CVCR built a mathematical model for optimizing the company's distribution network.

PROJECT RESULTS

The model's objective is to minimize the manufacturer's average transportation cost. This includes line-haul costs for truckloads to pool points and direct customers as well as the per-pound cost to ship to LTL customers. The model is capable of deciding, for a representative period of time, which of the 28 available pool points should be used and how much volume each pool point should handle. The model also indicates which customers should be served by direct truckload and which by LTL, and how truckload shipments should be scheduled throughout the network. The researchers aggregated Just Born's customers to the three-digit ZIP (postal code) level, and excluded customers that typically receive small or infrequent shipments. The resulting data set modeled roughly 85 percent of the manufacturer's average weekly volume.

The model revealed that Just Born's existing network was too costly and not as efficient as it could be. For example, there were too many pool points—the optimal number turned out to be 22, rather than 28, locations. But the researchers found that the shipper had some leeway in that regard; it could still achieve near-optimal results with anywhere from 20 to 24 pool points (Exhibit 3.1).

EXHIBIT 3.1	

Cost vs. Number of Pool Points Used

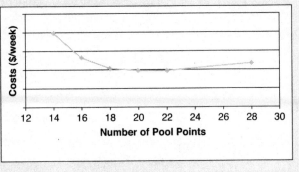

(Continued)

NEXT STEP—COLLABORATION

Just Born is now increasing the amount of freight shipped out of this DC by including other confectionery shippers to form a collaboration of like shippers delivering product to like customers. This collaborative arrangement is known as the "Confection Connection". It is estimated that this new solution will save the collaborating companies approximately 25 percent of their total transportation costs per year, as shown in Exhibit 3.2.

EXHIBIT 3.2

Estimated Combined Freight Spend Savings Is 25 Percent

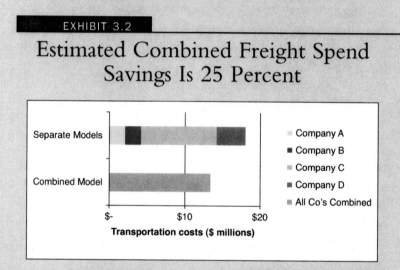

The concept of freight consolidation is not new, but it is tricky for companies to grasp when they are being asked to partner with competitors in a collaborative way. Yet for smaller confectioneries like Just Born, who are competing with giants like Mars, Nestle, and Hershey, collaborating is a way to achieve the critical mass to compete more effectively with these larger companies. Working with competitors makes sense, especially when their deliveries are going to the same retailers who prefer to have fewer trucks pulling in and out of their own distribution centers.

And partnering helps candy makers create ideal truckloads. For instance, Just Born makes huge shipments of marshmallow Peeps around holiday periods, but they are so light it is better to package

EXECUTIVE INSIGHT (*CONTINUED*)

them in trucks with heavier freight, achieving an optimal weight-to-cube ratio.

COLLABORATION VALUE ADD

Collaborative transportation management (CTM) demonstrates that opportunities to add value increase as multiple shipper networks are integrated, connecting a broader sphere of shippers, receivers, and carriers and enabling enhanced opportunities for communication and improved execution. Central to the effort to connect a network of collaborating parties is the development of a common information hub. In general, the level of information sharing increases with the level of collaboration. Exhibit 3.3 portrays the extension of value contribution as the collaborative network expands and information sharing increases.

EXHIBIT 3.3

Value Contribution as the Collaborative Network Expands

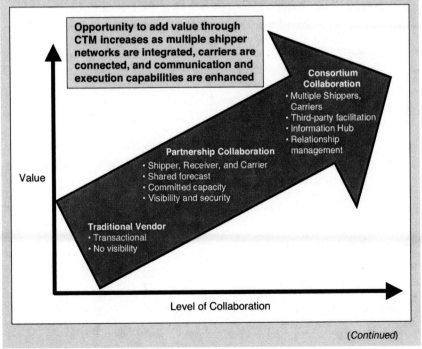

Opportunity to add value through CTM increases as multiple shipper networks are integrated, carriers are connected, and communication and execution capabilities are enhanced

Consortium Collaboration
- Multiple Shippers, Carriers
- Third-party facilitation
- Information Hub
- Relationship management

Partnership Collaboration
- Shipper, Receiver, and Carrier
- Shared forecast
- Committed capacity
- Visibility and security

Traditional Vendor
- Transactional
- No visibility

Value

Level of Collaboration

(*Continued*)

Key Enablers and Roadblocks to Collaboration

In order for collaborative initiatives to succeed, key enablers must be in place. These enablers support best practices in critical activity areas and help overcome the roadblocks to success that inevitably surround collaboration.

There are a number of key enablers that are equally important. Successful collaboration is a function of how well people work together both internally and with collaboration partners. The following enablers are related to the human side of CTM:

❶ *Common Interest*—All parties need to have a stake in the collaboration's outcome to ensure their ongoing commitment.

❷ *Openness*—For a relationship to work, the partners must openly discuss their practices and processes. Sometimes this means sharing information traditionally considered proprietary (though adherence to anti-trust guidelines remains prerequisite).

❸ *Recognizing who and what is important*—Not all prospective collaborators and supply chain activities are created equal. Choose those that will deliver the greatest benefits.

❹ *Clear expectations*—All parties need to understand what is expected of them and others in the relationship.

❺ *Leadership*—Without a champion to move collaboration forward, nothing significant will ever be accomplished.

❻ *Cooperation, not punishment*—When things go wrong in a relationship, punitive actions seldom make them better. The right approach is to solve the problem jointly.

❼ *Trust*—This basic human quality must be evident throughout the organization—at every management level and functional area.

❽ *Benefit Sharing*—In a true relationship, the partners need to share both the pain and the gain—use of a shared modular supply chain scorecard can help.

⑨ *Advanced IT*—IT is essential to enabling collaborative relations across the supply chain. Communication and process automation achieved through IT enables CTM by facilitating real-time, accurate data transfer.

In addition to enablers, firms seeking to implement CTM should recognize and avoid roadblocks to CTM success. Many of these roadblocks stem from behaviors, attitudes, and practices associated with traditional business operations. The following list summarizes primary potential roadblocks to successful collaboration, as identified at Lehigh University's Center for Value Chain Research.

① *Control and Trust*—How is knowledge shared in such relationships? Who owns and controls the intellectual property gained in such relationships and how is this shared?

② *Sharing of proprietary information*—How is information protected from getting into the hands of competitors?

③ *Ethical issues*—The very nature of collaborative relationships has not yet been clearly ironed out.

④ *Integration of systems and technology*—When sharing information and integrating systems, each company within the relationship must have accurate data to share.

⑤ *Going global*—Due to the size and scope of many businesses today, the complexity of global collaboration is something that has not yet been demonstrated.

⑥ *Measuring and documenting benefits*—While there are a number of different metrics in use today, there is no easy way to document total CTM benefits.

⑦ *Structure*—Establishing effective and implementable "standards" will be needed before such relationships can be successful and sustainable.

(Continued)

EXECUTIVE INSIGHT (*CONTINUED*)

SUMMARY

Collaboration is not meant for every situation. That is, collaborative efforts must result in gains for everyone involved. If outcomes involve only one party gaining, and the winner's gains are not shared to offset the losses of others, the collaboration should not be pursued. Therefore, no single party can only consider what it stands to gain from the effort. The initiative must represent a collective win.

The final requirement is ability. Having good opportunities and good intentions will only get you so far. The partners must individually and collectively have the skills and information capabilities to seize the opportunities. Management and analytical skills are necessary for finding the value and selling the prospects with internal and external parties.

While outside parties such as 3PL providers are not required of CTM, they can serve as facilitators of communication or execution. This is particularly true when potential for gains are found among trading partners but capabilities are lacking. The presence of an unbiased, capable intermediary can sometimes make collaboration possible when it might not exist otherwise.

Joel Sutherland is Managing Director, Center for Value Chain Research, and Adjunct Professor at Lehigh University. He is also president at Envoy Inc, a supply chain consulting company he founded in 1994. He has more than 30 years experience as a supply chain professional working for manufacturers, wholesale distributors, and third party service providers and is a frequent speaker at supply chain conferences.

Chapter Summary

The Make category includes the operations required to develop and build the products and services that a supply chain provides. Operations that are in this category are: product design; production management; and facility and management. The Deliver category of operations encompasses the activities that are part of receiving customer orders and delivering products to customers. The two main operations are order entry/fulfillment and product delivery. These two operations constitute the core connections between companies in a supply chain. The third operation in this category is return processing. This activity happens when customers need to return a product for any reason.

The relentless pressure on profit margins that free markets create is a driving force behind the growth of outsourcing. What may be considered as overhead for Company A may be a service that Company B can offer and make a profit doing so. Company B may be able to offer this service for a price lower than it costs Company A to do it in house. In that case Company A is going to consider outsourcing.

CHAPTER 4

Using Information Technology

After reading this chapter you will be able to

- Assess the technology that is available to support and enable effective supply chain operations
- Appreciate new technology trends and the business capabilities that they will enable
- Better understand how to apply this technology to your own supply chain operations

Information Systems that Support the Supply Chain

Information technology supports internal operations and also collaboration between companies in a supply chain. Using high-speed data networks and databases, companies can share data to better manage the supply chain as a whole and their own individual positions within the supply chain. The effective use of this technology is a key aspect of a company's success.

Although many readers of this book do not need to understand all the aspects and nuances of information technology (IT), every reader does need to understand the basic concepts that apply to using this technology effectively. Let's start with a simple reference model to describe IT. Then we'll use this model to classify and gain perspective on available technology and how it can be used.

All information systems are composed of technology that performs three main functions: data capture and communication; data storage and retrieval; and data manipulation and reporting. Different information systems have different combinations of capabilities in these three functional areas. The specific combination of capabilities is dependent on the demands of the job that a system is designed to perform. Information systems that are employed to support various aspects of supply chain management are created from technologies that perform some combination of these three functions.

Data Capture and Data Communications

The first functional area is composed of systems and technology that create high speed data capture and communications networks. We look at:

- The Internet
- Broadband
- Electronic Data Interchange (EDI)
- eXtensible Markup Language (XML)

The Internet

The Internet is the global data communications network that uses what is known as Internet Protocol (IP) standards to move data from one point to another. The Internet is the universal communication network that can connect with all computers and communication devices. Once a device is hooked into the Internet it can communicate with any other device that is also connected to the Internet, regardless of the different internal data formats that they may use.

Before the Internet, companies had to put in expensive dedicated networks to connect themselves to other companies and move data between their different computer systems. Now, with the Internet already in place, different companies have a way to quickly and inexpensively connect their computer systems. If needed, extra data protection and privacy can be provided by using technology to create virtual private networks (VPN), which utilize the Internet to create very secure communication networks.

Broadband

Basically, this means any communication technology that offers high-speed (faster than a 56Kb dial-up modem) access to the Internet with a connection that is always on. This includes technologies such as co-axial cable, digital subscriber line (DSL), metro Ethernet, fixed wireless, and satellite. Broadband technology is spreading and, as it does, it becomes possible for companies in a supply chain to easily and inexpensively hook up with each other and exchange large volumes of data in real time.

Most companies have connected themselves internally using local area network (LAN) technology such as Ethernet that gives them plenty of internal communication capability. Many companies have connected some or all of their different geographical locations using wide area network (WAN) technology such as T1, T3, or frame relay. What now needs to happen is high speed, relatively low-cost connections between separate companies, and that is the role that wireless broadband and cloud computing is playing (see pg. 133).

Electronic Data Interchange (EDI)

Electronic data interchange (EDI) is a technology that was developed to transmit common types of data between companies that do business with each other. Large companies in the manufacturing, automobile, and transportation industries deployed it in the 1980s. It was built to automate back office transactions such as the sending and receiving of purchase orders (known as an "850" transaction), invoices (an "810"), advance shipment notices (an "856"), and back order status (an "855") to name just a few. It originally was built to run on big, mainframe computers using value-added networks (VANs) to connect with other trading partners. That technology was expensive.

Many companies have large existing investments in EDI systems and find that it is very cost effective to continue to use these systems to communicate with other businesses. Standard EDI data sets have been defined for a large number of business transactions. Companies can decide which data sets they will use and which parts of each data set they will use. EDI systems can now run on any type of computer from mainframe to PC and can use the Internet for data communication as well as VANs. Costs for EDI technology have come down considerably.

Extensible Markup Language (XML)

XML (eXtensible Markup Language) is a technology that is being developed to transmit data in flexible formats between computers and between computers and humans. Where EDI uses rigid, predefined data sets to send data back and forth, XML is extensible and, once certain standards have been agreed upon, XML can also be used to communicate a wide range of different kinds of data and related processing instructions between different computer systems. XML can also be used to communicate between computers and humans because it can drive user interfaces such as web browsers and respond to human input. Unlike EDI, the exact data transactions and processing sequences do not have to be previously defined when using XML.

There are many evolving XML standards in different industries but as yet none of these standards has been widely adopted. The industry that has made the most progress in adopting XML standards is the electronics industry. It is beginning to implement the RosettaNet XML standards.

In the near term, XML and EDI are merging into hybrid systems that are evolving to meet the needs of companies in different supply chains. It is not cost effective for companies with existing EDI systems that are working well enough to replace them with newer XML systems all at once. So XML extensions are being grafted onto EDI systems. Software is available to quickly translate EDI data to XML and then back to EDI. Service providers are now offering Internet-based EDI to smaller suppliers who do business with large EDI-using customers.

In the longer term, EDI will be wholly consumed by XML as XML standards are agreed upon and start to spread. As these standards spread they will enable very flexible communication between companies in a supply chain. XML will allow communication that is more spontaneous and freeform, like any human language. This kind of communication will drive a network of computers and people interacting with other computers and other people. The purpose of this network will be to co-ordinate supply operations on a daily basis.

Data Storage and Retrieval

The second functional area of an information system is composed of technology that stores and retrieves data. This activity is performed by database technology. A database is an organized grouping of data that is stored in an electronic format. The most common type of database uses what is called "relational database" technology. Relational databases store related groups of data in individual tables and provide for retrieval of data with the use of a standard language called structured query language (SQL).

A database is a model of the business processes for which it collects and stores data. The model is defined by the level of detail in the data it collects. The design of every database has to strike a balance between highly aggregate data at one extreme and highly detailed data at the other extreme. This balance is arrived at by weighing the needs and budget of a business against the increasing cost associated with more and more detailed data. The balance is reflected in what is called the data model of the database.

As events occur in a business process, there are database transactions. The data model of the database determines which transactions can be recorded since the database cannot record transactions that are either more detailed or more aggregated than provided for in the data model. These transactions can be recorded as soon as they happen—called "real-time" updating—or they may be captured and recorded in batches that happen on a periodic basis—called "batch" updating.

A database also provides for the different data-retrieval needs of the people who use it. People doing different jobs will want different combinations of data from the same database. These different combinations are called "views." Views can be created and made available to people who need them to do their jobs. For instance, consider a database that contains sales history for a range of different products to a range of different customers. A customer view of this data might show a customer the different products and quantities they purchased over a period of time and show detail of the purchases at each customer location. A manufacturer view might show all the customers who bought their group of products over a period of time and show detail for the products that each customer bought.

Data Manipulation and Reporting

Different supply chain systems are created by combining processing logic to manipulate and display data with the technology required to capture, communicate, store, and retrieve data. The way that a system manipulates and displays the data that flows through it is determined by the specific business operations that the system is designed to support. Information systems contain the processing logic needed by the business operations they support. Chopra and Meindl define several kinds of systems that support supply chain operations:

- Enterprise Resource Planning (ERP)
- Procurement Systems
- Advanced Planning and Scheduling (APS)
- Transportation Planning Systems
- Demand Planning
- Customer Relationship Management (CRM) and Sales Force Automation (SFA)
- Supply Chain Management (SCM)
- Inventory Management Systems
- Manufacturing Execution Systems (MES)
- Transportation Scheduling Systems
- Warehouse Management Systems (WMS)

Enterprise Resource Planning

Enterprise Resource Planning (ERP) systems gather data from across multiple functions in a company. ERP systems monitor orders, production schedules, raw material purchases, and finished-goods inventory. They support a process-oriented view of business that cuts across different functional departments. For instance, an ERP system can view the entire order-fulfillment process and track an order from the procurement of material to fill the order to delivery of the finished product to the customer.

ERP systems come in modules that can be installed on their own or in combination with other modules. There are usually modules for finance, procurement, manufacturing, order fulfillment, human resources, and logistics. The focus of these modules is primarily on carrying out and monitoring daily transactions. ERP systems often lack the analytical capabilities needed to optimize the efficiency of these transactions.

Procurement Systems

Procurement systems focus on the procurement activities that take place between a company and its suppliers. The purpose of these systems is to streamline the procurement process and make it more efficient. Such systems typically replace supplier catalogs with a product database that contains all of the needed information about products the company buys. They also keep track of part numbers, prices, purchasing histories, and supplier performance.

Procurement systems allow people to compare the price and performance capabilities of different suppliers. This way the best suppliers are identified so that relationships can be established with these suppliers and prices negotiated. The routine transactions that occur in the purchasing process can then be largely automated.

Advanced Planning and Scheduling

Advanced Planning and Scheduling (APS) systems are highly analytical applications whose purpose is to assess plant capacity, material availability, and customer demand. These systems then produce schedules for what to make in which plant and at what time. APS systems base their calculations on the input of transaction-level data that is extracted from ERP or legacy transaction-processing systems. They then use linear programming techniques and other sophisticated algorithms to create their recommended schedules.

Transportation Planning Systems

Transportation Planning Systems are systems that calculate what quantity of materials should be brought to what locations at what times. The systems enable people to compare different modes of transportation, different routes, and different carriers. Transportation plans are then created using these systems. The software for these systems is sold by system vendors. Other providers—known as content vendors—provide the data that is needed by these systems, such as mileage, fuel costs, and shipping tariffs.

Demand Planning

Demand-planning systems use special techniques and algorithms to help a company forecast its demand. These systems take historical sales data and information about planned promotions and other events that can affect customer demand, such as seasonality and market trends. They use this data to create models that help predict future sales.

Another feature that is often associated with demand planning systems is revenue management. This feature lets a company experiment with different price mixes for its different products in light of the predicted demand. The idea is to find a mix of products and prices that maximizes total revenue to the company. Companies in the travel industry such as airlines, rental car agencies, and hotels are already using revenue management techniques. These techniques will spread to other industries.

Customer Relationship Management and Sales Force Automation

Systems of this type automate many of the tasks related to servicing existing customers and finding new customers. Customer Relationship Management (CRM) systems track buying patterns and histories of customers.

They consolidate a company's customer-related data in a place where it is quickly accessible to customer-service representatives and salespeople who use the data to better respond to customer requests.

Sales Force Automation (SFA) systems allow a company to better co-ordinate and monitor the activities of its sales force. These systems automate many of the tasks related to scheduling sales calls and follow-up visits and preparing quotes and proposals for customers and prospects.

Supply Chain Management

Supply Chain Management (SCM) systems are suites of different supply chain applications, such as those described here, that are tightly inte-grated with each other. An SCM system could be an integrated suite that contains advanced planning and scheduling, transportation planning, de-mand planning, and inventory planning applications. SCM systems rely on ERP or relevant legacy systems to provide them with the data to support the analysis and planning that they do. These systems have the analytical capabilities to support strategic-level decision making.

Inventory Management Systems

These systems support the activities described in Chapter 2 that are part of inventory management such as tracking historical demand patterns for products, monitoring inventory levels for different products, and cal-culating economic order quantities and the levels of safety inventory that should be held for each product. These systems are used to find the right balance for a company between the cost of carrying inventory and the cost of running out of inventory and losing sales revenue because of that.

Manufacturing Execution Systems

The focus is on carrying out the production activities in a factory. This kind of system is less analytical than an APS. It produces short-term production schedules and allocates raw materials and production resources within a single manufacturing plant. A Manufacturing Execution System (MES) is similar in its operational focus to an ERP system and frequently MES software is produced by ERP software vendors.

Transportation Scheduling Systems

Systems in this category are similar to ERP and MES applications in that they are less analytical and more focused on daily operational issues. A transportation scheduling system produces short-term transportation and delivery schedules that are used by a company.

Warehouse Management Systems

Warehouse Management Systems (WMS) support daily warehouse operations. They provide capabilities to efficiently run the ongoing operations of a warehouse. These systems keep track of inventory levels and stocking locations within a warehouse and they support the actions needed to pick, pack, and ship product to fill customer orders.

New Trends in Supply Chain Technology

The demands of our global economy are forcing companies and entire supply chains to adopt more flexible and responsive modes of operation. Both the interdependence of companies and economies, and the rapid and often unexpected pace of events call for responses from companies that are faster and also more well thought out than what was required in the past.

In order to rise to this challenge, companies must find ways to leverage the supply chain systems previously described, which they already have in place or that they are currently installing. They need to find ways to provide these systems with more timely and more accurate data and better coordinate the use of these systems. Companies need to achieve overall supply chain improvements and not just improvements in individual supply chain activities.

There are four promising technologies that can be used to complement existing supply chain systems. These technologies do not replace existing systems. In fact they require that there be an existing infrastructure of systems to provide the foundation upon which they can be installed.

Once installed, these technologies provide ways to better collect data needed by existing systems. They also provide better ways to share data among systems and to make that data visible and meaningful to people who need it. They also provide people with a way to devise well thought out and more effective responses to challenges and opportunities. These four technologies are:

1. Radio Frequency Identification (RFID)
2. Business Process Management (BPM)
3. Business Intelligence (BI)
4. Simulation Modeling

IN THE REAL WORLD

Markets and customer needs are evolving constantly and supply chains need to deliver new capabilities to enable companies to thrive. And often there is a pressing need to move quickly. Robert Meshew, a senior director at Microsoft (www.Microsoft. com), describes a project where he and his team delivered a new physical and digital supply chain in 90 days.

In advance of Microsoft's launch of Office 2010, our largest retail customer wanted to greatly reduce their on-hand inventory, decrease operations costs, and increase their product in-stock percentage. The retailer pushed our sales team to bring them solutions or risk not getting their full support around this important launch for Microsoft.

Our sales team urgently engaged our combined supply chain and IT team to determine how best to accomplish this very challenging goal. Our teams had historically been responsible only for delivering physical boxes of software to the retailers at the right times and in the right quantities. When we first looked at this new problem we saw the traditional solutions—such as collaborative forecasting and planning, lower packaging costs, and consigned inventory—but these solutions didn't deliver the dramatic improvements we wanted.

This problem required a whole new solution that we didn't have readily available. After evaluating possible alternatives, our team decided on a key card that could be activated at the retailer point of sale terminal as the best solution. These cards could be manufactured at a very low price, and would not be active until scanned. The customer could then go to a Microsoft web site to download a copy of the software at a later time. We would also work with the PC manufacturers to pre-load Office 2010 onto their machines to allow customers to instantly access the software with the key.

Benefits of the Point-of-Sale-Activated (POSA) card solution are the following:

1. Friendly to retailers on margin and turns—they don't pay for the cards up front

2. Support a consistent experience for all retailers across all Microsoft consumer products—single invoice and supply chain point of contact

3. Reduce Shrinkage and inventory risk for the retailers

4. Increase product add on sales with PCs sold—impulse buys at the cash register

5. Provide more consumer choice—retailers can afford a broader assortment of software since they aren't paying for inventory in advance, and the POSA cards don't take a lot of shelf space.

(Continued)

There were challenges for our team in building this POSA solution. First, the new version of Microsoft Office was nearing release and we needed to have the solution within 90 days. Secondly, the lead-time for servers in our crowded data center was greater than 90 days. Finally, we only had a limited amount of funding, as it was at the end of our fiscal year and budgets had been spent.

Given the constraints on the project, we decided that we needed to deliver the solution based on some guiding project principles:

1. We needed to deliver quickly and in iterative fashion, and would use the limited funding constraint as a friend to focus us only on the core elements of the solution—the most important system features. We would structure the work into a series of 30-day releases (blitzes) to achieve this.

2. We would co-locate our team. Given our tight timeline we needed to eliminate communication and decision delays. All business and IT people would work together in the same location.

3. We would look to the cloud to host the solution, as we didn't have the time to get physical hardware installed and configured without reprioritizing existing work in the pipeline.

4. We would use our existing billing, back office systems, and processes in manual mode until we had time to do the proper systems integration in a release soon after the launch of Microsoft Office.

The combined project team worked hard and narrowed scope to deliver the core solution. The POSA solution launched on time and exceeded the expectations of our business sponsors. In the first four weeks of service the system delivered thousands of keys successfully to customers, with minimal customer support issues and 100 percent uptime. Our retail partner exceeded their sales goals for the POSA product and it was highlighted as a key success for our sales team and the Office product group.

Since the initial launch we have implemented additional retailers and added more products, including Windows and Xbox games. We have continued to iteratively add more features to the system, and in addition to activation, we now support key delivery to in-store kiosks and we can print keys on receipts generated by store point-of-sale systems. The solution has been a huge success and has earned our supply chain and IT team a seat at the business management table. We have been called out of the "back office" to work closely with our business executives to define and design the future Digital Supply Chain for all of Microsoft's product groups.

SOLUTION OVERVIEW

Exhibit 4.1 illustrates how the POSA solution works. Tokens are printed on the cards and loaded into a database. The tokens are associated to keys that will unlock the software. When a POSA card is sold we receive a message from the retailer that sets a flag against the respective token and key pair in our database. We use this activation request to send a sales order event to our billing and financial system. These just-in-time retailer activations are then aggregated into a monthly invoice to the retailers.

The consumer at a later time goes to a Microsoft web site to retrieve the key. If a sale hasn't occurred there won't be a key associated with the token, and an error message will be returned if someone tries to activate a key they did not purchase. There is also a link to a download location on the web site for the product if it isn't already pre-loaded on the customer's PC.

Robert Meshew leads the Architecture and Production Support organization for Microsoft's Interactive Entertainment Division manufacturing, supply chain, and information solutions (MSCIS) group. Robert has 18 years of combined supply chain and IT experience and enjoys putting both disciplines into practice to architect and design solutions that help the business achieve sustainable and strategic advantage.

(Continued)

EXHIBIT 4.1

Process Flow for POSA Supply Chain Solution

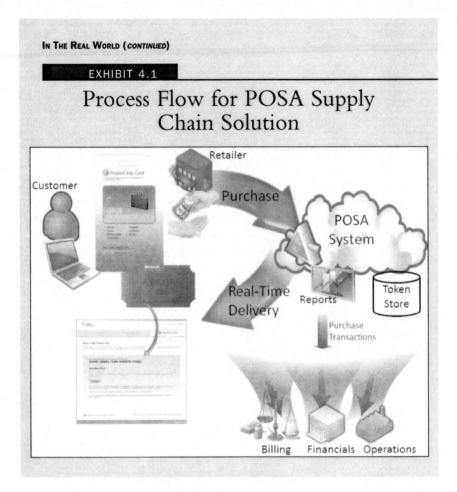

Radio Frequency Identification

This is a much-talked-about technology for supply chain management. What is new is the opportunity to start using this technology widely to track pallets, cases, and even individual items as they move through supply chains from manufacturers to end-use customers. Radio frequency identification (RFID) technology itself is not new and has been in use in specialized applications for more than 20 years. Now the technology is maturing and the related costs of using it are coming way down. Where the technology was once used to track movement of items within a facility or within a single company, it is now becoming cost effective to start using RFID to track products moving through supply chains that stretch all the way around the globe.

When we talk about RFID we need to understand that there are two parts to this discussion. The first part is about the technology itself, the electronic devices that make RFID systems a reality. The second part is about the information or the content this technology enables us to capture and share. It is important to understand both parts of RFID in order to appreciate how it can be such a powerful driver of supply chain efficiency.

RFID Technology RFID technology is composed of hardware such as RFID tags and the radio-frequency scanners and antennas that enable these hardware devices to communicate with each other. Let's start with the RFID tags. They come in two varieties—active and passive. Active tags have their own power source and continuously broadcast their information. Passive tags are tags where the tag has no energy of its own. When a passive RFID tag passes by a radio-frequency scanner the energy from the radio scanner activates passive tags and induces them to broadcast their data, which is then picked up by the antenna of a data reader.

The scanners operate at certain radio frequency levels and at certain power levels. The RFID tags, whether active or passive, broadcast their information on certain frequencies. There are standards published for these frequencies and power levels but the technology is still improving and standards are evolving.

Passive RFID tags are by far the most widely used. This is because their cost and complexity is much lower than that of active tags. Large companies, especially in the consumer-goods retail industry such as Wal-Mart, are mandating that their suppliers start using passive RFID tags on the products that they ship. Initially these tags are required only at the pallet and case level. As the technology matures, as people gain more experience in the use of the technology, and prices continue to come down, RFID tags will start being required on the individual items themselves.

RFID Information RFID information is composed of descriptive data about the product itself and of tracking data that traces the movement of the product through the supply chain. It makes sense for there to be a single worldwide standard for this information so that people all over the world in different companies and countries can read the data easily and not have to translate it from one standard to another. At present there is one organization that is setting standards for product information. This organization is called GS1 (www.gs1.org) and it is a combination of two previous organizations, the Uniform Code Council and EAN International. The Uniform Code Council was the originator of the Universal Product Code or UPC number. EAN International created the European Article Number or EAN.

The two item numbering schemes—UPC and EAN—were combined in 1997, and starting in 2005 all participants in a supply chain were required to handle product identification data that is in the combined format. This is referred to as the "14-digit UPC" in North America or the "13-digit EAN plus check digit" in Europe. The GS1 organization also introduced a new term for these item-numbering schemes. The term is Global Trade Item Number or GTIN and it refers to the fact that there is now just one unified 14-digit numbering scheme.

The GTIN is a part of a global item-numbering scheme that GS1 has introduced called the Electronic Product Code or EPC. The EPC consists of four components or data fields. Those components are: (1) the version code that tells what version of EPC is being used; (2) the manager code that tells what organization created the EPC number; (3) the object class that defines the type of item or service; and (4) the serial number that identifies a specific individual instance of the item or service. The GTIN already contains data for the manager code and the object class, so you can think of EPC as a GTIN (or a UPC or

EAN) with a serial number attached. Organizations can register with GS1. They will be assigned a manager code and can begin using the EPC standards.

At present most companies use systems based on the EPC information standards combined with passive RFID tags. In these systems a radio scanner activates a passive RFID tag that sends its EPC number to a data reader. The data reader sends the EPC number to an application system that uses the Internet to communicate with a system called the EPC Global Network. The EPC Global Network is a system designed by GS1 that enables companies to find out what kind of item an EPC number refers to and get more information about that specific item such as its manufacture date and its movement history through the supply chain. Exhibit 4.2 shows how this process works.

RFID Benefits and Problems The benefits of RFID are significant. To begin with, it offers a much lower-cost way to capture data about products and their movements through a supply chain. The data that is captured is also more accurate and it can go to great levels of detail. Data can go from the level of shipping containers to pallets to cases and down to individual items. This enables much more visibility of inventory and product flows in supply chains. The increased visibility makes it possible to operate supply chains more efficiently, leading to lower costs. And finally, because data is captured and stored so much more efficiently, it is also easier to share this data with other parties in a supply chain. This makes supply chain collaboration more effective and increases overall supply chain productivity.

There are problems with RFID as well. The technology itself is still improving and it can be difficult at times to get it to work as expected. As companies begin using the technology, they find that it takes time to set up systems of RFID tags and radio scanners so that there is a high enough read rate on the data readers. If passive RFID tags are blocked by metal or liquids or other tags then it can be difficult for data readers to accurately read all the RFID tags that flow past them. Data-read rates

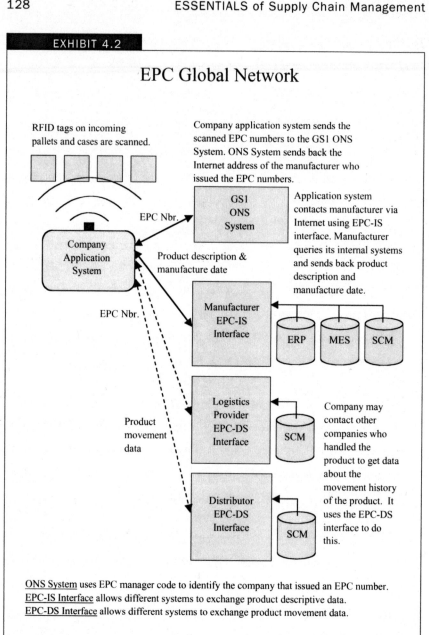

EXHIBIT 4.2

EPC Global Network

RFID tags on incoming pallets and cases are scanned.

Company application system sends the scanned EPC numbers to the GS1 ONS System. ONS System sends back the Internet address of the manufacturer who issued the EPC numbers.

EPC Nbr.

GS1 ONS System

Company Application System

Application system contacts manufacturer via Internet using EPC-IS interface. Manufacturer queries its internal systems and sends back product description and manufacture date.

Product description & manufacture date

EPC Nbr.

Manufacturer EPC-IS Interface

ERP   MES   SCM

Logistics Provider EPC-DS Interface

SCM

Company may contact other companies who handled the product to get data about the movement history of the product. It uses the EPC-DS interface to do this.

Product movement data

Distributor EPC-DS Interface

SCM

ONS System uses EPC manager code to identify the company that issued an EPC number.
EPC-IS Interface allows different systems to exchange product descriptive data.
EPC-DS Interface allows different systems to exchange product movement data.

can be very low at first and it takes time and trial and error to get read-rate percentages up into the high 90s.

The EPC Global Network and its various subsystems are also still works in progress. The goal is for any company anywhere that reads an

EPC number to be able to instantly access information describing the specific item and its supply chain movement. This is not always a reality. It will take a lot of work for product manufacturers to register their EPC numbers with the EPC Global Network and keep them constantly up to date. It will take work for other supply chain companies such as logistics and distribution companies to register with GS1 and record data that tracks product movements. In addition the EPC Global Network and the EPC standards must keep pace with global developments and evolve to meet changing needs in different regions of the world and in different industries.

Business Process Management

A process is a sequence of steps that lead to the delivery of a specified product or service. When you think about it you realize that business processes themselves are assets of an organization just as much as the organization's people, products, and information. The way that an organization uses its people, products, and information show up in the way its business processes operate.

Business process management (BPM) is a way for companies to carry out a continuous, incremental process of improving their operational performance. A company starts by mapping out its key processes. The company defines the steps in a process and uses BPM software to collect and display a continuous stream of data that shows the movement of transactions through each step. The BPM software can be used to automate many of the routine tasks such as moving different kinds of data from one task to another. It can also be set to detect certain error conditions and send automatic alerts to people who need to respond to these conditions quickly.

When used effectively, BPM software makes a business process visible to the people who are responsible for the efficient operation of that process. When people involved in the operation of a business process see what is happening as it is happening, they can take effective action to respond to problems and to improve productivity. The process-performance data that BPM software collects also provides a base of information that people can use to design new processes when existing ones are no longer able to meet business needs.

Business Intelligence

Because of the fast pace of change in markets and their supply chains, it is very important for people and organizations to stay current with events as they happen and understand what these events mean. Business intelligence (BI) systems help companies to understand what is happening within their own organizations and within the markets they serve.

BI systems collect, store, and analyze data. They collect data using many different sources. Data can be collected from sensors and RFID scanners. Data can be collected by BPM systems, or data can be obtained from the many transaction-processing systems in a company such as ERP systems, order entry systems, or CRM systems. Once the data is collected, it is stored in a database where people access it as needed. Often the database is updated with new data on a continuous or real-time basis.

When people access the data they use BI software tools that help them analyze the data and display the results. BI software tools run the range from simple spreadsheets and charts to complex multivariable regression analysis and linear programming. The proper mix of BI tools is determined by the needs of the people in a situation and their skill and training levels. Scientists doing molecular research have very demanding needs and they are also a highly skilled and educated group of people. Running an efficient supply chain is a very demanding job but people do not need the type of sophisticated BI tools called for in molecular research.

Successful BI systems are tailored to best support the people using them. In Chapter 5 we discuss the techniques and metrics for measuring supply chain performance. In light of these requirements, we then examine the structure of a BI system that is designed to meet the needs of people responsible for running a supply chain. This provides a good example of how BI is used to support supply chain operations (see pages 178–181).

Simulation Modeling

Simulation modeling software is a category of software that is growing rapidly. Because of the fast pace of change in business, companies are faced with the need to make important decisions more often and these decisions have significant consequences on company operations and profitability. Companies are faced with decisions such as where to build a new factory or distribution center and what is the best way to lay out and equip a new facility.

Simulation modeling software allows people to create a model of a factory or a supply chain or a delivery route and then subject that model to different inputs and different situations and observe what happens. A design that may seem good on paper could very well turn out to have problems that are not apparent until the design is modeled and its performance is simulated under a range of different conditions. It is much faster and cheaper to find this out through simulations than to find out the hard way through real experience (see Chapter 7 for more on this idea).

Companies that use BPM systems to manage their work processes can use the BPM process definitions to create models of their processes. Then they can use the data they collect in their BI systems to provide the input for simulating these processes under different business conditions. They can experiment with new ways to organize their work as business conditions evolve. By using simulation models and data from their BI systems, companies are able to test out new business models before they actually commit to them. And when new models are implemented there is much less risk because they have been tested. The models that are selected are shown to be the ones that offer the best performance and are much less likely to have serious problems.

The Impact on Supply Chain Operations

Although each of these new technologies is interesting and useful all by themselves, their true potential is realized when they are used in conjunction with each other. Just as Wal-Mart designed its supply chain based on the combination of four complementary practices (see Chapter 1 Executive Insight on page 18), companies once again have the opportunity to design extraordinary supply chains based on the use of combinations of these four new technologies (also see Chapter 7).

RFID technology can provide a steady stream of data that tracks individual items through a supply chain. This data can be monitored through the use of BPM systems and combined to provide a comprehensive end-to-end picture of the products flowing through a supply chain. BPM systems can update this picture on a real-time or near real-time basis and show people where the bottlenecks and disruptions are that need their attention.

Once people have identified the bottlenecks and disruptions in a supply chain, they can make use of BI databases and analytical software to investigate the situations and identify root causes of these problems. When root causes are identified, people can design ways to address these problems. Then by using simulation systems they can model potential supply chain process changes and see the probable impact of each different process change. In this way people quickly select the most effective changes and implement them with a high level of confidence that they will actually deliver the desired results.

Just as Wal-Mart rose to dominate its markets through the development of a highly efficient supply chain, there are opportunities once again for companies and alliances of companies to collaborate and create a new breed of supply chains that will be a key factor in achieving new levels of efficiency and responsiveness. This new level of supply chain performance will enable the rise of new companies and whole new industries. The potential of these new supply chains is further explored in the last chapter of this book.

A Combination of Technologies Creates Cloud Computing

Since the turn of this century, several different but related kinds of information technology have been evolving rapidly, and they are now combining to make it possible to deliver computing resources on demand to companies almost anywhere in the world. The combination of technologies, such as the Internet, Web browsers, server virtualization, parallel computing, and open source software, produces a whole new set of possibilities for delivering computing resources.

The term "cloud computing" is now used to describe the result of combining these technologies. IT vendors are offering combinations of these technologies to companies that want to outsource some or all of their traditional IT operations such as running data centers and operating traditional application packages, like ERP, CRM, and other business support applications.

The exact definition of cloud computing is still evolving. Cloud computing is both a model for delivery of business-computing services and a method for managing and operating computing hardware and software infrastructure. Different IT vendors put their own spin on their definitions, but they share more commonality in their definitions than differences. Here are two working definitions:

- "Consumer and business products, services, and solutions delivered and consumed in real time over the Internet" (Frank Gens,

"Defining "Cloud Services"—an IDC update," IDC Exchange, (September 30th 2009), http://blogs.idc.com/e/?p=422)

- "…a broad array of Web-based services aimed at allowing users to obtain a wide range of functional capabilities on a 'pay-as-you-go' basis that previously required tremendous hardware/software investments and professional skills to acquire." (Jeff Kaplan, "Simplifying the Term 'Cloud Computing'" Datamation.com Blog, (June 25, 2009), http://itmanagement.earthweb.com/netsys/article.php/3826921/Simplifying-the-Term-Cloud-Computing.htm)

There are three characteristics that everyone seems to accept when it comes to describing cloud computing. Everyone agrees that cloud computing has the characteristics of:

1. Practically Unlimited Computing Resources—Resources such as computing power, data storage space, and additional user sign-on IDs for applications are available on demand as needed, and this enables a high degree of agility and scalability in meeting evolving business needs.

2. No Long-Term Commitments—Computing resources are immediately available and they may be used as long as needed and then retired because they are acquired on a month-to-month or even a minute-to-minute basis.

3. Pay-as-You-Go Cost Structure—Because there are no long-term commitments, the cost of cloud computing resources is a variable cost, not a fixed cost; cost fluctuates depending on the amount of usage.

For a more detailed and far-reaching discussion of cloud computing and its impact on business operations please see my book *Business in the Cloud: What Every Business Needs to Know about Cloud Computing* (Hugos and Hulitzky, *Business in the Cloud*, John Wiley & Sons, Hoboken NJ, 2010).

Assessing Technology and System Needs

When evaluating different systems that can be used to support your supply chain it is important to keep in mind your goal—the reason for using any of these systems. What customers desire is good service and good prices. That is what guides them when they select companies to do business with. Technology is not an end in itself. It is only a means to enable a company to be of service to its customers. People and organizations that keep this in mind will do well.

Technology can be impressive, but in business, technology is only important insofar as it enables a company or an entire supply chain to profitably deliver valuable products and services to its customers. Do not let the complexity or the details of any technology or system be a distraction from this basic truth. Indeed, any technology that is highly complex or that is touted as being "state of the art" or "leading edge" is probably more suited for a research laboratory than it is for a business operation.

Success in supply chain management comes from delivering the highest levels of service at the lowest cost. Technology is expensive and it can quickly add a lot of cost to business operations. Keep in mind that it is a far better thing to use simple technology well than to use sophisticated technology in a clumsy manner.

E-Business and Supply Chain Integration

The widespread availability and use of the Internet offers companies opportunities that did not exist before. These opportunities are

Supply chain decisions are more vital than ever before and also more complex than ever before. How will companies address these challenges? One way is through the use of software and techniques for supply network design and simulation modeling. Tolga Yanasik and Thibault Quiviger specialize in the use of these tools and they describe some situations and the benefits they were able to deliver.

Consider the task faced by a large steel maker that is creating its five year investment plan. It must decide where to invest, which factories to revamp, and what production capacity to reduce in its 27 plants in Europe. Its product portfolio is made up of 16,000 different products, and many of them are processed on different production lines in different countries. The team in charge of this process is also concerned with the effect of different price policies contemplated for the different products and how this could modify their investment plan.

Or consider a carmaker that is going to re-engineer its global supply chain operations to build a competitive advantage against its competitors. The questions that both of these companies must answer are similar and are questions such as:

- Which product must be built on demand, which must be built on stock?
- Where to locate the different distribution centers?
- How much stock will be necessary to guarantee 95 percent service level to every customer with a delivery lead time of X days?
- Out of the total supply chain inventory, how much will be safety stock?

In another case, a company or port authority is planning to build a new container terminal. And it must decide about the new layout of the terminal, the number of cranes, the size of the parking lot for the waiting trucks, the number and location of weigh bridges and, most important, the number and layout of the customs gates it must negotiate with the country's government.

Simulation modeling can be used to answer the questions in all three of these situations. We will illustrate some tools and methodologies that can be used by companies to make rational decisions about their production and distribution strategies. We will address three different levels of planning: strategic, tactical, and operational. The difference between each level is the time horizon that drives different decision processes. For our discussion we will define these time horizons as follows:

- Strategic: One year to five years, depending on the industry dynamics.
- Tactical: One month to one year
- Operational: One day to one month

STRATEGIC SUPPLY CHAIN DESIGN

The purpose of strategic design is to minimize the total cost of the supply chain under capacity constraints. Using network design tools and quantitative methodologies, people can answer the following questions:

- Which product must be produced in which unit?
- Where should I build a new distribution center?
- Where to locate the inventories and how much to guarantee a certain service level?
- What is the most carbon efficient network?
- Is it better to build on demand or to build on stock?
- What is the impact of adding a new product in my Supply Chain?

(Continued)

- What if I reduce my product portfolio complexity in terms of total cost, customer service, and inventory level across the supply chain?

- At which stage of the supply chain should I hold safety stock? What about sharing this cost with my suppliers and customers and optimizing the overall inventory level?

Simulation software packages allow people to build a mathematical model representing the current and potential supply chain, with all of its products, production sites, and distribution sites that are relevant for the decision-making process. People can define the constraints on the supply chain (target service levels, maximum capacity of each plant, transport options, etc.) and quantify these constraints. Costs can then be entered into the model and used to help answer design questions. Exhibit 4.3 below shows the interrelationships between the physical and operating policy variables that must be modeled.

EXHIBIT 4.3

Physical and Behavioral Policies

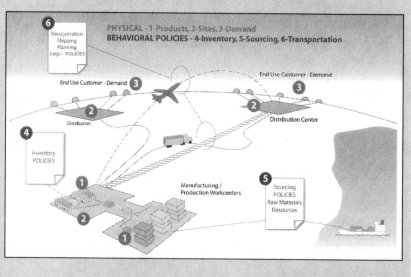

PHYSICAL - 1-Products, 2-Sites, 3-Demand
BEHAVIORAL POLICIES - 4-Inventory, 5-Sourcing, 6-Transportation

In this model, physical facilities and operating policies are put in place to tackle different problems such as:

- Factory production scheduling in the face of shifting product demand
- Managing production lead times that are longer than committed product delivery lead times to end customers
- Coping with supply uncertainty and demand uncertainty

For example, management of inventories to cope with demand uncertainty (also known as safety stocks), is complex because every stage in the supply chain usually builds up its own safety stock to guarantee a given service level. It can be mathematically demonstrated that this approach is not optimum and tends to build up too much inventory in the supply chain. One can show in simulations that it is possible to reduce the overall value of safety stock in the chain while increasing the service level to the supply chain end customers.

The further downstream in a supply chain, the higher is the value of the inventory and safety stock. And the more upstream safety stock is accumulated, the lower the value of these stocks. Yet safety stock held closer to the end customer guarantees a higher service level. The challenge is to find the optimum locations and quantities of different products and components to hold in the supply chain so as to guarantee target service level for the end customer and also minimize value of safety stocks. In many cases, simulations show how to reduce safety stocks by 30 percent or more while increasing service levels by 10 to 20 percent. Simulation shows this performance is achieved by reducing the safety stocks in the intermediate stages of the supply chain while increasing them in the final stage of the supply chain so as to increase service levels for the end customer.

USE OF SIMULATION FOR TACTICAL PLANNING

In tactical supply chain planning, uncertainty is mainly driven by demand uncertainty, but there may be other sources of uncertainty:

(Continued)

process times, availability of equipment, and complex interactions between workflows sharing limited resources (people, equipment, loading docks, etc.) making it hard to precisely know the overall system capacity. In these conditions, simulation can be of great help.

Simulators help managers to measure the consequences of these different sources of uncertainty in the supply chain operation. Let's consider here the example of a container terminal in Turkey. The container shipping business is booming in Turkey; a company is expanding its container terminal close to Istanbul in order to follow up on the container market demand. This company is already running another car export business, cars from the Renault Plant located close to the port and an import of steel slab for a neighboring plant. Exhibit 4.4 below shows a proposed layout for the facility. The proposed layout is overlaid on a Google Earth picture of the existing facility

EXHIBIT 4.4

Google Earth

Simulation is a powerful tool to study facility operations and workflows in scenarios of high variability. Logistics is very much subject to this variability because of the interactions between these

workflows which often cannot be controlled. When considering the different product flows, capacity computation is not simple because of factors such as: different product flows share some common resources (roads, custom tolls, weigh bridges); arrival of trucks is not constant during the day, nor during the week; weighing time and custom control times are very variable; and boat arrival times are unstable because of the crossing of the Bosphorus where many boats are queuing.

Using simulation, it was possible to verify:

- The current layout proposed was not optimal and could not absorb peak traffic
- No new investment was required: changing the layout to make it more flexible was enough to absorb the different traffic peaks
- Investment saved versus contemplated countermeasures: $4M

USE OF SIMULATION IN WAREHOUSE OPERATIONS

Very similar to manufacturing plants, simulation offers many benefits to warehouses. With the aid of simulation, logistics engineers can calculate how a new picking or replenishment strategy will affect the service levels or the utilization of lift trucks. Since logistics operations are exposed to more variation than factory production operations, it's crucial to monitor the behavior of these operations during extreme situations.

Simulation is a highly useful tool for calculating the effect of possible variations. It enables engineers to pinpoint zones of congestion and improve the layout of warehouses to respond to this congestion. Three-dimensional simulation is especially important when designing and installing automation systems such as conveyors, sorters, or palletizers in a warehouse (see Exhibit 4.5).

(Continued)

EXHIBIT 4.5

Three-dimensional Simulation

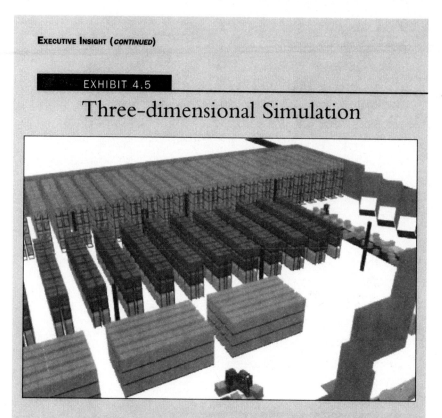

CONCLUSION

We have shown different techniques and uses of simulation to optimize supply chain investments and operations. We looked first at the strategic level because that's where the big money and big savings are to be found. Often supply chain managers are stuck in day-to-day operations. They tend to start from their daily experiences and try to extrapolate supply chain strategies. The difficulty of this approach lies in managers becoming focused on incremental changes to existing ways of working and failing to see the larger picture or try new ideas. Supply chains must be tailored to fit business strategy, not the other way around. Simulations of supply chain design and operations enable people to break out of preconceived ideas and try new approaches. Continuous simulation to find new ways to structure and operate supply chains is made possible because it is now so easy and relatively inexpensive for companies to connect to the Internet. Once connected, companies can send data to and receive data from other companies that they do business with, regardless of the particular computers or software that individual companies may be using to run their internal operations. Based on this data sharing, opportunities exist to achieve tremendous supply chain efficiencies and significant increases in customer service and responsiveness. These are the results of better supply chain integration.

E-business encompasses the evolving set of principles and practices that companies are employing to gain the benefits inherent in better supply chain integration. In the words of professors Hau Lee and Seungjin Whang of Stanford University, e-business specifically refers to "the planning and execution of the front-end and back-end operations in a supply chain using the Internet."

In a white paper titled "E-Business and Supply Chain Integration" published by the Stanford Global Supply Chain Management Forum, professors Lee and Whang lay out four key dimensions of the impact of e-business on supply chain integration. These four dimensions create a sequence of greater and greater integration and coordination among supply chain participants. This sequence culminates in the creation of whole new ways to conduct business. The four dimensions are:

1. *Information Integration*—Is the ability to share relevant information among companies in a supply chain. This includes data such as: sales history and demand forecasts; inventory status; production schedules; production capacities; sales promotions; and transportation schedules. This data should be available to the people who need it in a real-time, on-line format via the Internet or private network.

2. *Planning Synchronization*—Refers to the joint participation of companies in a supply chain in the demand forecasting and inventory replenishment scheduling. It also includes the collaborative design, development, and bringing to market of new products.

3. *Work-Flow Coordination*—Is the next step after planning synchronization. It is the streamlining and automation of ongoing business activities across companies in a given supply chain. This includes activities such as purchasing and product design.

4. New Business Models—Can emerge as a result of supply chain integration made possible by the Internet. Roles and responsibilities of companies in a supply chain can be redesigned so that each company can truly concentrate on the activities that are its core competencies. Noncore activities can be outsourced to other companies. New capabilities and efficiencies will become possible.

Companies are looking at how to achieve efficiencies in a broad range of supply chain operations such as product design, demand forecasting, inventory management, and customer service. The key to realizing these efficiencies is information sharing between companies in a supply chain. Many current e-business developments are working on methods and standards to share information across multiple companies. Information sharing is the foundation, and then cross-company coordination is what will deliver the desired efficiencies. Once information integration is in place, the next three dimensions: planning synchronization; workflow coordination; and new business models can evolve much more rapidly. E-business and supply chain development has only just begun.

Chapter Summary

The use of supporting technology is necessary for effective supply chain operations. All information systems are composed of technology that performs three main functions. These three functions are: (1) data capture and communication; (2) data storage and retrieval; and (3) data manipulation and reporting. Different supply chain information systems have different combinations of capabilities in these functional areas. Systems such as ERP, CRM, and MES are all examples of systems that consist of combinations of these three functions.

New technologies are having a strong impact on supply chain management. Some technologies that are changing the way businesses manage their supply chains are RFID, BPM, BI, and simulation modeling. These technologies do not replace older systems, but instead build upon the foundation of system functionality provided by existing systems such as ERP, CRM, and MES. The combined effect of these new technologies gives a company the ability to closely monitor supply chain operations and make adjustments quickly and cost effectively.

The Internet makes it possible for companies in a supply chain to make electronic connections with each other for purposes of exchanging information about the products they sell. These connections also enable close coordination between companies as they carry out the various activities that drive the supply chains they participate in. As these electronic connections become more widespread and commonplace, they are enabling a whole new level of cooperation that leads to greater business efficiency and responsiveness.

CHAPTER 5

Metrics for Measuring Supply Chain Performance

After reading this chapter you will be able to

- Employ a useful model for assessing markets and the supply chains that support them
- Define a concise set of metrics for measuring the performance of a company's supply chain operations
- Discuss ways to collect and display supply chain performance data
- Use performance data to spotlight problems and opportunities

Supply chains are fluid and are continuously adjusting to changes in supply and demand for the products they handle. To get the performance desired from supply chains requires a company to monitor and control its operations on a daily basis. This chapter introduces four performance categories that each supply chain participant should measure. It then discusses the performance metrics that can be used in each of these performance categories. The chapter also explores some of the technology that can be used to collect, store, and present performance data.

Useful Model of Markets and Their Supply Chains

A supply chain exists to support the market that it serves. To identify the performance that a supply chain should deliver, we need to evaluate the market being served. In support of this analysis we will employ a simple model. The model allows us to categorize a market and identify the requirements and opportunities that each kind of market presents to its supply chains. Reality is, of course, more subtle and more complex than any model can represent but this model can point you in the right direction and guide you through an investigation of the markets your company serves.

Let us start by defining a market using its two most basic components—supply and demand. A market is characterized by its combination of supply and demand. This model defines four basic kinds of markets, or market quadrants. In the first quadrant is a market where both supply and demand for its products are low and unpredictable. Let's call this a *developing* market. In the second quadrant is a market where supply is low and demand is high. This is a *growth* market. The third quadrant contains a market where both supply and demand are high. There is a lot of predictability in this market so call this a *steady* market. In the fourth quadrant, this kind of market supply is higher than demand. This is a *mature* market.

In a developing market, both supply and demand are low and also uncertain. These are usually new markets that are just emerging. These markets are created by new technology becoming available or by social and economic trends that cause a group of customers to perceive some new set of needs. Opportunities in a developing market are in the areas of partnering with other players in the supply chain to gather intelligence about what the market wants. Cost of sales is high in this market and inventories are low.

Growth markets are markets where demand is higher than supply and so supply is often uncertain. If a developing market solidifies and builds up momentum, it can suddenly take off and for a time there is a surge in demand that suppliers cannot keep up with. Opportunities in a growth market are in providing a high level of customer service as measured by order fill rates and on-time deliveries. Customers in a market like this value a reliable source of supply and will pay premium prices for reliability. Cost of sales should be low since customers are easy to find and inventories can be higher because they are increasing in value.

In a steady market both supply and demand are high and thus relatively predictable. This is an established market where market forces have been at work for a while and have pretty well balanced supply and demand. Opportunities here lie in fine tuning and optimizing internal company operations. Companies should focus on minimizing inventory and cost of sales while maintaining high levels of customer service.

In a mature market, supply has overtaken demand and excess supply capacity exists. Demand is reasonably stable or slowly falling but because of the fierce competition due to oversupply, demand seems uncertain from the point of view of any one supplier in this market. Opportunities in this market are in the area of flexibility as measured by an ability to respond quickly to changes in product demand while maintaining high levels of customer service. Customers in a market like this value the convenience of "one stop shopping" where they can purchase a wide variety of related products at low prices. Inventories should be minimized and the cost of sales are somewhat higher due to the expense of attracting customers in a crowded market.

Market Performance Categories

Markets in each quadrant have their own mix of opportunities for the supply chains that support them. A different mix of performance characteristics is required of companies in the supply chains of each kind of market. In order to thrive, the companies in a supply chain must be able to work together to exploit the opportunities available in their markets. The highest profits go to the companies that can successfully respond to the opportunities their markets offer. Companies that are unable to respond to opportunities as effectively will fall behind.

TIPS & TECHNIQUES

Each Market Quadrant Presents Different Opportunities

MATURE	**STEADY**
Supply exceeds demand	Established market, supply and demand are balanced
Opportunities lie in coordinating with supply chain partners to provide a wide range of products to the market and accommodate wide fluctuations in product demand while maintaining high levels of customer service.	Opportunities lie in each company fine tuning and optimizing their internal operations to get maximum efficiency and best overall supply chain profitability.
DEVELOPING	**GROWTH**
New market and new products, supply and demand are low	Demand exceeds supply
Opportunities lie in partnering with other companies in the supply chain to gather intelligence about what the market wants and build and deliver products that will be attractive to the market.	Opportunities lie in building market share and recognition through working with supply chain partners to provide high levels of customer service as measured by order fill rate and on-time delivery.

SUPPLY ↑

DEMAND ⟶

What are the markets your company serves? What quadrants are they in? How can your company respond to the opportunities in these markets?

In Chapter 1 we introduced two characteristics that describe supply chain performance—responsiveness and efficiency. We all intuitively know what these two characteristics imply, but now we need to define them in more precise terms so that they can be measured objectively. We will use four measurement categories:

1. Customer Service
2. Internal Efficiency
3. Demand Flexibility
4. Product Development

Customer Service

Customer service measures the ability of the supply chain to meet the expectations of its customers. Depending on the type of market being served, the customers in that market will have different expectations for customer service. Customers in some markets both expect and will pay for high levels of product availability and quick delivery of small purchase quantities. Customers in other markets will accept longer waits for products and will purchase in large quantities. Whatever the market being served, the supply chain must meet the customer service expectations of the people in that market.

Internal Efficiency

Internal efficiency refers to the ability of a company or a supply chain to operate in such a way as to generate an appropriate level of profitability. As with customer service, market conditions vary and what is an appropriate level of profit varies from one market to another. In a risky developing market, the profit margins need to be higher in order to justify the investment of time and money. In a mature market where there is little uncertainty or risk, profit margins can be somewhat lower. These markets offer the opportunity to do large volumes of business and to make up in gross profit what is given up in gross margin.

Demand Flexibility

This category measures the ability to respond to uncertainty in levels of product demand. It shows how much of an increase over current levels of demand can be handled by a company or a supply chain. It also includes the ability to respond to uncertainty in the range of products that may be demanded. This ability is often needed in mature markets.

Product Development

This encompasses a company and a supply chain's ability to continue to evolve along with the markets they serve. It measures the ability to develop and deliver new products in a timely manner. This ability is necessary when serving developing markets.

A Framework for Performance Measurement

There are other demands that real-world markets place on their supply chains; however, by using these four performance categories we can create a useful framework. This framework describes the mix of performance required from companies and supply chains that serve the four different market quadrants. When a company identifies the markets it serves it can then define the performance mix required by those markets in order to best respond to the opportunities they provide.

Markets in the first quadrant, developing markets, require their supply chains to excel in product development and customer service. Growth markets require very high levels of customer service, particularly as measured by order fill rates and on-time delivery. Steady markets require internal efficiency as well as an even broader scope of customer service. Mature markets require all the internal efficiency and customer service called for by steady markets. They also require the highest levels of demand flexibility.

The most profitable companies and supply chains are those that deliver the performance called for by their markets. These organizations are the most profitable because they are the ones most able to respond effectively to the opportunities offered by their markets. Companies should collect and track a handful of performance measures that cover these four areas. This will give them valuable information about how well they are responding to their markets.

The metrics that measure performance in the four areas are applicable to individual companies and also to entire supply chains. It is harder to gather these metrics for entire supply chains because companies are reluctant to share data that may be used against them by their competitors or by their customers or suppliers. There are issues of trust and incentive to work out before these metrics can readily be collected for an entire supply chain. Nonetheless, when these issues are worked out, these metrics will help to guide the behavior of the entire supply chain and should benefit all the participants in that chain over the long term.

Customer Service Metrics

In the words of Warren Hausman, a professor at Stanford University, "Service relates to the ability to anticipate, capture, and fulfill customer demand with personalized products and on-time delivery" (Hausman, Warren H., 2000, "Supply Chain Performance Metrics," Management Science & Engineering Department, Stanford University). The reason that any company exists is to be of service to its customers. The reason that any supply chain exists is to serve the market it is attached to. These measures indicate how well a company serves its customers and how well a supply chain supports its market.

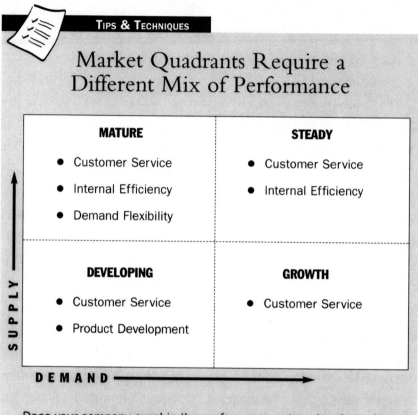

Market Quadrants Require a Different Mix of Performance

MATURE
- Customer Service
- Internal Efficiency
- Demand Flexibility

STEADY
- Customer Service
- Internal Efficiency

DEVELOPING
- Customer Service
- Product Development

GROWTH
- Customer Service

SUPPLY

DEMAND

Does your company excel in the performance categories that relate to the markets you serve? Profit opportunities lie in being a leader in the mix of performance categories that your markets call for.

There are two sets of customer service metrics, depending on whether the company or supply chain is in a build-to-stock (BTS) or build-to-order (BTO) situation. Popular metrics for a build to stock situation are:

- Complete Order Fill Rate and Order Line Item Fill Rate
- On-Time Delivery Rate
- Value of Total Backorders and Number of Backorders

- Frequency and Duration of Backorders
- Line Item Return Rate

Popular metrics for a build-to-order situation are:

- Quoted Customer Response Time and On-Time Completion Rate
- On-Time Delivery Rate
- Value of Late Orders and Number of Late Orders
- Frequency and Duration of Late Orders
- Number of Warranty Returns and Repairs

Build to Stock

A build-to-stock (BTS) situation is one where common commodity products are supplied to a large market or customer base. These are products such as office supplies, cleaning supplies, building supplies, and so on. Customers expect to get these products right away any time they need them. Supply chains for these products must meet this demand by stocking them in inventory so they are always available.

In a BTS environment a customer wants their complete order to be filled immediately. This may be expensive to provide if customer orders contain a wide range and number of items. It is costly for companies to carry all those items in stock so they may have backup plans to provide expedited delivery of items not in stock or substitution of upgraded items for those not in stock. The order-fill rate measures the percentage of total orders where all items on the order are filled immediately from stock. The line-item fill rate is the percentage of total line items on all orders that are filled immediately from stock. Used together, these two measures track customer service from two important perspectives.

Build to Order

A build-to-order (BTO) situation is one where a customized product is ordered by a customer. This is any situation where a product is built based on a specific customer order and is configured to meet a unique set of requirements defined by the customer. An example of this is the way Boeing builds airplanes for specific customers and their requirements or the way Dell Computer assembles PCs to fit individual customer orders and specifications.

In a BTO environment it is important to track both the quoted customer response time and the on-time completion rate. It is easier for a company to achieve a high on-time completion rate if it quotes longer customer response times. The question is whether the customer really wants a short response time or will accept a longer response time. The quoted response time needs to be aligned with the company's value proposition and competitive strategy.

Internal Efficiency Metrics

Internal efficiency refers to the ability of a company or a supply chain to use their assets as profitably as possible. Assets include anything of tangible value such as plant, equipment, inventory, and cash. Some popular measures of internal efficiency are:

- Inventory Value
- Inventory Turns
- Return on Sales
- Cash-to-Cash Cycle Time

Inventory Value

This should be measured both at a point in time and also as an average over time. The major asset involved in a supply chain is the inventory contained throughout the length of the chain. Supply chains and the companies that make them up are always looking for ways to reduce inventory while still delivering high levels of customer service. This means trying to match inventory availability (supply) with sales (demand) and not have excess inventory left over. The only time a company would want to let inventory exceed sales is in a growth market where the value of the inventory will increase. However, markets change and as a rule it is best to avoid excess inventory.

Inventory Turns

This is a way to measure the profitability of inventory by tracking the speed with which it is sold or turned over during the course of a year. This measure is often referred to as "turn and earn" (T&E). It is calculated by the equation:

Turns = Annual Cost of Sales / Annual Average Inventory Value

Generally, the higher the turn rate the better, although some lower-turning inventory needs to be available in order to meet customer service and demand flexibility.

Return on Sales

Return on sales is a broad measure of how well an operation is being run. It measures how well fixed and variable costs are managed and also the gross profit generated on sales:

Return on Sales = Earnings before Interest and Tax / Sales

Again, as a rule, the higher the return on sales the better. There are times though when a company may deliberately reduce this number in order to gain or defend market share or to incur expenses that are necessary to achieve some other business objective.

Cash-to-Cash Cycle Time

This is the time it takes from when a company pays its suppliers for materials to when it gets paid by its customers. This time can be estimated with the following formula:

Cash-to-Cash Cycle Time = Inventory Days of Supply + Days Sales Outstanding – Average Payment Period on Purchases

The shorter this cycle time the better. A company can often make more improvements in their accounts payable and receivable areas than they can in their inventory levels. Accounts receivable may be large due to late payments caused by billing errors or selling to customers who are bad credit risks. These are things a company can manage as well as inventory.

Demand Flexibility Metrics

Demand flexibility describes a company's ability to be responsive to new demands in the quantity and range of products and to act quickly. A company or supply chain needs capabilities in this area in order to cope with uncertainty in the markets they serve. Some measures of flexibility are:

- Activity Cycle Time
- Upside Flexibility
- Outside Flexibility
- Activity Cycle Time

The cycle time measures the amount of time it takes to perform a supply chain activity such as order fulfillment, product design, product assembly, or any other activity that supports the supply chain. This cycle time can be measured within an individual company or across an entire supply chain. Order fulfillment within a single company may be fast but that company may only be filling an order from another company in the supply chain. What is important is the cycle time for order fulfillment to the ultimate end-use customer that the entire supply chain is there to serve.

Upside Flexibility

It is the ability of a company or supply chain to respond quickly to additional order volume for the products they carry. Normal order volume may be 100 units per week for a product. Can an order be accommodated that is 25 percent greater one week or will the extra product demand wind up as a backorder? Upside flexibility can be measured as the percentage increase over the expected demand for a product that can be accommodated.

Outside Flexibility

This is the ability to quickly provide the customer with additional products outside the bundle of products normally provided. As markets mature and technologies blend, products that were once considered outside of the range of a company's offerings can become a logical extension of its offerings. There is danger in trying to provide customers with a new and unrelated set of products that has little in common with the existing product bundle. However, there is opportunity to acquire new customers and sell more to existing customers when outside flexibility is managed skillfully.

Product Development Metrics

Product development measures a company or a supply chain's ability to design, build, and deliver new products to serve their markets as those

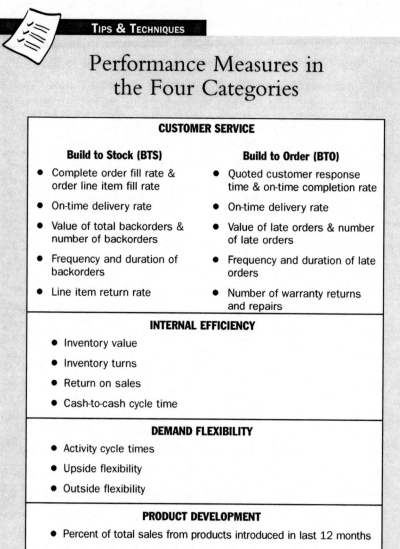

TIPS & TECHNIQUES

Performance Measures in the Four Categories

CUSTOMER SERVICE

Build to Stock (BTS)

- Complete order fill rate & order line item fill rate
- On-time delivery rate
- Value of total backorders & number of backorders
- Frequency and duration of backorders
- Line item return rate

Build to Order (BTO)

- Quoted customer response time & on-time completion rate
- On-time delivery rate
- Value of late orders & number of late orders
- Frequency and duration of late orders
- Number of warranty returns and repairs

INTERNAL EFFICIENCY

- Inventory value
- Inventory turns
- Return on sales
- Cash-to-cash cycle time

DEMAND FLEXIBILITY

- Activity cycle times
- Upside flexibility
- Outside flexibility

PRODUCT DEVELOPMENT

- Percent of total sales from products introduced in last 12 months
- Percent of total SKUs that were introduced in last 12 months
- Cycle time for new product development and delivery

Companies need to track some or all of these metrics to get an accurate picture of their capabilities in the four performance categories.

markets evolve over time. Technical innovations, social change, and economic developments cause a market to change over time. Measurements in this performance category are often overlooked, but companies do so at their own peril. A supply chain must keep pace with the market it serves or it will be replaced. The ability to keep pace with an evolving market can be measured by metrics such as:

- Percentage of total products sold that were introduced in the last year
- Percentage of total sales from products introduced in the last year
- Cycle time to develop and deliver a new product

Operations that Enable Supply Chain Performance

In order for an organization to meet the performance requirements of the markets it serves, it must look to measure and improve its capabilities in the four categories of supply chain operations:

1. Plan
2. Source
3. Make
4. Deliver

EXECUTIVE INSIGHT

Supply chains created in the last several decades often focused on producing and delivering products at the lowest price. That worked best when product life cycles were longer and sales forecasts were more accurate. But now, due to the rate of technical and economic change in our global economy, product life cycles

(Continued)

are measured in months, prices of component parts, fuel, and labor fluctuate constantly, and sales forecasting is much harder. Supply chains need to focus on responding to constant change. Shoshanah Cohen, Director Emeritus of PRTM Management Consulting, explains why supply chains must balance needs for efficiency and low cost with needs for responsiveness and high customer service.

Traditional supply chain metrics focus on efficiency and productivity, whereas financial metrics focus on cost, revenue, and profitability. While it's not uncommon to find supply chain performance management programs that use both operational and financial metrics, many companies don't do this particularly well.

As an example, a leading manufacturer of personal computer peripherals relied on a business strategy based on ongoing innovation and frequent new product introductions. Product managers were measured on their ability to design, develop, and release a constant stream of profitable new products, while growing market share for their particular categories. A make-to-stock supply chain supported this strategy so that customers could order and receive products immediately after they were released. Supply chain metrics tracked on a regular basis included material and product costs, delivery performance, fill rate, and transportation costs.

Because the company expected every product to maximize its potential margin, the supply chain was optimized to manufacture at the lowest possible unit cost. That meant developing low-cost material suppliers and setting up production in low-cost countries, including several relationships with large original design manufacturers (ODMs) in Asia and a large company-owned plant in China. Standard product costs were established based on anticipated material prices, planned production schedules, and ocean shipment for virtually all products. Standard product margins, therefore, reflected best-case scenarios for procurement, production, and distribution, and variances were due to fluctuations in selling price.

Although most manufacturing sites were in Asia, most of the company's business was in North America and Europe. Standard ocean shipment meant that products took up to five weeks to reach regional distribution centers, making the strategic objective of fast order fulfillment a major challenge. "We're very dependent on an accurate forecast," explains the company's Vice President of Global Supply Chain, "but the peripherals market is pretty volatile. Plus we have constant product introductions and phase-outs and a lot of slips in the product development schedule, even though product release dates rarely shift to accommodate them."

Expediting was one of the few levers available to increase flexibility amid the combination of complexity and forecast inaccuracy—and was used frequently. Shipping raw materials and finished goods by air rather than sea nearly tripled transportation costs, but was necessary to maintain targeted customer-service levels. When necessary, the company also reworked products at regional distribution centers to align availability with current demand. "We recognize that this is also a very expensive option," notes the Supply Chain VP, "especially since our whole cost model is based on producing in locations with low labor rates. But this is the only way we can meet our fill-rate and on-time delivery objectives."

The resulting costs were charged to the supply chain group, appearing in quarterly financial reports as unplanned/incremental expenses. While this had a significant impact on the perceived performance of the supply chain organization, product management didn't see these added costs as an issue. Because they were not added to the product standard cost, they were virtually invisible to product managers.

Of course, the total cost of managing the supply chain increased significantly as the organization struggled to provide the required flexibility. "We got pummeled every time the quarterly financial reports came out," the Supply Chain VP explains, "it looked like our spending was out of control. We needed to find a way to get the rest of the

(Continued)

company to understand that it wasn't just a supply chain issue, even though the way we were measuring performance made it look that way. We needed a better balance of financial and operation metrics."

To address this problem, the company modified its enterprise resource planning (ERP) cost module so that expedite and rework costs could be allocated to each major product group and their impact analyzed. "We would have liked to have been able to do this on a product-by-product basis," notes a financial analyst, "but the cost of putting that level of granularity in place was prohibitive." But even at a product-group level, the impact was clear: for many products, the costs of accommodating development delays and forecast inaccuracy through air shipment and local reconfiguration was enough to wipe out profitability for some products.

Product managers were not happy with the new means of measurement. "We hadn't changed anything we were doing," explains one Product Manager, "but suddenly it looked like our margins were degrading." The executive management team stood firm despite numerous complaints from the product groups, and directed them to focus more attention on forecasting and compliance with established product-development schedules. The new metrics became the catalyst needed to move forward with several major initiatives: improving the forecasting process, increasing product modularity and configurability, and updating systems and processes to enable increased parts commonality.

Of course changing the way costs are allocated does nothing in and of itself to reduce costs or optimize a supply chain. But simply increasing visibility can drive changes in behavior that can lower the overall cost of managing a supply chain.

This example is not unusual. As this company found, measuring operational metrics in isolation can be a counterproductive way to use performance-related data. A more effective approach is to start with the company's strategic goals, identify the supply chain configuration necessary to support the strategy, and then derive operational and financial performance metrics that support those goals.

EXECUTIVE INSIGHT (*CONTINUED*)

Shoshanah Cohen is Director of the Stanford Global Supply Chain Management Forum, a research institute in partnership with industry and the Graduate School of Business at Stanford University. The Forum's mission is to advance the theory and practice of excellence in global supply chain management through, research, development, and dissemination of best practices within a dynamic and increasingly global business environment. She is also co-author of *Strategic Supply Chain Management: The Five Disciplines for Top Performance* (McGraw-Hill, 2005).

The efficiency with which these activities are carried out will ultimately determine how well a company performs as measured by things such as order and line-item fill rate, on-time delivery, inventory turns, and cash-to-cash cycle time. Certain activities are directly related to certain performance categories. For instance, inventory management will directly affect a company's order and line-item fill rate and its inventory turns. Its procurement activity will directly affect its return on sales and upside ability. A company needs to collect data about its activities in these four operational areas and monitor results.

The Supply-Chain Council's supply chain operations reference (SCOR) model suggests the kind of operational data that should be collected. This data is referred to as "Level 2 Performance Metrics." In the plan operation, useful measures are the cost of planning activities, inventory financing costs, inventory days of supply on hand, and forecast accuracy. In the sourcing operation, it is useful to have data on material acquisition costs, sourcing cycle times, and raw material days of supply. Useful measures in the make operation are the number of product defects/complaints, make cycle times, build-order attainment rates, and product quality. Suggested delivery operation measures are fill rates, order-management costs, order lead times, and item-return rates.

This data should be collected regularly and trends should be watched. When performance targets start to be missed, the next step is to investigate the business operations that support that performance. Again, the SCOR model suggests more detailed data that can be collected and analyzed in each of the four supply chain operating areas. This more detailed data is referred to as "Level 3 Diagnostic Metrics."

Diagnostic metrics can be used to analyze the complexity and configuration of the supply chain and also to study specific practices. In the plan operation, complexity measures are the number and percentage of order changes, number of stock keeping units (SKUs) carried, production volumes, and inventory carrying costs. Configuration measures track things such as product volume by channel, number of channels, and number of supply chain locations. Measures of management practices in the plan operation are such things as planning cycle time, forecast accuracy, and obsolete inventory on hand.

In the source operation, measures of complexity and configuration are number of suppliers, percentage of purchasing spending by distance, and purchased material by geography. Some practice measurements are supplier delivery performance, payment period, and percentage of items purchased by their associated lead time.

The make operation has measures of complexity and configuration such as number of SKUs, upside production flexibility, manufacturing process steps by geographical location, and capacity utilization. Management practice measurements are value-added percentage, BTO percentage, BTS percentage, percentage of manufacturing order changes due to internal issues, and work in process inventory.

In the fourth supply chain operation, deliver, there are complexity measures that include number of orders by channel, number of line items and shipments by channel, and percentage of line items returned. Configuration measures are delivery locations by geography and number of channels. Practice measures cover things like published delivery lead times, percentage of invoices that contain billing errors, and order entry methods.

Business Operations Support Company Performance

PERFORMANCE CATEGORIES / BUSINESS OPERATIONS	CUSTOMER SERVICE — As measured by: Fill Rate; On-Time Delivery; Product Returns	INTERNAL EFFICIENCY — As measured by: Inventory Turns; Return on Sales; Cash-to-Cash	DEMAND FLEXIBILITY — As measured by: Cycle Times; Upside Flex; Outside Flex	PRODUCT DEVELOPMENT — As measured by: New Prod. Sales; % Revenue; Cycle Time
PLAN Demand Forecasts	X	X	X	
Product Pricing	X	X		
Inventory Management	X	X	X	
SOURCE Procurement		X	X	
Credit & Collections	X	X		
MAKE Product Design	X			X
Production Scheduling		X	X	
Facility Mgmt.	X	X		
DELIVER Order Management	X	X		X
Delivery Scheduling	X	X		
Return Processing	X			X

Every business operation indirectly affects overall supply chain performance but certain operations have a strong effect on specific categories of performance. This table shows the performance categories that are most strongly affected by each business operation.

Collecting and Displaying Performance Data

Historically, companies based their management decisions on periodic, standard reports that showed what happened during some period in the past. In stable and slow-moving business environments this worked well enough. However, there are not many companies that work in stable and slow-moving environments any more. Working from traditional, periodic, accounting-oriented reports in a fast-paced world is somewhat like trying to drive a car by looking into the rearview mirror.

The business environments we live in are characterized by shorter product life cycles, mass markets dissolving into smaller niche markets, and new technology and distribution channels constantly opening up new opportunities. The pace of change is both exhilarating and relentless. A company must keep up. To do this, a company needs to build a business intelligence (BI) system that presents data at three levels of detail:

- *Strategic*—to help top management decide what to do
- *Tactical*—to help middle management decide how to do it
- *Operational*—to help people *actually* do it

Three Levels of Detail

In a supply chain management context, strategic data consists of current actual, as well as plan and historical numbers that show the company's standing in the four performance categories: customer service; internal efficiency; demand flexibility; and product development. In the Supply-Chain Council SCOR model, data of this type is referred to as "Level 1" data. This data is summarized by major business units and for the company as a whole. Strategic data also consists of data from outside the company such as market sizes and growth rates, demographics, and economic indicators such as GNP, inflation rates, and interest rates. There should also be benchmark data from industry

TIPS & TECHNIQUES

Supply Chain Performance Metrics and Diagnostic Measures (Supply-Chain Council SCOR Model)

	LEVEL 2	LEVEL 3		
	Performance Metrics	Complexity Measures	Configuration Measures	Practice Measures
P L A N	• Planning costs • Financing costs • Inventory days of supply	• % of order changes • # of SKUs carried • Production volume • Inventory carrying costs	• Product volume by channel • # of channels • # of supply chain locations	• Planning cycle time • Forecast accuracy • Obsolete inventory on hand
S O U R C E	• Material acquisition costs • Source cycle time • Raw material days of supply	• # of suppliers • % of purchasing spending by distance	• Purchased material by geography • % of purchasing spending by distance	• Supplier delivery performance • Payment period • % of items purchased by their associated lead times
M A K E	• # of defects or complaints • Make cycle time • Build order attainment • Product quality	• # of SKUs • Upside production flexibility	• Manufacturing process steps by geography • Capacity utilization	• Value add % • Build to order % • Build to stock % • % mfg. order changes due to internal issues • WIP inventory
D E L I V E R	• Fill rates • Order management costs • Order fulfillment lead times • Line item return rates	• # of orders by channel • # of line items and shipments by channel • % of line items returned	• Delivery locations by geography • # of channels	• Published delivery lead times • % invoices containing billing errors • Order entry methods

trade associations and studies that show the operating standards and financial performance levels that are standard for companies in the markets being served.

Tactical data consists of actual, plan, and historical numbers in the four performance categories displayed at the branch office level of detail.

This data also includes the performance metrics labeled "Level 2" in the SCOR model. These metrics monitor the plan, source, make, and deliver operations that every company in a supply chain must perform.

Operational data consists of the measures labeled "Level 3" in the SCOR model. These measurements help people who are charged with getting a job done to understand what is happening and to find ways to make improvements where needed to meet the performance targets that have been set. The SCOR model refers to these measurements as diagnostic measures.

We are awash in data. It is important to present it in such a way that it is useful. If people are overwhelmed with data they cannot use it. By organizing data into these three levels, people can quickly access what they need to do their jobs. Upper management uses strategic-level data to assess market conditions and set business-performance objectives. They can drill down to the tactical level or even the operational levels when necessary. Middle managers use tactical data to do planning and resource allocation to achieve the performance objectives set by upper management. Line managers and their staffs use operational data to solve problems and get things done.

The Data Warehouse

To collect this data requires the creation of a data warehouse. This data warehouse is a central repository of data that is drawn from a variety of operating systems and accounting systems in a company. It is important to collect the needed data at its source. Tap into relevant systems within a company and capture needed data automatically as a by-product of daily operations. Avoid having people do manual entry to get data into the data warehouse.

A data warehouse is composed of a database software package and the automated connections to other systems needed to collect the relevant data on a regular and timely schedule. Working in conjunction with the database software is software that allows for the creation of standard predefined reports and graphic displays which people can use to monitor operations. In addition to predefined reports and displays, the software must also allow people to do ad hoc queries of the data in the data warehouse, permitting detailed investigations when necessary.

When designing and building a data warehouse it is best to start quickly with something that is simple and on a smaller scale. This way people can get experience in using data more actively to do their jobs. As they gain experience and can clearly describe the additional features they would like, larger and more complex data warehouses can be built. Remember, the most important component in any data warehouse system is not the technology, or even the data, but the people who use the system and their ability to use the system effectively to learn from the data and become more efficient at their jobs. Chapter 7 goes into further detail about the design and building of these kinds of systems.

In addition to helping people inside a company become more efficient in performing their supply chain management jobs, a data warehouse can also be the foundation for collaboration with other companies in the supply chain. Whatever information is shared between companies in a supply chain should be made available to those other companies electronically. This often takes the form of reports that can be retrieved on demand by other companies, who access a company's data warehouse over the Internet using features of the same data-reporting software that people inside the company use (see Exhibit 5.1).

Spotlighting Problems and Finding Opportunities

Depending on the type of markets a company serves, senior management needs to define a handful of key performance targets in the areas of customer service, internal efficiency, demand flexibility, and product development. The task then becomes one of figuring out how to

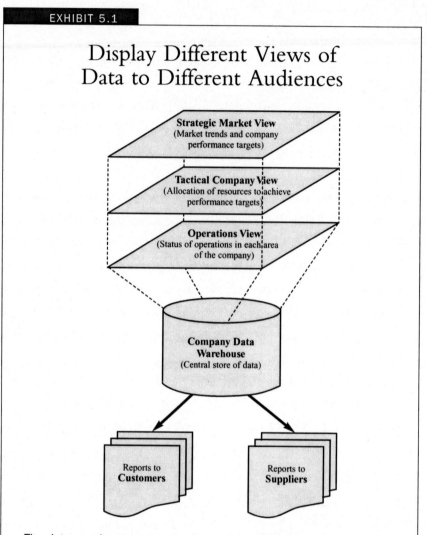

EXHIBIT 5.1

Display Different Views of Data to Different Audiences

Strategic Market View
(Market trends and company performance targets)

Tactical Company View
(Allocation of resources to achieve performance targets)

Operations View
(Status of operations in each area of the company)

Company Data Warehouse
(Central store of data)

Reports to **Customers**

Reports to **Suppliers**

The data warehouse supports views of data at the strategic, tactical, and operational levels. This makes it easy for management and staff in a company to get quick access to the data they need to do their jobs. The data warehouse also supports the sharing of data with customers and suppliers needed to coordinate supply chain activities.

manage operations to achieve the target numbers. The point of collecting performance data is to help monitor and control daily, weekly, and monthly operations.

People in a company need access to a one-page display of the key operating or financial measures that they are responsible for achieving. These one page displays are known as "dashboards" because they show a person at a glance the data that is most important to them. The data that is displayed on a senior management dashboard is different from that on an operating manager's dashboard and the data on the dashboard of a staff person in one department is different from a staff person's in another department.

Senior management sets company performance targets and they need access to a dashboard report that shows them the company's current performance against these targets. If things are going well and performance is meeting expectations, then no further attention is called for, but if performance is falling short against one or more of the performance targets, then the senior manager knows right away where more attention is needed.

Middle managers are responsible for managing their operations to achieve one or more of the company's performance targets. Their dashboards need to show them the plan and actual data on company performance targets they are responsible for. They need to see quickly if operations are on target or not and direct their attention accordingly. Once alerted by their dashboard that there is a problem in a particular area, the manager can then drill down into further detail in that area.

Staff people in various departments need dashboards that track and illuminate the specific business operations that they are responsible for such as purchasing, credit, inventory management, and so on. These displays should highlight issues needing their attention.

For the most part, people run their businesses or do their jobs by keeping track of a handful of key indicators. These indicators tell them where to direct their attention and help them steer through a complex and changing world. When a data warehouse and software reporting tools are in place in a company, people need to experiment with the design of their dashboard displays or reports. As they get better at using their dashboards to guide their actions, the overall effect will be for the company as a whole to become more efficient and more responsive to its markets.

Since very few companies work in stable and slow-moving markets anymore, there is a great need to learn to use data effectively to make decisions and act. Speed is a major competitive advantage. The faster a company can spot problems and fix them or see opportunities and respond to them, the more profitable the company will be. It will also have a much better chance of survival over the long term. Companies that can see their markets change and adjust and follow those markets most efficiently are the ones that will stay in business. Companies that do not notice problems soon enough or that do not see how their markets change are the ones that will get into trouble (see Exhibit 5.2).

Markets Migrate from One Quadrant to Another

Markets migrate from one quadrant to another during the course of their life cycle. Over time, market forces are always pushing a market toward an equilibrium where supply meets demand. At the same time, other forces also influence a market so it fluctuates back and forth around the equilibrium point. At times demand outstrips supply and at other times there is more supply than there is demand.

Companies in the supply chains that supply a market must be able to adjust their operations over time as their markets migrate from one quadrant to another in order to remain competitive. For instance, in growth markets, supply chains that do the best are the ones that have the highest levels of customer service as measured by order-fill rate and on-time delivery. All the companies in the supply chain must focus on delivering this performance in order to succeed.

As a growth market moves on to a steady market, the most profitable companies will be those that are able to maintain high levels of existing customer service and also broaden the scope of their customer services.

EXHIBIT 5.2

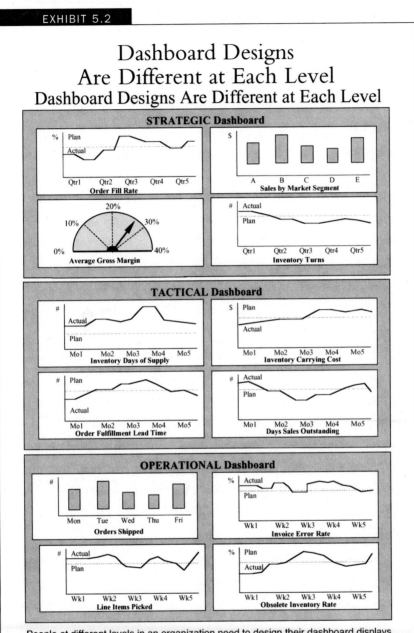

Dashboard Designs
Are Different at Each Level
Dashboard Designs Are Different at Each Level

People at different levels in an organization need to design their dashboard displays so that they get quick and easy access to the data they need to do their jobs and monitor their progress.

In addition, profitable companies will be the ones that achieve the best levels of internal efficiency. They can no longer focus only on customer service.

As steady markets become mature markets, the supply chains that serve them must again develop their performance in another category. Mature markets require companies to develop the capabilities needed to accommodate high levels of demand flexibility. Then in the midst of mature markets, new developing markets can appear and the ability to create new products and bring them to market becomes critical.

Adaptability itself is now as important to survival and success as the four performance categories. Market evolution is now often measured in years and sometimes in months. Gone are the days when markets changed more slowly over decades. No company has the luxury of being able to focus on optimizing any single mix of performance capabilities over the long term.

A company may become very skilled at internal efficiency and customer service as called for in a steady market. The company needs to remember though that its markets will change. The company will have to add skills in the area of demand flexibility as some of its markets mature. The company may even need to de-emphasize some of its internal efficiency policies in order to emphasize its performance in product development so that it can participate in a promising developing market. The key here is that a company needs to know when to shift its emphasis from one mix of performance categories to another.

A ship at sea needs to watch the wind and the waves and respond appropriately when the weather changes. So too must a company watch the supply and demand situation in its markets and respond appropriately when one of its markets enters a new quadrant. If the collection and display of market and company performance data alert a company to respond sooner to a market change than its competitors, then the company has indeed developed an important tool for its success and survival (see Exhibit 5.3).

EXHIBIT 5.3

Market Conditions Shift Over Time

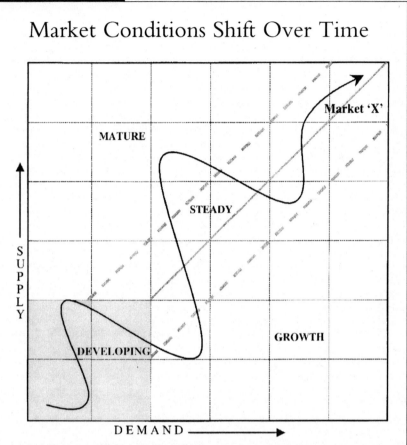

A market (call it Market 'X') follows a life cycle. It develops and then it goes on to become a growth market which leads to a steady market and then a mature market and so on. Over time the forces of supply and demand are always pushing the market toward a steady state where supply and demand are equal yet at the same time other forces disrupt this balance.

The supply chains that support Market 'X' need to be able to provide first one kind of performance and then another as the market moves through its life cycle. The companies that are most successful in supplying this market are those that can adapt their performance appropriately to follow the market as it changes.

Sharing Data Across the Supply Chain

As markets migrate from one quadrant to another, there are great demands placed on the supply chains that support them. In fact, it is sometimes the operation of the supply chain itself that can push a market from one quadrant to another. A case in point is illustrated by the beer game simulation described in Chapter 6. This simulation shows how a slight change in demand by the end customer or the market can cause wildly escalating product demand forecasts to be sent to companies further down the supply chain. This "bullwhip" effect results in the production of large quantities of inventory which can then outstrip the real demand in the market. This event becomes the event that pushes a market out of the steady quadrant and into the mature quadrant. As excess inventory gets used up, it gradually brings the market back into the steady quadrant.

The cure for the bullwhip effect is better sharing of data among all the companies in a supply chain. Companies need to work through their concerns about sharing data that many of them might consider confidential. There are serious questions to be answered. What data is it reasonable to share? How can privacy of critical data be maintained? What are the benefits of sharing data and how can they be quantified?

Hau Lee is a professor at Stanford University's business school and director of the Stanford Global Supply Chain Management Forum. He envisions the supply chain as an "intricate network of suppliers, distributors, and customers who share carefully managed information about demand, decisions, and performance, and who recognize that success for one part of the supply chain means success for all."

If each company had demand information from the other companies in its supply chain, it would help everyone to make the best decisions about how much manufacturing capacity to build and how much inventory to hold. Companies need to see demand information from their immediate customers and also from the end customers that the supply chain ultimately supports.

In addition to sharing demand data across the supply chain, companies need to share decisions they make that have supply chain implications. A company could be unaware of decisions made by one of its customers or one of its customer's customers that will have a big impact on product demand. For instance, a chain of retail stores may decide to run a special promotion on a certain group of products. An analysis of past seasonal sales data would not predict the spike in demand that will result from running this promotion. So if the retail store chain does not share this decision with its suppliers, there is a very good chance they will be caught short and not be able to deliver enough product to support the promotion.

It is also important for companies to let each other know how well they are doing in the performance of their supply chain activities. These metrics can then be combined to provide a holistic picture of the performance of the entire supply chain. When each company in a supply chain sees how the supply chain is working overall, then each company can make better individual decisions about where performance improvements are needed.

At present, companies are most likely to share demand information with each other. There is already a lot of precedent for doing this. However, companies are much less likely to share their decisions or performance metrics because they are afraid that if this information gets out, it could wind up in the hands of their competitors and be used against them. The need for sharing this information continues to grow though. Customers continue to demand more and more from their supply chains. In an interview with *CIO Magazine* for an article titled "The Cost of Secrecy," Professor Hau Lee said, "If you are late because your distributor is late, your customers will go to a competitor whose distributor isn't late. That is more than a company-to-company

EXHIBIT 5.4

Benefits of Data Sharing across the Entire Supply Chain

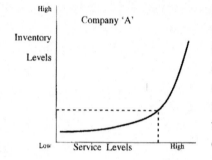

An individual company can achieve high levels of customer service to its customer. However, this customer may not be the end use customer that the supply chain ultimately serves, in which case, the company may find that its success is short lived.

Company 'A' may be part of a supply chain (Supply Chain 'Y') that actually maintains higher levels of inventory across the entire supply chain to deliver the required level of customer service. A competing supply chain that does not maintain as much inventory will be more profitable and can take more market share.

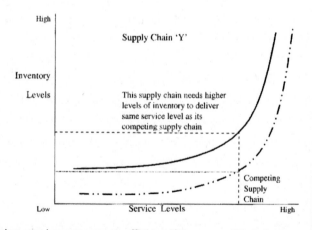

Whole supply chains can become more efficient if they are able to better coordinate their operations. As supply and demand conditions change, coordination of inventory levels is critical to business success.

competition. We're going to see more supply-chain-to-supply-chain competition."

Companies that can work together to create efficient supply chains are going to be the ones that do the best over the long term. Companies that can figure out how to share data effectively will be the ones to create the most competitive supply chains. Customers are attracted to efficient supply chains and they gain market share at the expense of less efficient supply chains (see Exhibit 5.4).

Chapter Summary

A useful model of markets can be constructed using the basic components of supply and demand. Using these two components results in a model that defines four market quadrants:

1. *Developing*—New markets and new products where both supply and demand are low and uncertain
2. *Growth*—Markets where demand is higher than supply and supply is uncertain
3. *Steady*—Established markets where supply is high and demand is high and both are stable and predictable
4. *Mature*—Markets where supply exceeds demand and where demand can be unpredictable

The markets in each quadrant have a unique set of performance requirements that they place on their supply chains. Developing markets require performance in the areas of customer service and product development. Growth markets demand customer service above all else. Steady markets call for customer service and for internal efficiency, and mature markets require customer service, internal efficiency, and demand flexibility. In order to succeed, companies and supply chains must excel in the performance areas that are required by the markets they serve.

Customer service performance is measured by metrics such as order- and line-item fill rate, on-time delivery, and item-return rates. Internal efficiency refers to the ability of a company or supply chain to use its assets as profitably as possible. Popular measures of internal efficiency are metrics such as inventory value, inventory turns, and return on sales. Demand flexibility describes the ability of a company or supply chain to be responsive to sudden market demands for greatly increased quantities of product or for additional products outside the normal bundle of products provided. Product development measures an organization's ability to design, build, and deliver new products to serve their markets as those markets evolve over time. Performance in this area is most important in developing markets.

CHAPTER 6

Supply Chain Coordination

After reading this chapter you will be able to

- Understand a common supply chain dynamic that is a major contributor to the "boom to bust" business cycle

- Appreciate the factors that contribute to this supply chain dynamic

- Gain an overview of the Global Data Synchronization Network (GDSN) and see how it can help improve supply chain coordination

- Evaluate methods such as collaborative planning, forecasting, and replenishment (CPFR) to improve coordination and combat the bullwhip effect

The spread of high-speed data communication networks and computer technology has made it possible to manage supply chains with a level of precision just not feasible even as recently as the 1990s. Those organizations that learn to use the techniques and technologies that are now available can build supply chains that have a competitive advantage in their markets.

Because the capability exists to react much more quickly to changes in market demand, this capability is now a point of competition. Business competition based on supply chain efficiency is becoming a central fact in many markets. To develop this capability, individual companies and entire supply chains need to learn new behaviors and they need to enable these new behaviors with the use of appropriate technology.

The Bullwhip Effect

One of the most common dynamics in supply chains is a phenomena that has been dubbed "the bullwhip effect." What happens is that small changes in product demand by the consumer at the front of the supply chain translate into wider and wider swings in demand experienced by companies further back in the supply chain. Companies at different stages in the supply chain come to have very different pictures of market demand and the result is a breakdown in supply chain coordination. Companies behave in ways that at first create product shortages and then lead to an excess supply of products.

This dynamic plays out on a larger scale in certain industries in what is called a "boom to bust" business cycle. In particular this affects industries that serve developing and growth markets where demand can suddenly grow. Good examples of this can be found in the industries that serve the telecommunications equipment or computer components markets. The cycle starts when strong market demand creates a shortage of product. Distributors and manufacturers steadily increase their inventories and production rates in response to the demand. At some point either demand changes or the supply of product exceeds the demand level. Distributors and manufacturers do not at first realize that supply exceeds demand and they continue building the supply. Finally the glut of product is so large that everyone realizes there is too much. Manufacturers shut down plants and lay off workers. Distributors are stuck with inventories that decrease in value and can take years to work down.

This dynamic can be modeled in a simple supply chain that contains a retailer, a distributor, and a manufacturer. In the 1960s a simulation game was developed by the Massachusetts Institute of Technology's

Sloan School of Management that illustrates how the bullwhip effect develops. The simulation game they developed is called the "beer game." It shows what happens in a hypothetical supply chain that supports a group of retail stores that sell beer, snacks, and other convenience items. The results of the beer game simulation teach a lot about how to coordinate the actions of different companies in a supply chain.

Peter Senge in his book, *The Fifth Discipline* (Senge, Peter M., 1990, *The Fifth Discipline: The Art and Practice of the Learning Organization,* New York: Doubleday/Currency, Chapter 3), devotes a chapter to exploring how the bullwhip effect gathers momentum and what can be done to avoid it. The beer game starts with retailers experiencing a sudden but small increase in customer demand for a certain brand of beer called Lover's Beer. Orders are batched up by retailers and passed on to the distributors who deliver the beer. Initially, these orders exceed the inventory that distributors have on hand so they ration out their supplies of Lover's Beer to the retailers and place even larger orders for the beer with the brewery that makes Lover's Beer. The brewery cannot instantly increase production of the beer so it rations out the beer it can produce to the distributors and begins building additional production capacity.

At first the scarcity of the beer prompts panic buying and hoarding behavior. Then as the brewery ramps up its production rate and begins shipping the product in large quantities, the orders that had been steadily increasing due to panic buying suddenly decline. The glut of product fills up the distributors' warehouses, fills all the retailers' unfilled back orders, and exceeds the actual consumer demand. The brewery is left with excess production capacity, the distributors are stuck with excess inventory, and the retailers either cancel their beer orders or run discount promotions to move the product. Everybody loses money. Exhibit 6.1 illustrates how each company sees product demand and the distortion that causes such havoc.

The costs of the bullwhip effect are felt by all members of the supply chain. Manufacturers add extra production capacity to satisfy

EXHIBIT 6.1

Product Demand Distortion
"The Bullwhip Effect"

Inventory levels in supply chain over time illustrating the wild swings that develop as product demand distortion moves from customer to retailer to distributor to manufacturer. Swings in product demand appear more pronounced to companies further up the supply chain. This distortion makes effective supply chain management very difficult.

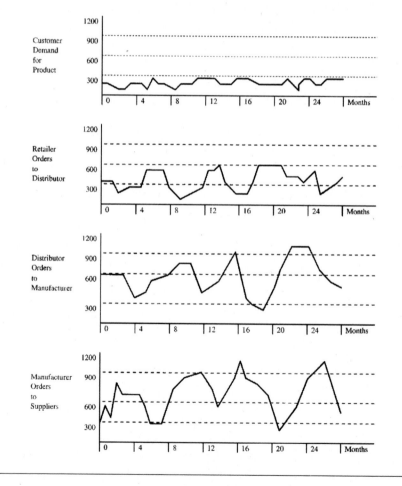

an order stream that is much more volatile than actual demand. Distributors carry extra inventory to cover the variability in order levels. Transportation costs increase because excess transportation capacity has to be added to cover the periods of high demand. Along with transportation costs, labor costs also go up in order to respond to the high demand periods. Retailers experience problems with product availability and extended replenishment lead times. During periods of high demand, there are times when the available capacity and inventory in the supply chain cannot cover the orders being placed. This results in product rationing, longer order replenishment cycles, and lost sales due to lack of inventory.

Coordination in the Supply Chain

Research into the bullwhip effect has identified five major factors that cause the effect. These factors interact with each other in different combinations in different supply chains, but the net effect is that they generate the wild demand swings that make it so hard to run an efficient supply chain. These factors must be understood and addressed in order to coordinate the actions of any supply chain. They are:

1. Demand Forecasting
2. Order Batching
3. Product Rationing
4. Product Pricing
5. Performance Incentives

Demand Forecasting

Demand forecasting, based on orders received instead of end user demand data will inherently become more and more inaccurate as it moves up the supply chain. Companies that are removed from contact with the end user can lose touch with actual market demand if they view their role as simply filling the orders placed with them by their immediate customers. Each company in a supply chain sees fluctuations in the orders that come to them that are caused by the bullwhip effect. When they use this order data to do their demand forecasts, they just add further distortion to the demand picture and pass this distortion along in the form of orders that they place with their suppliers.

Clearly, one way to counteract this distortion in demand forecasts is for all companies in a supply chain to share a common set of demand data from which to do their forecasting. The most accurate source of this demand data is the supply chain member closest to the end-use customer (if not the end-use customers themselves). Sharing point-of-sales (POS) data among all the companies in a supply chain goes a long way toward taming the bullwhip effect because it lets everyone respond to actual market demand instead of supply chain distortions.

Order Batching

Order batching occurs because companies place orders periodically for amounts of product that will minimize their order-processing and transportation costs. As discussed in the section on inventory control in Chapter 2, companies tend to order in lot sizes determined by the economic order quantity (EOQ). Because of order batching, these orders vary from the level of actual demand and this variance is magnified as it moves up the supply chain.

The way to address demand distortion caused by order batching is to find ways to reduce the cost of order-processing and transportation. This will cause EOQ lot sizes to get smaller and orders to be placed more frequently. The result will be a smoother flow of orders that distributors and manufacturers will be able to handle more efficiently. Ordering costs can be reduced by using electronic ordering technology. Transportation costs can be reduced by using third-party logistics suppliers (3PLs) to cost effectively pick up many small shipments from suppliers and deliver small orders to many customers.

Product Rationing

This is the response that manufacturers take when they are faced with more demand than they can meet. One common rationing approach is for a manufacturer to allocate the available supply of product based on the number of orders received. Thus if the available supply equals 70 percent of the orders received, the manufacturer will fill 70 percent of the amount of each order and backorder the rest. This leads distributors and retailers in the supply chain to raise their order quantities artificially in order to increase the amount of product that gets rationed to them. This behavior greatly overstates product demand and it is called "shortage gaming."

There are several ways to respond to this. Manufacturers can base their rationing decisions on the historical ordering patterns of a given distributor or retailer and not on their present order sizes. This eliminates much of the motivation for the shortage gaming that otherwise occurs. Manufacturers and distributors can also alert their customers in advance if they see demand outstripping supply. This way product shortages will not take buyers by surprise and there will be less panic buying.

Product Pricing

Product pricing causes product prices to fluctuate, resulting in distortions of product demand. If special sales are offered and product prices are lowered, it will induce customers to buy more product or to buy product sooner than they otherwise would (forward buying). Then prices return to normal levels and demand falls off. Instead of a smooth flow of products through the supply chain, price fluctuations can create waves of demand and surges of product flow that are hard to handle efficiently.

Answers to this problem generally revolve around the concept of "everyday low prices." If the end customers for a product believe that they will get a good price whenever they purchase the product, they will make purchases based on real need and not other considerations. This in turn makes demand easier to forecast and companies in the supply chain can respond more efficiently.

Performance Incentives

These are often different for different companies and individuals in a supply chain. Each company can see its job as managing its position in isolation from the rest of the supply chain. Within companies, individuals can also see their jobs in isolation from the rest of the company. It is common for companies to structure incentives that reward a company's sales force on sales made each month or each quarter. Therefore as the end of a month or a quarter approaches, the sales force offers discounts and takes other measures to move product in order to meet quotas. This results in product for which there is no real demand being pushed into the supply chain. It is also common for managers within a company to be motivated by incentives that conflict with other company objectives. For instance, a transportation manager may take actions that minimize transportation costs at the expense of customer service or inventory carrying costs.

Alignment of performance incentives with supply chain efficiencies is a real challenge. It begins with the use of accurate activity-based costing (ABC) data that can highlight the associated costs. Companies need to quantify the expenses incurred by forward buying due to month-end or quarter-end sales incentives. Companies also need to identify the effect of conflicting internal performance incentives. The next step is to experiment with new incentive plans that support efficient supply chain operation. This is a process that each company needs to work through in its own way.

EXECUTIVE INSIGHT

Eliyahu Goldratt wrote a book titled, *The Goal*, about a factory manager's quest to save his factory from being closed down for lack of profitability. It chronicles the process that the manager and his staff go through as they learn how to save their factory. What they learn is how to apply the principles of what Mr. Goldratt calls the "Theory of Constraints."

Mr. Goldratt and others have realized that the theory of constraints applies equally well to the operation of a whole supply chain as to the operation of a single factory within a supply chain. Lawrence Fredendall and Ed Hill in their book, *Basics of Supply Chain Management* (Fredendall, Lawrence D., and Ed Hill, 2001, *Basics of Supply Chain Management*, Boca Raton, FL: St. Lucie Press), have put forth a clear explanation for how to apply the theory of constraints to synchronize the operations of a supply chain.

The theory of constraints provides a useful model to conceptualize and manage the supply chain within a single company or across a collection of companies. The theory of constraints is based upon the idea that all systems have at least one constraint and that it is better to manage constraints than to try to eliminate them. This is because when one part of a system ceases to be a constraint, a different constraint will occur in another part of the system. This is inevitable because the capacities of each part of a system are not all the same. So instead of forever reacting to new constraints or bottlenecks as they appear, why not choose a small group of constraints and manage them deliberately and efficiently?

To apply this model, the first step is to define the goal and decide what measurements will be used to measure progress toward the goal. Mr. Goldratt's definition of the goal for a manufacturing company also works for a supply chain. The goal is defined as

(Continued)

"Increase throughput while simultaneously reducing both inventory and operating expense." Throughput is the rate at which sales to end customers occur.

Once a goal has been defined and there is agreement on how to measure progress toward the goal, it is possible to apply the five focusing steps. These steps help clarify the situation being investigated and lead to the decisions necessary to reach the goal. The five steps are:

Identify the System's Bottlenecks or Constraints—Trace out the workflows and the paths that materials travel in a factory or a supply chain. Find out where slowdowns and backups occur.

Decide How to Exploit These Bottlenecks—Figure out how to maximize the operation of those activities that are bottlenecks. The rate of throughput for the entire system is set by the rate of throughput achieved by the bottlenecks. Ensure the bottlenecks operate at maximum capacity by providing them with enough inventory so that they can continue to operate even if there are occasional slowdowns elsewhere in the system.

Subordinate Everything Else to the Above Decision—Do not try to maximize the operation of a non-bottleneck operation. Additional productivity achieved by non-bottleneck operations that exceeds the capacity of the bottlenecks to process will be neutralized anyway by the slowdowns and backups caused at the bottlenecks. Synchronize all system operations to the rates that can be efficiently processed by the bottleneck operations.

Elevate the System's Bottlenecks—Add additional processing capacity to the bottleneck activities. Since the rate of throughput of the entire system is set by the throughput of the bottlenecks, improvements in the bottlenecks will increase the efficiency of the entire system and provide the best return on investment.

If, in a Previous Step, a Bottleneck Has Been Broken, Go Back to Step 1—As the capacity of one system bottleneck is elevated,

EXECUTIVE INSIGHT (*CONTINUED*)

it may cease to be a bottleneck. The bottleneck may transfer to another operation that could keep up before but now cannot keep up with the new increase in capacity. Watch the entire system to see where slowdowns and backups occur; they may shift from one area to another. If this occurs, start again at Step 1.

The theory of constraints says that the throughput of the whole system is set by the capacity of the bottlenecks. Exhibit 6.2 shows a sample diagram of workflows and bottlenecks in a factory. This model of workflows in a factory can be applied to the workflows in a supply chain. One constraint or bottleneck in every supply chain is the demand that is generated by the market that the supply chain serves. In many cases, market demand is the only constraint because supply of products equals or exceeds demand. In cases where demand exceeds supply there will be some other constraints elsewhere in the supply chain. If we apply this model to a supply chain, we get a powerful method to organize and manage supply chain operations.

EXHIBIT 6.2

Flow of Work and Inventory through a Factory

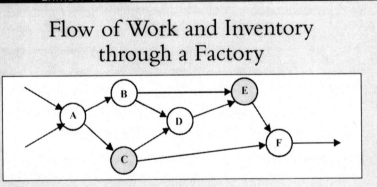

FLOW OF WORK AND INVENTORY THROUGH A FACTORY

The bottlenecks or constraints in the flow of work through this factory are operations C and E in Exhibit 6.2. The productivity set by these two operations sets the pace for the *entire* factory. Productivity improvements in the other operations will not result

(*Continued*)

in any improvement in the productivity of the factory as a whole. Apply the five focusing steps to manage this system and move it toward the goal defined for it.

A very effective response to the bullwhip effect is to manage the entire supply chain as a single entity and to synchronize it to the timing of actual market demand. Exhibit 6.3 illustrates this idea. This can happen if the supply chain participants closest to the end-use customers share their sales numbers and their sales forecasts with the other companies in the supply chain. Each company can then manage their actions based on the most accurate data about market demand.

Buffers in the supply chain are determined by the degree of uncertainty about future market demand and the service levels required by the market. The lower the uncertainty about demand, the smaller the buffers can be and still maintain high service levels. Companies can manage their buffers by using either productive capacity or inventory, whichever is most cost effective for them.

Synchronized supply chains avoid the volatile waves of demand that are generated by the bullwhip effect. And increased predictability makes the productivity of each company easier to manage and the supply chain as a whole becomes more efficient and profitable.

FLOW OF INVENTORY THROUGH A SYNCHRONIZED SUPPLY CHAIN

This model is called "drum-buffer-rope." Market demand is the constraint on the system and it sets the drumbeat or pace of the supply chain. Individual companies manage uncertainty in their stage of the supply chain by using a buffer of either inventory or productive capacity. Buffers are kept low because uncertainty is minimized by sharing market demand data. This data is the rope that ties the participants together and allows them to synchronize their actions.

EXHIBIT 6.3

Flow of Inventory through a Synchronized Supply Chain

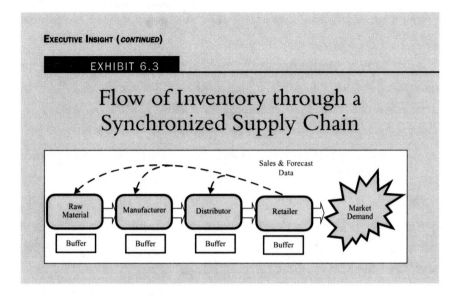

Supply Chain Product Data Standards

Historically, companies have assigned their own part numbers to the items that they buy and sell. This worked well enough in a slower time when supply chains were less complex and when products themselves were less complex. Those were times we now refer to as the "good old days." Increasing competition and demands from customers to deliver products faster and cheaper shapes the world we live in today. At the same time, the array and complexity of products in our economy have increased dramatically and that trend will clearly continue and even accelerate.

In order to be competitive and also profitable, companies need to find ways to reduce or eliminate costs associated with routine and repetitive business transactions. Those transactions often fall in the areas of purchasing, billing, accounts receivable, and accounts payable. It is in these areas that the confusion caused by translating part numbers is most noticeable. Time spent translating one part number to another part number for the same item adds very little, if any, value to the transaction. The errors that result from errors in translation are the cause of many problems in invoicing and making payments. These problems consume people's time and slow down cash flow. All these expenses simply eat away at profit margins that are already thin enough.

In addition to the operating problems caused by using different part numbers for the same item, another consequence is a lack of accuracy and clarity in sales history data. Part number translation errors result in sales of some items being undercounted and sales of other items being overcounted. And sales of many items are simply not counted at all or they are lumped under a miscellaneous part number such as the famous "9999" part number. Sales history data is usually the basis for forecasting future demand and this fuzziness in the data hampers efforts to improve demand forecasts, production scheduling, and inventory management.

In order for companies to coordinate effectively, they need to have a single part number that stays with a part as it makes its way through the supply chain. That number is the electronic product code (EPC) number. Companies that do business together need to be able to tag every item that they buy and sell with an EPC number. They can still use their internal part numbers for internal operations if they wish. But when they communicate with each other they need to use EPC numbers so as to eliminate the need to do part-number translations. There are more valuable and profitable things that can be done with the time and money that now goes into translating part numbers and dealing with translation-related problems.

Global Data Synchronization Network

The Global Data Synchronization Network (GDSN) is a network of independently owned and operated databases that can exchange data with each other and the GS1 Global Registry. The GS1 Global Registry acts as a central coordinator between all the other databases to provide for timely and traceable distribution of verified product descriptive information between all the databases. It is the locator and routing mechanism for finding source data and sending requested data between databases.

GS1 is a global, not-for-profit organization of member organizations, including GS1 US, representing more than 100 countries around the world. GS1 is based in Brussels, Belgium. GS1 US is the former Uniform Code Council and consists of the EAN UCC System, UCCnet, EPCglobal US, RosettaNet, and UNSPSC. GS1 US is based in New Jersey, USA (www.gs1us.org).

Companies join the GS1 Global Registry to keep connected to their trading partners that also join the Global Registry. Parties in a supply chain—manufacturers, logistics providers, distributors, retailers—then subscribe to the database of their choice and through these databases they can both publish data about their products to other parties as well as request and receive data from other companies about their products. This is illustrated in Exhibit 6.4.

The GDSN is being administered by GS1 and increasingly is being used by companies in consumer goods retail and related areas. It allows data about products to be continuously updated as new products are released, existing products evolve, and obsolete products are discontinued. The benefits are significant beginning with the fact that each company needs only to make a single connection to their selected database or "data pool" as GDSN calls them. Once they do this they can send and receive data to and from any other company that is connected to any other data pool that is part of the GDSN.

Other benefits include things such as elimination of the need for companies to maintain massive cross-reference tables to translate between the different part numbers for the same product that are used by different supply chain partners. This reduces many ordering and billing errors that consume people's time and result in delays in product deliveries and cash flows between companies. It also simplifies order tracking and tracing individual items as they move through a supply chain.

EXHIBIT 6.4

Global Data Synchronization Network (GDSN)

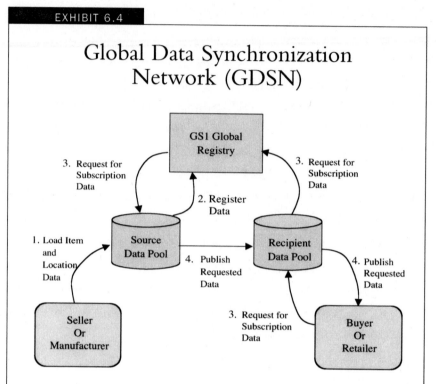

1. **Load Item and Location Data** – the seller or manufacturer registers with a GS1 certified data pool and uploads item and location data to their data pool.

2. **Register Data** – a small subset of item and location data is sent by the data pool to GS1 Global Registry.

3. **Request for Subscription Data** – the buyer or retailer subscribes to a data pool and to categories of products or to particular suppliers to receive the related item and location data. Buyer requests data from their data pool. The data pool requests this data from the GS1 Global Registry and the Global Registry sends the request to the data pool containing this data.

4. **Publish Requested Data** – the seller's data pool provides requested item and location data to the data pool of the buyer and the buyer's data pool sends the data to the buyer. Buyer updates its systems with this data. Buyer and seller now have identical item and location data—data synchronization is complete.

Source: GS1 US (formerly known as Uniform Code Council Inc)

Product Classification

Products that move through a supply chain need to be identified and traced so that people know how many products are moving through their supply chains. Products also need to be classified so that people know what types of products they are handling. All supply chains handle a mix of different product types and that mix changes over time. As the product mix changes, the supply chain itself must change.

There are two major standards presently in use for product classification. The first one is the United Nations Standard Products and Services Code (UNSPSC). The United Nations Development Program (UNDP) and Dun & Bradstreet Corporation (D&B) jointly developed the UNSPSC in 1998. The UNSPSC is a hierarchical classification with five levels. These levels allow analysis by drilling down or rolling up to analyze expenditures and product usage at each level. Each level in the hierarchy has its own unique number. Starting with the highest level, the five levels are segment, family, class, commodity, and business function.

The second major product classification standard presently in use is the GS1 Global Product Code or GPC. The GPC was developed by GS1 and is used in the GDSN to identify different types of products. The GPC is also a hierarchical classification scheme and it has four levels: Segment; Family; Class; and Brick. These two product-classification schemes are not mutually exclusive and they can be used together. It does require all parties to agree on the rules they will use to translate product codes between UNSPSC numbers and GPC numbers.

Collaborative Planning, Forecasting, and Replenishment

To facilitate the coordination that is needed in supply chains, an industry group known as the Voluntary Interindustry Commerce Standards (VICS) (www.vics.org) has set up a committee to investigate collaborative planning, forecasting, and replenishment issues (CPFR). This committee documents best practices for CPFR and creates guidelines to follow for CPFR.

Supply chains where people use technology to support a CPFR process are the most efficient supply chains, because they can best manage the factors that give rise to the bullwhip effect.

The CPFR process is divided into the three activities of planning, forecasting, and replenishment. Within each activity there are several steps:

Collaborative Planning

- Negotiate a front-end agreement that defines the responsibilities of the companies that will collaborate with each other
- Build a joint business plan that shows how the companies will work together to meet demand

Collaborative Forecasting

- Create sales forecasts for all the collaborating companies
- Identify any exceptions or differences between companies
- Resolve the exceptions to provide a common sales forecast

Collaborative Replenishment

- Create order forecasts for all the collaborating companies
- Identify exceptions between companies
- Resolve the exceptions to provide an efficient production and delivery schedule
- Generate actual orders to meet customer demand

CPFR in Action

For an example of how CPFR can work let's return to the example of Nimble Co. In the section on product design in Chapter 3, we saw how Nimble Co. developed a home entertainment system that was much simpler to manufacture than a competitor's system. This simpler design is in turn supported by a less-complex supply chain that reduces production costs and increases responsiveness to market demands. All of this is central to the competitive success that Nimble Co. is enjoying.

Nimble Co. has collaboration agreements in place with its supply chain partners and has an ongoing planning, forecasting, and replenishment process in place with these partners. Nimble Co. receives point of sale (POS) data that shows the actual sales of its systems in retail stores. From these same retailers, Nimble Co. receives regular updates of their sales forecasts and their inventory levels of Nimble Co. home entertainment systems. Nimble Co. uses this data to plan its production schedule and it also shares this data with the component manufacturers who provide parts for its home entertainment system. This way the component manufacturers can plan their own production schedules.

In looking at the sales data and forecasts, Nimble Co. sees that demand for their product is growing faster than anticipated in their yearly plan, and they need to increase production. Nimble Co. revises its production schedule for the year and takes the new plan to its key component suppliers to negotiate additional purchases of their components. It turns out that one component supplier cannot quickly ramp up their production but a second supplier has a component that could fill the need with just a slight modification to the design of one part of Nimble Co.'s home entertainment system. Because all affected parties know what is going on and have enough lead time, the design changes are made and production schedules are increased to meet the rise in product demand without any retailers running out of inventory.

The benefits illustrated in this scenario are numerous. To begin with, the bullwhip effect is diminished because all companies in the supply chain can see real-time sales data and share sales forecasts. This allows everyone to optimize their production schedules, inventory levels, and delivery schedules. Next there are the benefits associated with Nimble Co. being able to quickly see a real rise in customer demand

and coordinate with its suppliers to increase production schedules over previously planned levels. Even though one component supplier was not able to accommodate Nimble Co.'s increased production schedule, another supplier had a workable substitute. Changes were made to the product design, production was increased, and no retailer lost sales revenue due to running out of inventory.

Those companies that can create collaborative supply chains will have a significant competitive advantage. Collaboration is not easy to implement and it will take time to become more common in business. However, prominent companies are already beginning to lead the way. Companies such as Wal-Mart, Dell, and Procter & Gamble share POS data with all the other companies in their respective supply chains. The companies in these supply chains are also starting to share inventory data with each other. Sharing this kind of information provides a basis for each company to make decisions about its own activities that will yield better efficiencies and profits for itself and for the supply chain as a whole.

How to Start Supply Chain Collaboration

The best place to start in any effort to promote collaboration is to measure the bullwhip effect within your company. Over a period of time such as a quarter or a year, compare the volume and frequency of orders you receive from your customers with the volume and frequency of orders you place with your suppliers. Plot them out on a graph so everyone can see the divergence between incoming customer orders and your outgoing supplier orders. What is the extent of this divergence? Where is your company located in the supply chain—is it toward the front of the chain close to the end customer or is it further toward the back of the chain? Remember, the distortion caused by divergence of incoming orders with outgoing orders increases as it moves back through the supply chain.

Many companies are not aware of the cost of the bullwhip effect on their supply chains. Traditionally, demand variability caused by the bullwhip effect was taken as a given and companies worked on their own to develop better capabilities to respond to fluctuations in demand. It may instead be far more efficient for companies to work together to actually reduce the fluctuations in demand. A company can either try to optimize its individual response to fluctuating demand or it can collaborate with other companies to reduce the fluctuations themselves.

Once you have established the magnitude of the bullwhip effect in your company, then get some estimates of the cost consequences in different areas of the company. What is the effect of this demand variability on production costs and scheduling? What is the effect on transportation costs and shipping and receiving costs? What inventory levels are needed to maintain service levels in such a volatile situation and what is the associated carrying cost? What is the effect on product availability and order lead times—are sales lost because of lack of inventory? These estimates show the cost to the company of dealing with demand fluctuations. This is the basis upon which to discuss what it might be worth to fix the bullwhip effect.

EXECUTIVE INSIGHT

The Tao of Supply Chains: Effective supply chain collaboration requires that the people involved be able to see accurate and timely data showing inventory levels at different stages in the supply chain. What follows is a story about creating a simple supply chain visibility system that enabled very effective collaboration.

Sun Tzu was a Taoist philosopher who lived in China about 2,500 years ago. He wrote a book called *The Art of War*. It isn't so much a book about war as it is a book about the art of competition and collaboration—whether in business, politics, the military, or even

(Continued)

sports. I've puzzled through this book several times, and the concepts that I've taken away have helped me develop and preserve a reputation for IT agility.

For six years I was the chief information officer (CIO) of Network Services Company. Network Services is a nationwide distribution cooperative that provides foodservice items, janitorial supplies, and printing paper. It is wholly owned by its 80+ member companies. They each have their own facilities and internal IT systems and they have their own local customers. They also work together to serve national account customers. The members' collective revenue was then more than $7 billion, and Network's total national account revenue was more than $500 million, growing by double-digit percentages every year. We provided customers with a tailored package of products and supply chain services to lower their overall operating costs.

One of our biggest national account customers was a chain of stores that each holiday season used specially printed paper items to promote its holiday theme. Those items were used in the customer's 4,500 stores during November and December, and when January arrived any remaining inventory had to be written off. The same holiday print designs were never used two years in a row. In years past, there had been excess inventory of around 4 percent, amounting to almost $600,000 in costs that had to be written off by the customer.

This retail chain hired a new purchasing manager who decided we could all do better than in prior holiday seasons. He called us out to the company's headquarters that summer for a meeting. There he announced his intention to reduce excess inventory of the specially printed holiday items by 50 percent or more. We still had to maintain 100 percent product availability for all of its stores and minimize expensive movements of inventory from one region to another to meet unexpected demand. He asked us how we were going to work with him to make that happen. I told him we understood what he wanted and that we'd be back in touch with the specifics in a few weeks.

As we flew home, our sales director on the account told me this was a high-visibility project with the customer, and we had to figure out how to do it. He reminded me that it was already halfway through the summer, so we had to be ready to go in 90 days because we would begin stocking inventory in our distribution centers by October. And, of course, we couldn't spend lots of money on this because margins were tight. In addition, all the parties in this supply chain used different enterprise resource planning (ERP) systems. And even within Network Services, the 26 member companies that served the account used different ERP systems. Several times on that flight, I experienced a sudden falling sensation in my stomach, and it wasn't due to air turbulence.

At times like these my identity as IT Agility Man hangs in the balance. Can I rise to the challenge, or will I flee in panic? Agility means doing three things: First, taking a deep breath; second, taking another deep breath; then, remembering *The Art of War* and asking, "What would Master Sun Tzu do?"

The concepts that I've been able to absorb from Master Sun tell me that apparent complexity is really composed of simple underlying patterns. If I can discern those underlying patterns, then I can devise simple and effective responses. So what was the pattern here? As I saw it, the need was to track daily product usage, constantly update demand forecasts, move inventory so as to cover demand, and use it all up by the end of the season.

That meant effective collaboration among all parties in the supply chain to respond as actual demand unfolded. If our initial assumptions about demand were not entirely accurate (and they never are), we needed to be able to reposition inventory among distribution centers earlier and more efficiently. No sudden air freighting of paper goods to stores across the country. So, I asked myself, "What can IT provide that will enable this collaboration?" Obviously, what was needed was a continually updated, end-to-end view of product in the supply chain that was visible at all times to people at my company, the manufacturers, and

(Continued)

the customer. That would be the basis for our collaboration and decision making.

I knew of several fine software vendors' products that could do that, but they cost more money than I had to spend and took more time to install than I had available. So much for the orthodox ideas. What else could I do? Master Sun says, "Therefore, those skilled at the unorthodox are infinite as heaven and earth, inexhaustible as the great rivers." Wow. What unorthodox ideas could I come up with?

Master Sun says, "There are only five notes in the musical scale, but their variations are so many that they cannot all be heard. There are only five basic colors, but their variations are so many that they cannot all be seen." Does this mean that there is a combination of basic IT components that I could use to quickly create my end-to-end supply chain picture and keep it constantly updated?

What basic IT components do all parties in this supply chain have easy access to, and how could I combine them into the system I needed? I'm not going to give you the whole answer because then you wouldn't get to practice your own agility and figure it out for yourself. But I will give you some hints. The components are spreadsheets, text files, e-mail, a few Web pages, a relational database, and some Java programs that took about three weeks to write and test.

We assembled these components into a system that collected data from all members of the supply chain. The data consisted of inventory amounts that were in production, in warehouses, and on order. It also included invoice data that showed our deliveries to the customer's stores, which allowed us to track actual demand at the store levels and regional levels.

The system was up and running by October. It was extremely cost effective to build. We used it to facilitate conference calls that increased in frequency as the season progressed. On those calls, we all reviewed the numbers and projected run-out dates. We made decisions and continued to tweak the system to incorporate new views of the data and new calculations.

We reduced excess inventory from 4 percent in prior years to 1.3 percent that year on increased total sales, and the dollar value of the excess inventory dropped to less than $200,000. As we reviewed the holiday season results in January, the new purchasing manager said he was quite pleased with our performance. We worked with him and the manufacturers to document what we learned, make further improvements, and extend the system to cover the rollout of other new products—not just holiday items. Thank you, Master Sun.

If you want to know more about how I designed and built this supply chain visibility system you can contact me by e-mail at: mhugos@yahoo.com and I'll be glad to share the details with you.

Sales and Operations Planning

Sales and operations planning (S&OP) is, to a large degree, a further elaboration of the planning process described in Chapter 2 (page 42). It also shares elements in common with the CPFR process described in this chapter (page 199). As companies develop effective S&OP processes internally and collaboratively with their supply chain partners, they will see significant improvements in their supply chain management capabilities.

The Association for Operations Management (APICS, formerly American Production and Inventory Control Society), endorses a definition of sales and operations planning provided by Tom Wallace in his book *Sales & Operations Planning*:

Sales & Operations Planning (S&OP) is a business process that helps companies keep demand and supply in balance. It does that by focusing on aggregate volumes—product families and groups—so that mix issues—individual products and customer orders—can be handled more readily. It occurs on a monthly cycle and displays information in both units and dollars. S&OP is cross functional, involving General Management, Sales, Operations, Finance, and Product Development. It occurs at multiple levels within the company, up to and including the executive in charge of the business unit, that is, division president, business unit general manager, or CEO of a smaller corporation. S&OP links the company's Strategic Plans and Business Plan to its detailed processes—the order entry, master scheduling, and purchasing tools it uses to run the business on a week-to-week, day-to-day, and hour-to-hour basis. Used properly, S&OP enables the company's managers to view the business holistically and gives them a window into the future. (Tom Wallace, *Sales & Operations Planning*, T.F. Wallace & Co., Cincinnati, OH, 2000.)

The purpose of S&OP is to routinely review customer demand for different products and the sources of supply for those products, and then re-plan or adjust existing plans to best match supply with demand. The process focuses on changes to earlier supply and demand forecasts and helps managers understand how well the company is doing in the process of balancing supply and demand. The primary aim is to continuously adjust company operating procedures so as to accomplish its strategic goals and annual sales targets in light of expected future conditions.

The continuous adjustment of sales and operations plans as forecasts change is the method by which a company takes steps each month to best meet its annual sales targets. The S&OP process can be thought of as having five main steps as shown in Exhibit 6.5 below.

S&OP takes a phased and iterative approach to the planning and operations in a company. Instead of attempting to do one master plan each year and then spend the rest of the year following that one plan, S&OP takes the approach of continuously reevaluating demand and supply conditions and continuously adjusting plans in light of changing

EXHIBIT 6.5

Sales & Operations Planning Cycle

Sales Forecasting	Demand Planning	Supply Planning	Reconcile Plans	Finalize Plans & Implement
Collect sales data, analyze trends, make forecasts	Check forecasts, review demand variability, adjust inventory and customer service policies	Review supply capacity and schedule operations to meet demand	Match supply and demand and assess financial implications	Finalize plans and schedule production

This planning cycle is done on a monthly basis, and increasingly, it needs to be done on a weekly or even daily basis in order to respond effectively as conditions change.

conditions. It is a process of constantly responding to change. Fixed annual plans worked better in the slower and more predictable industrial economy of the last century. The real-time unpredictable nature of the economy of this century makes it critical for companies to constantly respond to changing conditions.

Companies are encouraged to take an "outside-in" approach to their S&OP planning. People should begin their forecasting and planning by considering the effect of events that are largely outside of their control such as the actions of customers, partners, and competitors. These actions typically have the greatest impact, either positive or negative, on a company's ability to meet its sales and operating targets. Collaboration with customers and partners (if not with competitors) provides for more accurate information about these possible actions and thus makes the S&OP process more effective. This is where practices from CPFR can be beneficial to S&OP.

In a world now awash in data thanks to computers, the Internet, and the global reach of telecommunication networks, it is important for people in the S&OP process to know the data they need and find ways to get that data quickly and accurately. The collection of massive amounts of unnecessary data or inaccurate data will slow down the planning process and prevent people from making effective decisions in a timely manner. Good S&OP practice defines the minimum amount of data needed to make certain decisions and focuses on getting that data quickly and guaranteeing its accuracy.

Chapter Summary

One of the most common dynamics in supply chains is a phenomenon that has been dubbed "the bullwhip effect." What happens is that small changes in product demand by the consumer at the front of the supply chain translate into wider and wider swings in demand, as experienced by companies further back in the supply chain. Companies at different stages in the supply chain come to have very different pictures of market demand and the result is a breakdown in supply chain coordination. Companies behave in ways that at first create product shortages and then lead to an excess supply of products.

Many companies are not aware of the cost of the bullwhip effect on their supply chains. Traditionally, difficulties in predicting demand caused by the bullwhip effect were taken as a given and companies worked on their own to develop better capabilities to respond to these hard-to-predict fluctuations in demand. It may instead be far more efficient for companies to work together to actually reduce the fluctuations in demand or more accurately predict those changes in demand. A company can use CPFR to better forecast changes in demand and supply and it can use S&OP to optimize its individual response to fluctuating demand and supply conditions.

The GDSN is a network of interoperable databases that allows all parties in a supply chain to continuously update and request data about different products. The GDSN is administered by the GS1 organization. GS1 is a global not-for-profit organization devoted to setting standards and providing for efficient data transfer between all parties in global and regional supply chains. Efficient transfer of up-to-date and accurate information is a basic requirement for supply chain coordination.

CHAPTER 7

Supply Chain Innovation for the Real-Time Economy

After reading this chapter you will be able to:

- Consider trends that make coordination and collaboration key requirements for success in twenty-first century supply chains.

- Discuss the potential of real-time simulation and massively multi-player online games as a source of ideas for new supply chain operating models.

- Appreciate the need for universal, easy, and inexpensive data connections between all parties in a supply chain and see why these connections will improve supply chain performance and profitability.

- Start to assess the potential for using social media to enhance supply chain capabilities.

Coordination and Collaboration in Supply Chains

Innovation in supply chains starts with the realization of how much has changed over the last 20 years or so and how that affects the way supply chains need to be organized and operated. In complex and high-change environments like our real-time global economy it is hard for a single company to forecast demand and act effectively in isolation. In this environment, coordination is more powerful than control. Profits come from being able to plug into supply chain networks and then develop a reputation in those networks for having the best service and best products at good prices. Companies do not need to have the lowest prices, they just need to be "in the ballpark" or within a few percentage points of the market average, because most customers are looking for something in addition to low prices.

The relentless price-driven pursuit of cost savings alone doesn't produce the profits it once did because this focus causes companies to optimize efficient production of existing products at the expense of their ability to change and create new products as markets evolve. Companies optimized for efficiency are like cars optimized for speed. They go fast and win races as long as the road is straight and flat; but when the road twists and turns they cannot handle the corners and go flying off the road and crash. Winding roads need cars that are responsive, not just fast. And that is why coordination and collaboration are so important.

There is an inescapable tension between efficiency and responsiveness. They're at opposite ends of a spectrum; companies need to position themselves at a point on the continuum between those two that best meets their present circumstances. And as circumstances change, they need to keep repositioning themselves. Failure to do this has been the downfall of many fine industrial-age companies in the last decade; they stayed at the efficiency end of the continuum for too long while their markets evolved and customers went elsewhere.

Traditional Pursuit of Efficiency Is Now Less Profitable

This traditional tendency to focus too much on efficiency is apparent when senior managers of a company are quoted saying things such as, "Clients turn to us to eliminate cost and increase efficiency in their supply chains". Such companies often go on to announce they are employing a system that is described as, "an integrated extension of our clients' multi-channel, global supply chains aimed at improving global operating efficiency and time to market, while reducing cost." (What exactly does that mean?)

These phrases are corporate code words for systems designed to assist companies in implementing traditional efficiency-oriented low-price strategies. Big-clout companies attempt to implement systems like this to give themselves control over their suppliers in the name of achieving greater efficiency. And what happens is these systems shift profits from the suppliers to the big-clout companies. Big-clout companies then become complacent with their profits and the suppliers lose their motivation to do anything new because they aren't making any money. So then when the market changes, everybody (the whole supply chain) flies off the road and crashes as demand for existing products drops and new products have not been developed to take their place.

Wealth is now created by supply chains that enable companies to better collaborate and coordinate their activities so as to keep up with changing markets and keep delivering new products that customers want and will pay profitable prices to acquire. Successful and profitable companies understand that customers want a good price but that doesn't mean they want the lowest price as long as they get other features they want. People want products that keep responding to their changing desires and circumstances.

As a case in point, consider what happened to that once-simple product called the mobile phone. In the late 1990s Motorola owned the market and their StarTac phone was a popular, low-cost, and high-quality product. But Motorola focused too much on a low-cost approach and optimized itself and its supply chain to make low-cost, high-quality mobile phones that eventually nobody wanted to buy anymore. Customers moved on to other mobile phones that responded to their changing desires. First Nokia came out with colorful and stylish phones and customers bought them even though they cost more and had some quality problems. Then Blackberry came along and combined e-mail with a mobile phone and every business exec wanted one even though they cost more and had some quality problems. Now everybody wants an iPhone or something that competes with it such as an Android. Customers are paying more and accepting some quality problems in order to get what they want. Low price is not the deciding factor in how most customers select these products.

The iPhone is a rapidly changing mix of tangible and intangible values and features delivered via a mix of hardware and software that is responsive to evolving desires of its growing customer base. There are profits to be made by everybody in the iPhone supply chain because customers will pay more for the product. The iPhone is a like a symphony orchestra; Apple is the conductor of the orchestra but it's only one party in the process that creates the success the product is enjoying. Companies in the iPhone orchestra pay attention to Apple and coordinate their actions with each other to keep up with the fast pace of change because they are all making money (or at least believe they soon will be).

Apple isn't trying to create all the innovation itself; everybody is innovating and coordinating with each other to keep the ball rolling because iPhone is more than a mobile phone; it's a growing ecosystem of products and services that is taking on a life of its own. The phone is actually just one of many applications that run on the iPhone platform.

Time to Get Agile and Reinvent Traditional Supply Chain Operations

As more and more products follow a trajectory similar to the mobile phone, there's a huge opportunity to provide collaboration platforms for all parties in a supply chain to come together and get better and better at doing what they do to create and deliver new products. There's an opportunity to reinvent supply chains by supplementing traditional supply chain practices with collaboration and coordination practices.

Single companies using their own factories once designed and made the products of the industrial economy; now it is supply chains of inter-related companies working together to evolve products in a process of constant response to market change. Responsive supply chains trump merely efficient supply chains because only responsive supply chains provide the motivation needed for innovation and continuous change (see Chapter 10, Exhibit 10.1 "Strengthening Supply Chain Alliances").

What would happen if traditional supply chain operations were combined with practices from collaborative planning, forecasting, and replenishment (CPFR) and with approaches taken from sales and operations planning (S&OP) as discussed in Chapter 6? What would happen if we looked at supply chains as responsive and agile collections of collaborative projects instead of continuing to try to manage them as centrally controlled assembly-line style operations optimized for efficiency? Centrally controlled assembly lines optimized for efficiency worked well in the slower moving and more predictable industrial economy of the last century where product life cycles were measured in years or decades instead of months or quarters. In the real-time economy of this century, conditions change too fast for efficiency to be the only focus. As soon as a supply chain is optimized for one set of circumstances, those circumstances change and what was optimal is no longer optimal.

Massively Multi-Player [Serious] Supply Chain Games

There is a class of online computer games known as massively multi-player online role playing games (MMORPGs). In these massively multi-player online games, also known as MMOs, players from all over the globe log into virtual worlds via the Internet; they learn different roles and skill sets, and come together in self-selecting teams to carry out daring missions in pursuit of common goals. Question: How is this any different from the challenges that we face in designing and operating supply chains in the global real-time economy we now live in?

Another way to look at these MMOs is to call them real-time simulation modeling systems because that is literally what they are. The word "game" makes MMOs seem as if they are merely toys and that is unfortunate. Popular MMOs such as World of Warcraft, EVE-Online, or EverQuest bring together hundreds of thousands of simultaneous online players from countries around the globe to interact in complex, realistic three-dimensional worlds based on themes from Star Wars science fiction to Lord of the Rings epics.

MMOs are not to be confused with single-person shooter games where individual players blast aliens and tough guys, steal cars, and get into street fights. Those games develop fast eye-hand coordination but not much else. And neither are we talking about virtual social worlds such as Second Life.

What we are talking about is online games where there are rules and politics and opportunities to collaborate with others and build your reputation and your fortune. To play these games, players have to interact with each other and build relationships and put together plans and go on missions. They join guilds or corporations that exist in these games; they develop specific skills related to the roles they play (roles like pilot, trader, wizard, warrior, hunter, and priest); and they develop reputations and rating levels based on their successes and failures.

These are games that provide what is known as an "unscripted emergent experience". These games start from an initial set of conditions and then depending on the actions and interactions of the players, there is the potential for an almost infinite number of outcomes—just like in the real world. In Chaos Theory this is known as "The Butterfly Effect". In the world of MMOs this interaction between players is referred to as "The Sandbox". (This concept is eloquently illustrated in a short video created by the makers of the MMO called EVE Online. You can view this video on YouTube; to find it do a search on "EVE Online: The Butterfly Effect".)

The potential for using MMOs to develop skills people need to succeed in the global economy is starting to get serious attention. A study titled "Virtual Worlds, Real Leaders" was done by IBM and some professors from Stanford University and MIT who work together at a company named Seriosity (http://www.seriosity.com/downloads/GIO_PDF_web.pdf). They focused their study in particular on the MMO named World of Warcraft and came up with some interesting insights.

Consider what could happen if a massively multi-player online game (like World of Warcraft or EVE Online) was used to monitor and co-ordinate the operation of a real-world business process like operating global supply chains. Games aren't just for kids anymore as the median age of gamers (presently 36) continues to rise, and games aren't just for entertainment anymore either. There is a rapidly growing category of games called "serious games" used to deliver training and skills development for real world situations (militaries around the world make heavy use of such games).

Operating a global supply chain is a game with some pretty challenging dynamics. Players need to figure out how to deliver products where and when they are needed to meet demand while at the same time minimizing inventory levels and holding down transportation and manufacturing costs. If people succeed in keeping down inventory levels and costs but fail to meet product demand, they lose. And if they always deliver the products but fail to keep the other factors under control, then costs get out of hand and people don't make any money. So how do people and companies learn to excel in this kind of risky business environment?

MMOs provide an engaging and unifying framework to combine several technologies discussed in Chapter 4: business intelligence

(BI), simulation modeling, and business process management (BPM). MMOs take advantage of real-time reporting of actual supply chain status (business intelligence) and display this data in a manner that is easy for players to understand and respond to. Then people can use gaming to try out different plans of action to see the probable result (simulation modeling). And they can then select the best plan and coordinate with each other to carry out the plan successfully (business process management). MMOs for supply chain operation can be delivered to people all over the world using cloud computing and wireless broadband Internet connections.

Learning by Trial and Error Alone Is a Lot Riskier than It Used to Be

In the old days, companies had to learn mostly by trial and error, making mistakes, and hoping to learn fast enough so they didn't go out of business before they got good at what they did. But the learning curve is much steeper now. The rising costs of fuel oil and other raw materials are forcing companies around the world to rethink and redesign the supply chains built up over the last 25 years. Supply chains must continually adjust as prices and product demand forecasts change. With profit margins so thin and markets evolving so quickly, learning by trial and error alone is an increasingly risky proposition.

Supply chains can be defined as collections and combinations of just four things: facilities, routes, vehicles, and inventory. Suppose companies could use a simulation game that provided a map of the world where people from different companies working together in a supply chain could design and evaluate different supply chain options. They could point and click on the map to define facilities (factories, warehouses, stores, airports, harbors, etc.) and their locations. They could then define routes (roads, rails, air routes, sea routes, etc.) to move inventory between facilities and define vehicles (trucks, trains, airplanes, ships, etc.)

that will use these routes to move inventory. Then suppose companies could also define the production volumes of the factories, storage capacity of the warehouses, and movement capacity of the different modes of transportation.

Once these facilities and transportation routes are defined, people could associate operating costs with each facility and each mode of transportation. And people could specify expected inventory demand at the locations where end customers supplied by the supply chain purchase finished products. Simulations can be run to assess the ability and operating costs of a given supply chain to meet expected demand for products.

Users can experiment with different supply chain designs and run simulations to assess their effectiveness. Simulations will identify the most efficient supply chain designs for each study. These supply chains could then be put into production in the real world.

For each facility, users could define operating parameters to use in monitoring daily operations. These parameters monitor things such as the inventory levels of individual products at each facility, the expected demand for products that each facility must meet, and the operating costs. This real-time system (this serious game modeled on a MMO) then collects actual performance data every day from each of the facilities in the supply chain and updates the status of inventory and operating costs on a daily basis.

The daily monitoring of supply chain operations enables all authorized parties to see status of inventory and product usage. The system sends alerts to appropriate parties when actual inventory, demand, and costs exceed acceptable operating parameters as defined for each facility.

As a companion to this book I have collaborated with a group of people to create a MMO to use for gaining a better understanding of the dynamics that underlie supply chains and their operations. This game allows people from all over the world to collaborate in the design and operation of supply chains. It can be used to model real or imaginary supply chains and simulate their operations. It will show the performance characteristics and operating costs of these supply chains under different circumstances. The purpose of this game is to engage people in an interactive experience that accelerates their learning and increases their mastery of the skills involved in supply chain management.

The game is titled "SCM Globe" and it can be accessed through my website at www.MichaelHugos.com.

A Sequence of Screens Illustrates These Capabilities

The first screen shown in Exhibit 7.1 shows a design for a pharmaceutical supply chain; facilities and routes that move inventory between them are shown. A pharmaceutical manufacturing facility is located in Pittsburgh and a route connects it to Newark International Airport. From Newark there are two air routes that move material to Heathrow Airport in the United Kingdom and Barcelona Airport in Spain. From Heathrow Airport a route is defined to move product to a hub facility in Stuttgart in Germany. From this hub, product is moved to patient sites in Warsaw and Budapest. Also shown are routes to move product to a site in Manchester directly from Heathrow Airport. From Barcelona Airport, routes are shown to move products to sites in Lyon and Lisbon.

The next screen shown in Exhibit 7.2 illustrates how the system simulates the operation of this supply chain. Shown on the screen are some of the facilities and routes and a data display in the upper part of the screen provides a readout of relevant variables that measure the operation of this particular supply chain. The data display shows daily values for inventory and costs of operation. This enables users to see the characteristics of a supply chain design and to modify the facilities, routes, and vehicles used until an optimal design is achieved.

EXHIBIT 7.1

Supply Chains are Combinations of
Facilities, Routes, Vehicles, and Inventory

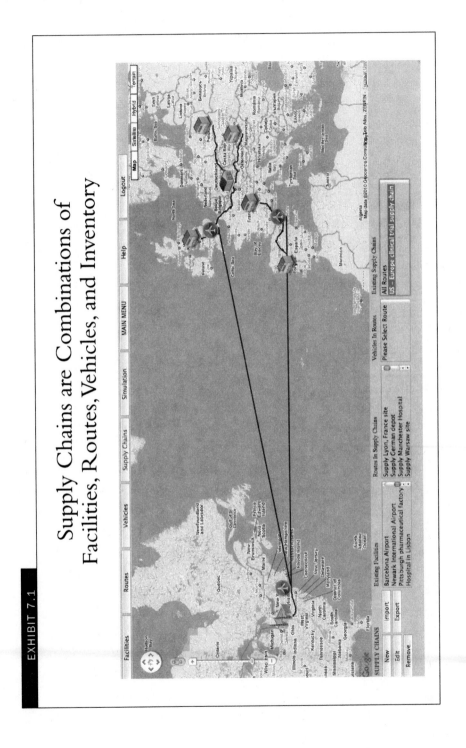

EXHIBIT 7.2

Based on Simulation Results, Modify Design to Achieve Desired Cost and Performance

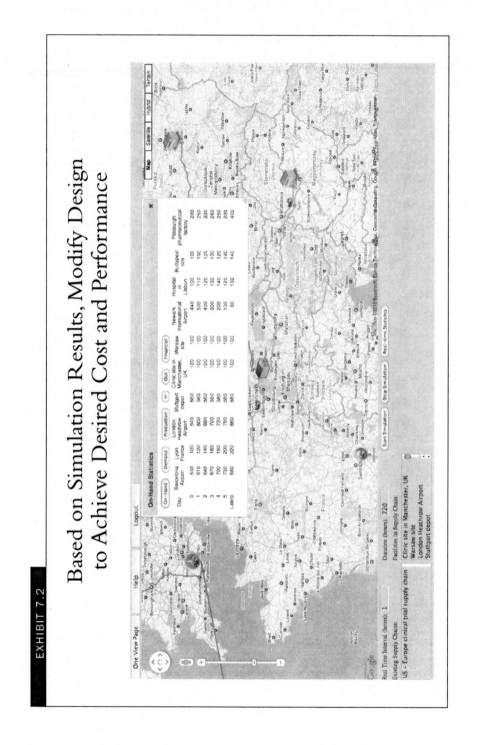

Once a supply chain is put into operation, the system could use simple data interfaces with the existing systems of the facilities and vehicles in the supply chain to collect data on a daily or even hourly basis and display the status of inventory at each facility. As shown in Exhibit 7.3, system users can click on any facility and get a data display showing current status of inventory at that facility.

Support for Collaborative Operations and Decision Making

As the users of this system (this MMO sandbox) collaborate to design effective supply chains to respond to changing conditions, the system could constantly keep track of the operating characteristics of the supply chains that were created and the users could select those designs that provided the best results. And then once that supply chain was in operation, the system itself would collect live data feeds from the actual facilities and parties in the supply chain and display real time status of ongoing operations. This would be a powerful inter-company collaboration platform. This platform combines the practices of collaborative planning, forecasting, and replenishment (CPFR) and sales and operations planning (S&OP) as described in Chapter 6. It would be a serious game whose object is for its players to monitor and manage their supply chains so as to best respond to changing business conditions.

As demand for products fluctuates, and as operating costs for factories, warehouses, and transportation modes change, companies and their supply chain partners could constantly test out different ways to meet demand while minimizing cost. If inventory planners and supply chain operators could literally draw supply chain configurations on an electronic map display and then simulate those configurations over some time period, they would quickly learn what combinations produce the best results. They would become immersed and completely involved.

EXHIBIT 7.3

Simple Data Connections Collect Continuous Data from Facilities and Vehicles

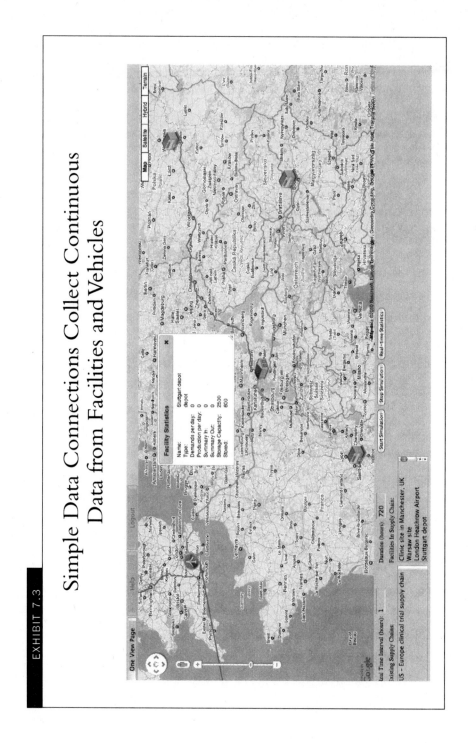

People would develop very accurate intuition about how best to respond to changing business conditions. They would be able to constantly adjust their supply chains to maintain the highest service levels at the lowest costs. And companies using this supply chain system would continuously learn and adjust their supply chains while incurring less risk and less cost than companies that learned only in the real world by trial and error alone.

(Readers can use a version of this system at www.MichaelHugos. com by clicking on the link for "SCM Globe". Companies wanting to explore using this system in their business can contact me about a more full-featured version to collaborate with their customers and suppliers.)

Supply Chains and Simple Data Connections

In all supply chains there are five drivers: production, inventory, location, transportation, and information. And the goal is to manage them so as to "Increase throughput while simultaneously reducing inventory and operating expense" as Eliyahu Goldratt so eloquently put it in his book *The Goal.*

Accomplishing this goal requires constant adjusting of the first four drivers to get the right balance of efficiency and responsiveness as the world unfolds. The key to achieving this balance is to have timely and accurate information and act effectively based on what it tells you. Information is the central leverage point for running any good supply chain.

Continuous Balancing between Efficiency and Responsiveness

One ever-present challenge in running an efficient supply chain is to cope with the effects of a dynamic called "The Bullwhip Effect," a illustrated in Exhibit 7.4. Small changes in demand for products at the front of a supply chain create increasing distortion in the perceived demand for those products as you move toward the back of the supply chain.

Demand forecasting and the related S&OP tasks are the basis for running efficient supply chains, but in high change and unpredictable times like these, it's hard to do these tasks well. It takes good data and requires people in different companies to collaborate to do these tasks well, because a supply chain isn't just one company, it's a network of companies. This is illustrated in Exhibit 7.4.

Efficient supply chains reduce inventory and operating expense, but it takes responsive supply chains to increase throughput. And to increase throughput, supply chains have to provide what customers want. Throughput is also known as sales, so to increase sales (as well as profits) companies need to do more than just offer basic products at low prices. They need to respond to opportunities to wrap their basic products in blankets of value-added services (from e-business services to customer service) that are tailored to fit customers' evolving needs and desires. This is illustrated in Exhibit 7.5.

Good Supply Chain Strategy Is Based on Timely and Accurate Data

Because accurate and timely information is the central supply chain driver, good strategy starts with improving the accuracy and flow of data between companies working in a supply chain. All other strategic decisions and tactical actions depend on this. Effective strategies support creation of a "virtuous cycle" of continuous improvement, and good information is what makes that possible. Exhibit 7.6 shows how this virtuous cycle comes into being.

Most supply chains still do not have the accurate and timely data they need because they lack effective electronic data connections between companies. Electronic data interchange (EDI) systems are used by many large companies, but those systems are expensive and complicated. In some instances EDI has been replaced by extensible markup language (XML), yet those systems too are expensive and complicated.

EXHIBIT 7.4

Supply Chains Need to Respond to Continuous Fluctuations in Supply and Demand

Efficient Supply Chain

"Bullwhip Effect"

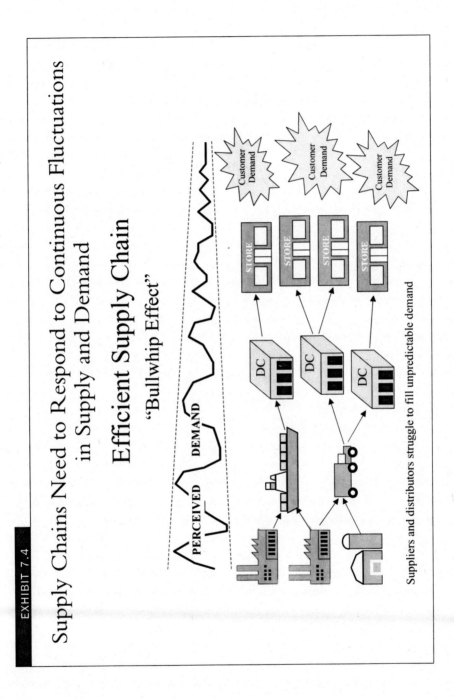

Suppliers and distributors struggle to fill unpredictable demand

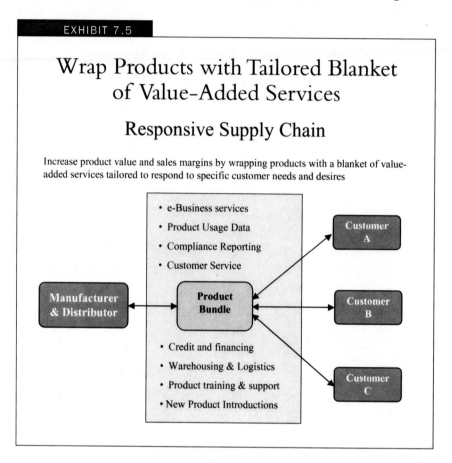

EXHIBIT 7.5

Wrap Products with Tailored Blanket of Value–Added Services

Responsive Supply Chain

Increase product value and sales margins by wrapping products with a blanket of value-added services tailored to respond to specific customer needs and desires

In most supply chains the big Tier 1 brand-name companies are a minority, most companies are the smaller Tier 2, Tier 3, and so on companies, and they still use e-mail, faxes, and spreadsheets to move data between each other because they can't afford the complex and expensive systems used by Tier 1 companies. Until simple data-connection solutions are found, it will continue to be a problem to get timely and accurate information to manage supply chains (Gatepoint Research, *Pulse Report Survey of Critical Supply Chain Trends: Summary Results*, December 2009).

As data flows through these simple data connections it is then possible to do comparisons between different data sets and display

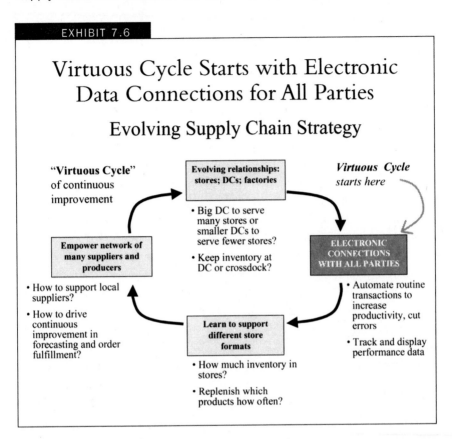

EXHIBIT 7.6

Virtuous Cycle Starts with Electronic Data Connections for All Parties

Evolving Supply Chain Strategy

"Virtuous Cycle" of continuous improvement

Evolving relationships: stores; DCs; factories

Virtuous Cycle *starts here*

- Big DC to serve many stores or smaller DCs to serve fewer stores?
- Keep inventory at DC or crossdock?

Empower network of many suppliers and producers

ELECTRONIC CONNECTIONS WITH ALL PARTIES

- How to support local suppliers?
- How to drive continuous improvement in forecasting and order fulfillment?

Learn to support different store formats

- Automate routine transactions to increase productivity, cut errors
- Track and display performance data

- How much inventory in stores?
- Replenish which products how often?

continuously updated score cards that show performance of the supply chain overall and performance of each of the companies in that supply chain. A sample score card is shown in Exhibit 7.7. When everybody can see those score cards every day, they have the information they need to start and maintain a virtuous cycle of continuous improvement.

This visibility created by universal data connections is the basis for effective supply chain management. These simple solutions and the systems they support are better than the present complex solutions because simple systems using good data a deliver better results than complex systems using bad data (there is an old saying in the computer world that goes like this, "garbage in, garbage out").

EXHIBIT 7.7

Scorecard for Supply Chain Performance Provides Real-time Transparency

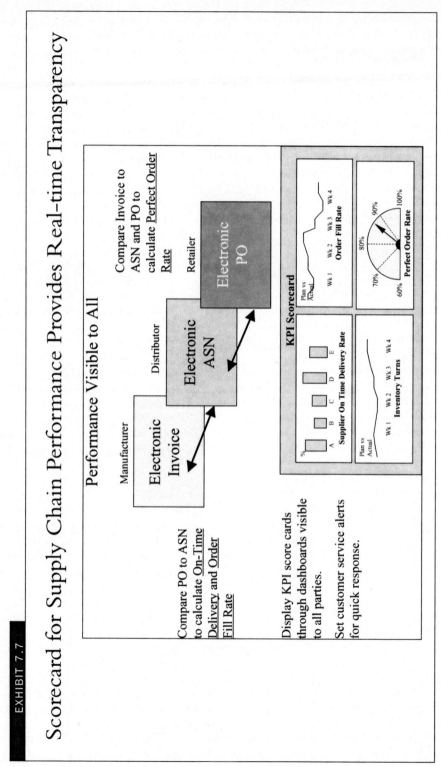

A huge opportunity exists right now in global and local supply chains to electronically connect all companies from the largest to the smallest. And since simple solutions are the only ones that will work for everybody, they are the only ones that will work at all.

I built a simple data connection and scorecard system like this to connect more than 80 smaller companies in a national distribution cooperative with the much larger companies of their customers and manufacturers (see Chapter 9, "Conceptual Design for E-Business Systems Infrastructure"). It connects the different ERP systems of these companies, supports billions of dollars in commerce, and enables other applications such as business intelligence, business process management (BPM) and S&OP.

EXECUTIVE INSIGHT

Many strategic experiments in organizations are enabled by information technology (IT) and organizations that employ a mindful approach to experimentation and their use of IT are likely to be in a better position to achieve the benefits they are looking for. Associate professor C. Ranganathan at the University of Illinois at Chicago believes that mindfulness at the individual level is characterized by openness to novelty, alertness to distinction, sensitivity to different contexts, awareness of multiple perspectives, and an orientation to the present.

The idea of mindfulness has been extended to organizations, and research finds that mindfulness enhances an organization's innovative ability as it fosters exploring a problem from multiple perspectives and focusing on business processes and ways to improve those processes. Organizational mindfulness is also associated with adaptive management of stakeholder expectations as unexpected events occur. Mindful organizations practice continuous learning where organizational actions are based on

(Continued)

what they have learned about themselves and their environment. Mindful organizations apply insights from their learning to their strategic IT experimentation.

Singapore-based YCH Group is one such mindful organization. They are a leading logistics and supply chain management company which provides integrated, end-to-end supply chain solutions to some of the world's largest companies including Dell, Motorola, LG, Pfizer, and Unilever. With more than 500 million square-feet of warehouse space, YCH Group handles more than $50 million worth of goods for its multinational corporation (MNC) customers.

YCH Group's intention is to help improve the business of their customers so that as their customers do well, YCH Group will also do well. To this end, YCH group engaged in strategic IT experimentation to integrate three supply chain flows in a single, integrated process. Those three flows are: 1) physical flows of inventory from one point to another; 2) information flow of data about the inventory; and 3) financial flow of ownership and related documents about the inventory.

YCH group pioneered using RFID for liquid and other controlled products in a bonded warehouse environment. A bonded warehouse is a licensed area that is used to store controlled items such as alcohol or cigarettes for re-export or local consumption. YCH group not only had to strictly adhere to the customs guidelines, but also ensure integrity and security of data at any point of time. They developed a unique "One-Touch" strategy using RFID technology. The One-Touch strategy uses two key components. The first component is a software that ensures data is clean and error-free at the point of collection and that data integrity is maintained seamlessly thereafter (hence, "one-touch"). And the second component is technology that ensures that the data filtered at the source is accurate. Chief Operating Officer James Loo explains further, "We were able to capture right data at the source, and manage this data through its lifecycle. One-Touch ensures that despite multiple modifications, enhancements, and process flows, the core set of data is kept secure and intact. Data remains accurate and available for appropriate users in the value chain."

Exhibit 7.8 depicts a typical process flow in a YCH bonded warehouse. When bonded goods arrive at the main distribution center, each pallet gets a radio frequency identification (RFID) tag. The tag contains product information as well as data on arrival time and designated storage location. Handheld readers are used to record and retrieve information from these tags. Forklift operators pick up the pallet and make their way to the designated storage location. The reader emits a light when this location is reached so that the operator knows the exact spot for storage. On receiving orders from customers, the RFID reader is used to help staff locate the goods. This also makes it easier for customs officials to conduct spot checks; otherwise they have to walk all over the warehouse and move up the racks to find the pallet they are looking for.

The forklift driver then removes the goods from the storage area into the outbound (or staging) area. While the goods are en-route to the staging area, the RFID reader will send a signal to prompt the computer system to start printing the relevant documentation. By the time the forklift arrives with the goods, all relevant paperwork and labels are ready, making it easier to load the shipment onto the trucks with minimal delay. Before RFID was implemented, staff had to wait for the goods to arrive at the outbound area before preparing the dispatch documentation.

Through RFID, YCH group also gained end-to-end visibility of stocks as they pass through the supply chain. YCH can now ensure that the pallets and cartons comply with the picking and transfer order requirements. YCH can also track goods in the storage area as well as their movement throughout the supply chain. YCH's stock-taking and verification have become error-free and easier. Each RFID gantry has an LED panel so that the forklift driver knows that the goods

(Continued)

EXHIBIT 7.8

Process Flow in YCH-bonded Warehouses

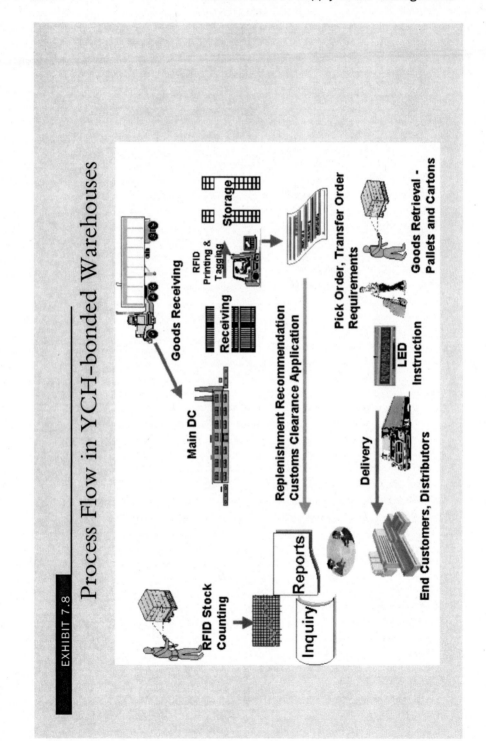

Executive Insight (*continued*)

have been captured by the reader and recorded in the warehouse management system. With this, YCH is able to offer visibility of the cargo for customs purposes and to facilitate planning throughout the distribution process. Custom clearance application forms and recommendations for replenishment are also automatically generated.

Adapted from a paper by **Teo, T.S.H.**, **Srivastava, S.C.**, **Ranganathan C.**, and **Loo, J.W.K.** "A Framework for Stakeholder Oriented Mindfulness: Case of RFID Implementation at YCH Group, Singapore", in *European Journal of Information Systems*, 2010.

Social Media and Real-Time Feedback

Facebook is defining a genre of software that will become as generic and widespread as the spreadsheet and word processing. And that means Facebook is probably not the last word in this genre. Maybe it's only an early incarnation. For example, the first popular spreadsheet was called Visicalc; it introduced the world to this genre of application. Then Visicalc was succeeded by Lotus 1-2-3, and then Lotus was surpassed by the current market leader, Excel.

Perhaps MySpace was the first popular incarnation of this new genre. Then MySpace was succeeded by Facebook. And maybe there is another contender now in the works that will surpass Facebook. Things happen fast these days. Software vendors are introducing systems that are cloud-based, software-as-a-service (SaaS) applications that have simple user interfaces much like Facebook but also come with additional features businesses need that Facebook and other current social media applications lack—like better security, better administrative control, and better user analytics (applications like Jive and Yammer are examples).

There may be a bigger and more compelling case for businesses to build and spend time maintaining their social networks than there is for individuals to do this. If maintaining social media sites was part of a paying job and if it was shown to generate measurable benefits for companies that did it well, there would be lots of demand for this activity.

Social media and related SaaS applications provide excellent real-time communication and collaboration platforms for companies that do business together. They provide real-time feedback that companies can use to continually communicate with their supply chain partners and adjust their daily operations to fit real-world circumstances.

Business-oriented social media can be used for everything from providing customer service and technical support to managing supply chains and executing joint marketing and sales campaigns. Business-oriented social media could well become, as Steve Jobs, CEO of Apple once put it, "the next insanely great new thing". It could enable companies to monitor and manage their business ecosystems in real time as our global economy continues to evolve.

If companies defined their target audience and then crafted appropriate messages, they could practically read their customers' minds. They would always know what customers wanted and could deliver the right products at the right prices at the right time.

How is this possible? It's possible if companies that do business together "friended" each other on Facebook or other similar types of social media platforms. For instance, if companies linked their company Facebook pages with those of their repeat customers and their main suppliers, they would have a powerful real-time communication platform in place to work with all the companies in their extended supply chain.

Once they had this real-time communication platform in place, the next thing companies could do is use it to "communicate with" instead of just "talk at" their customers and suppliers. Meaningful communication starts by asking relevant questions. Instead of a company telling its customers what it has for sale, it could ask customers what they would like to see the company sell. Companies could ask customers what their problems are and find ways they might be able to help. Companies could suggest ideas for products and services and see how customers reacted.

Social media is a two-way medium. The power of social media is that it puts out messages and also returns messages and does so in real time. And that capability is what creates the feedback loops that enable companies to understand what their customers want so they can stay close to them over time as the world changes. This is how companies can have the right product at the right price at the right place and right time.

Social media used this way connects companies with their best customers and their most important suppliers. It makes possible the two-way communication that generates the feedback they need to sense and respond to constantly evolving situations and desires of customers and suppliers.

Chapter Summary

Collaboration and coordination are the keys to effective supply chain performance and profitability in this century. In the slower moving and more predictable economy of the last century, most companies placed their emphasis on the use of centralized command and control to achieve performance and profitability goals, but command and control techniques do not perform well in fast-paced and unpredictable markets like those we live with now. Practices from CPFR can be used to improve collaboration and the S&OP process provides ways to improve coordination within and between companies.

A category of online computer games known as MMOs provides technology and innovative ideas for creating the kind of real-time simulation and monitoring systems that companies can use to work together in global and regional supply chains. Because profit margins are thin and supply chains are complex it is increasingly risky for supply chain practitioners to learn by trial and error alone; they are prone to making expensive mistakes that can threaten a company's viability. Using MMOs, people can take advantage of real-time reporting of actual supply chain status (BI); they can try out plans of action to see the probable result (simulation modeling); and they can then select the best plan and coordinate with each other to carry out the plan successfully (BPM).

The larger companies that have been in existence for a while often use EDI or XML to make electronic connections and send supply chain data to each other. These technologies work well for those that can afford them, but they are expensive and complicated and smaller and newer companies often do not have the capability or desire to work with those technologies. They use simple methods such as e-mail and faxes to send data to their supply chain partners, which causes delays in data transmission and is the source of many errors in the data.

The spread of cloud computing and wireless broadband Internet connections makes it possible to offer an inexpensive and easy-to-use data connection technology. Such a system will not be able to do everything that more complex EDI and XML systems can do, but it will still deliver better results. This is because simple systems that deliver accurate data in a timely manner will outperform complex systems hampered by data that is not timely or accurate.

The use of social media to assist in the coordination of business activities is only starting to be explored. There is an emerging class of software that is patterned on social media but which also has additional features such as better data security and better administrative monitoring and control features. This kind of social media software used in business can provide a real-time communication capability that companies can use to stay close to the changing desires of their customers and the changing trends in their markets.

CHAPTER 8

Defining Supply Chain Opportunities

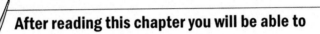

After reading this chapter you will be able to

- Apply the market-analysis framework to define the type of markets your company serves and identify the performance capabilities most valuable to those markets

- Define performance targets for your company to succeed in the markets you serve—the goal

- Create a strategy and define the objectives needed to reach the goal

- Estimate the budget needed for this effort and calculate the return on investment (ROI)

- Create the high-level project plan that will guide the effort

Now that conscious design and real-time management of a company's supply chain is possible, how does a company use this ability to its competitive advantage? A well designed and managed supply chain will enable a company to offer high levels of customer service and at the same time hold its inventories and cost of sales to levels lower than its competitors. This chapter will lay out a process to use for defining the supply chain management opportunities available to a company.

The Supply Chain as a Competitive Advantage

As companies such as Wal-Mart and Dell Computer have so clearly shown, if a company can design and build a supply chain that is responsive to market demands, it can grow from a small company to become a major player. Efficient supply chain operations are central to being able to satisfy market demands and to do so in a way that is profitable. Where once markets were shaped by the availability of product, now they are shaped by the evolving demands (some might say whims) of the end-use customers. Availability of most products is now taken for granted. So in addition to the product itself, the market has a host of other requirements in the areas of customer service, demand flexibility, and product development. A company needs to understand where it fits in the supply chains of the markets it serves. Then it needs to decide which activities it will focus on to deliver value.

Supply chains that deliver the best value to their end-use customers generate a strong demand for products and services. They are good places for producers, logistics providers, distributors, and retailers to do business. The efficiency of the entire supply chain greatly affects each company's ability to prosper, so standards of performance evolve in these supply chains over time. New companies cannot enter unless they can meet these standards. What this means is that companies who are good at their core supply chain operations work together in self-selecting supply chains to deliver the greatest value to the end-use customer.

It also means that there is great profit potential to be had for companies in a supply chain that learn to cooperate to generate efficiencies and cost savings for all. Skilled companies in specific markets that learn to work together to achieve new levels of efficiency and cost savings will create supply chains that grow faster than other supply chains in their markets.

We may even begin to look at a market in terms of the competing supply chains that support it instead of just the competing supplier companies within the market. Just as we now rate individual companies by their profitability and customer-service levels, we may begin to measure entire supply chains on their overall performance in these areas.

Identify the Business Opportunity and Define the Goal

Supply chain opportunities generally come in one of two categories. The first category is to fix or improve something already in place. The second category is to build something new. In both categories you have to first define the goal and then set about accomplishing that goal. Depending on which type of opportunity you are pursuing, the way to accomplish the goal will be different.

If you are pursuing an opportunity that is in the category of "fix or improve something already existing," then use Mr. Goldratt's theory of constraints as your guidelines for taking action. These guidelines are summarized in an executive insight section in Chapter 6 (see page 191). If you are going after an opportunity in the "build something new" category, then use the process outlined in this chapter.

New markets emerge, existing markets evolve, and mature markets fade away. A market creates a demand for a bundle of products and services to support it. Over the life span of a market, its supply chain evolves in response to the forces of supply and demand. Companies that supply a market must evolve along with the demands of that market. What are the markets your company serves and who are the end-use customers in these markets? Who are the producers in these markets? Who are the distributors, the logistics providers, and the retailers? What are the products and services demanded by this market?

What is the supply and demand situation in the markets you serve? The supply chain opportunities available to a company depend on which quadrants the markets it serves are in. Use the market-analysis framework to determine which market quadrants your company deals with. Which quadrants are your markets in today? Which quadrants do you think they will be in two years from now? Compare your organization against competing organizations in your markets. Identify whether you lead, equal, or lag your competitors in the areas of:

- Customer Service
- Internal Efficiency
- Demand Flexibility
- Product Development

Each market is best served by some combination of performance in these four areas. Define whether your company needs to lead, equal, or even excel in each of these areas. Identify the position your company needs to take in the four areas to best align itself with the demands of the markets it serves.

As discussed in Chapter 5, a company must lead in demand flexibility if its customers are in a mature market, and it must lead in internal efficiency if its customers are in steady markets. A company must excel in product development if it serves developing markets, and companies must meet high customer service standards in all of the markets they serve. Set the performance targets your organization needs to achieve alignment with the markets it participates in. These performance targets influence the goals a company selects and they become the measures of its success.

Create the Strategy

Once a business goal is defined and the related performance targets are set, the next step is to create a strategy to accomplish this. Strategy can be defined as simply, "the use of means to achieve ends." In other words, a strategy uses the business operations (means) of an organization to achieve its goals (ends).

To define the strategy, begin by looking at the supply chain operations that are performed in your company. Achieving the performance targets that have been set will require improvements in one or more of the four categories of business operations that are used to manage the supply chain:

1. Plan

2. Source

3. Make

4. Deliver

Use Brainstorming to Generate Ideas

Brainstorm a large list of improvement ideas for the operations under each of the four categories. Ask the question, "What seems impossible to do, but if it could be done, would dramatically change the way we do business?" Look for ways to change the business landscape—ways to give your organization a significant competitive advantage by doing something new and different. Where no new ideas are found, look for ways to significantly improve existing operations to get greater performance and increased cost savings. Better efficiencies in existing operations will rarely provide huge business wins, but they help ensure the company's survival.

Take the time to work up a large list of ideas. These ideas are the raw material from which the business strategy will emerge. When a sufficiently large body of ideas has been generated, review the lists and select three to six or so of the ideas that seem to have the most impact. These are ideas that will deliver improvements in multiple operations or performance categories. They are also ideas that promise the greatest payback and have the highest likelihood of success. These are the ideas that now need to get further attention. They will be the foundation upon which the strategy is based (see Exhibit 8.1).

EXHIBIT 8.1

Improve Selected Business Operations to Meet Performance Targets

PERFORMANCE CATEGORIES BUSINESS OPERATIONS	CUSTOMER SERVICE As measured by: Fill Rate; On-Time Delivery; Product Returns	INTERNAL EFFICIENCY As measured by: Inventory Turns; Return on Sales; Cash-to-Cash	DEMAND FLEXIBILITY As measured by: Cycle Times; Upside Flex; Outside Flex	PRODUCT DEVELOPMENT As measured by: New Prod. Sales; % Revenue; Cycle Time
PLAN Demand Forecasts	(X)	X	(X)	
Product Pricing	(X)	X		
Inventory Management	X	X	X	
SOURCE Procurement		X	X	
Credit & Collections	X	(X)		
MAKE Product Design	X			X
Production Scheduling		X	X	
Facility Mgmt.	X	X		
DELIVER Order Management	(X)	X		X
Delivery Scheduling	X	X		
Return Processing	X			X

Network Services set a goal and performance targets that called for improvements in the categories of customer service and demand flexibility. To excel in these two categories, Network Services Co. had earlier made major improvements in its credit and collections operations. Next, it decided to improve its demand forecasting, product pricing, and order management operations.

Examine this handful of most promising ideas that have been selected. How will these ideas play out over the next few years? How do these ideas work together to form a big-picture sequence of events that will take the organization from where it presently is to where it wants to go—the accomplishment of its business goals? What things have to be done, what new operating procedures and information systems need to be created in order to carry out these ideas? What are the best guesses as to the time it will take to create these new operating procedures and systems?

Look to see how these ideas relate to each other. Does the implementation of one idea build upon the implementation of a previous idea? What sequence should be followed in the implementation of these ideas? What kind of changes in operations, technology, and staffing are called for to implement each idea and how can these changes be done in a manageable way? How can the implementation of these ideas be broken up into phases that can each be completed in three to nine months? A phase needs to create deliverables that provide value in their own right and that can be put to use as soon as the phase is completed (see Exhibit 8.2).

It is important to both see the big picture that stretches over a period of several years and also to segment this big picture into smaller phases. This way the company is able to begin receiving tangible benefits from its work in a relatively short period of time. It can also respond to new developments in the business environment in a timely manner by adjusting its strategy, as necessary, as it completes each phase. There is a saying that sums up this approach very nicely: "Think big, start small, and deliver quickly."

Create a Conceptual System Design

The strategy to achieve the business goals is expressed in the conceptual design. The conceptual design is the high-level outline of a system or a set of systems. Generate several different conceptual designs for systems

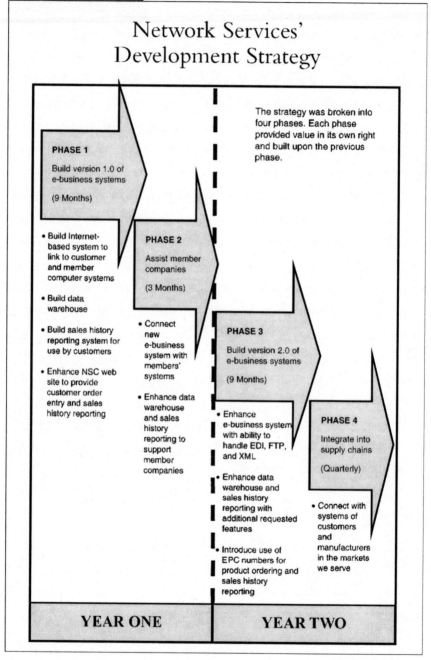

Network Services' Development Strategy

The strategy was broken into four phases. Each phase provided value in its own right and built upon the previous phase.

PHASE 1

Build version 1.0 of e-business systems

(9 Months)

- Build Internet-based system to link to customer and member computer systems
- Build data warehouse
- Build sales history reporting system for use by customers
- Enhance NSC web site to provide customer order entry and sales history reporting

PHASE 2

Assist member companies

(3 Months)

- Connect new e-business system with members' systems
- Enhance data warehouse and sales history reporting to support member companies

PHASE 3

Build version 2.0 of e-business systems

(9 Months)

- Enhance e-business system with ability to handle EDI, FTP, and XML
- Enhance data warehouse and sales history reporting with additional requested features
- Introduce use of EPC numbers for product ordering and sales history reporting

PHASE 4

Integrate into supply chains

(Quarterly)

- Connect with systems of customers and manufacturers in the markets we serve

YEAR ONE   **YEAR TWO**

that will meet the desired performance criteria. Approach the conceptual design first from the perspective of the business processes that are supported. Sketch out the different operations that are performed and note the kind of information that is required by and created by each operation.

Then add further definition to these process flows by specifying the data flows into and out of each operation. For each operation, estimate the volume and frequency of the data flows and also the source and destination of each data flow. In addition, for each operation, define the types of people (if any) who will perform this work. How many people will there be? What are the skill levels of the different types of people? This kind of business process diagram is illustrated in Exhibit 8.3.

Next, decide which operation will be automated, which will be manual, and which will be part automated and part manual. As a rule, people will like systems that automate the rote and repetitive tasks and empower them to do the problem-solving and decision-making tasks more effectively. People really are the most valuable resource of any company, so design systems that make maximum use of their skills. Technology's role is to support the people who use it, not the other way around.

Evaluate the existing computer system's infrastructure in your organization. Look for ways to build on that infrastructure. The most cost-effective systems are those that deliver valuable new capabilities to an organization quickly and with a minimum of effort.

Select the simplest combinations of technology and business processes that will meet the specified performance criteria. Balance the need for simplicity with the ability to increase the capacity of the system to handle greater volumes of data and to add new functionality as the business operations grow in volume. And remember that markets move over time from one quadrant to another, so build a supply chain infrastructure that is flexible enough to change with the

EXHIBIT 8.3

Diagram of the Business Process Flows

Network Services: E-Business Process Flows

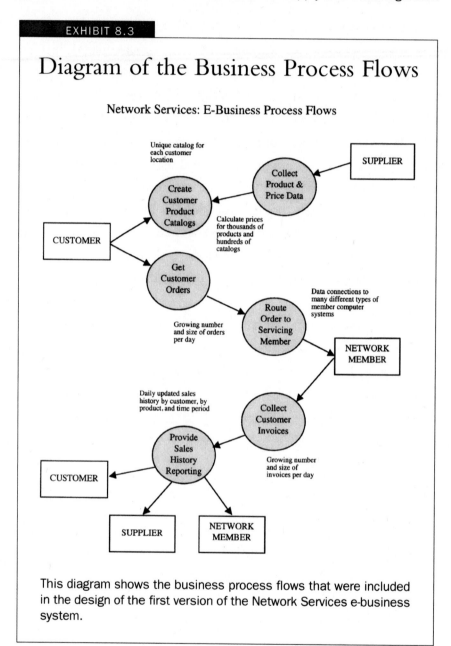

This diagram shows the business process flows that were included in the design of the first version of the Network Services e-business system.

needs of the markets your company serves. Do not design a system that locks the company into one way of operating and that is not capable of evolving to support new operations.

Create high-level schematic diagrams to illustrate each conceptual system design. In these diagrams use simple shapes like cubes and cylinders and spheres to represent different components of the design. Connect these shapes with lines and arrows to show the direction of data flow and activity. Do not get too technical or detailed in these diagrams. Their purpose is to quickly communicate the basic structure of the proposed designs. See Exhibit 8.4 on page 256 for an example of a conceptual system design.

These schematic diagrams are invaluable in communicating the features of the different designs to a wide audience of people. Reviews and comments should be sought from people who will use the new system, people who will pay for it, and people who will build it. Thoughtful input from a wide audience of people is very helpful in selecting the best design and then in adjusting that design to increase the likelihood that it will succeed.

Strategic Guidelines for Designing Systems

Designing supply chain systems or any other kind of system can quickly become a very complex undertaking. The business manager can come to feel overwhelmed by the possible choices and be tempted to leave this activity to the technical experts. Do not give in to this temptation. Business management must remain actively involved with the technical people in creating the conceptual design for the system. It is in this activity that the business manager can exercise very effective control over the strategy that the company will take to accomplish its goal. This activity cannot be left entirely to technical people because they usually do not have the depth of business knowledge that is needed to make the best decisions.

The best approach is for business and technical people to work together and generate a number of possible conceptual designs. Evaluate the goodness of each conceptual design by applying the seven guidelines for the design of new systems. These guidelines provide a basis to compare different designs and to select the conceptual design that has the best chance of success. A design that respects all seven of these guidelines is the best. It may still be a workable design if one or two of these guidelines are violated (as long as it is not the first of the seven guidelines shown). If guidelines are violated, there need to be very good reasons for doing so and specific compensations made to cover those violations. If three or more guidelines are broken, then the conceptual design is seriously flawed and it is very unlikely that the design can be successfully built.

The seven system design guidelines are:

1. *Closely Align System Designs with the Business Goals and Performance Targets They Are Intended to Accomplish*—For any systems development project to be a success it must directly support the organization to achieve one or more of its goals. No new system can be effective until you have first identified or created the business opportunity that will make the system worth building, and no new system will bring any sustained benefit to your company unless it supports the efficient exploitation of the business opportunity it was built to address.

2. *Use Systems to Change the Competitive Landscape*—Ask yourself what seems impossible to do today, but if it could be done, would fundamentally change what your company does in a positive way. Put yourself in your customers' shoes. In the words of the Nordstrom's motto, think of what would "surprise and delight" your customers. Look for opportunities to create a transformation or value shift in your market. Find ways to do things that provide dramatic cost savings or productivity increases. Place yourself in your competitor's shoes and think of what course you could take that would be the least likely to be foreseen or quickly countered or copied. As long as you are

able to do something of value that your competitors cannot, you have an advantage. If you are going to take bigger risks and incur larger costs to develop a system, then make sure it is a system that will change the competitive landscape. This is the kind of system that can deliver benefits that might justify bigger risks and costs.

3. *Leverage the Strengths of Existing Systems Infrastructure*—When existing systems have proven over time to be stable and responsive, find ways to incorporate them into the design of new systems. The purpose of strategy is to best use the means available to the organization to accomplish its goal. The design of a system is the embodiment of the strategy being used. Build new systems on the strengths of older systems. That is what nature does in the evolutionary process. New systems provide value only insofar as they provide new business capabilities. Time spent replacing old systems with new systems that do essentially the same things will not, as a general rule, provide enough value to justify the cost.

4. *Use the Simplest Possible Combination of Technology and Business Procedures to Achieve the Maximum Number of Performance Targets*— A simple mix of technology and process that can achieve several different performance targets increases the probability that at least some performance targets can actually be achieved. This is because simple combinations of technology and business process reduce the complexity and the risk associated with the systems. Using a different combination of technology and business process to achieve each different performance target multiplies the cost and the complexity of the entire undertaking and reduces the overall probability of success.

5. *Structure the Design so as to Provide Flexibility in the Development Sequence Used to Create the System*—Break the system design into separate components or objectives and, as much as possible,

run the work on individual objectives in parallel. Try not to make the achievement of one objective dependent on the prior achievement of another objective. In this way, delays in the work toward one objective will not impact the progress toward other objectives. Use people on the project who have skills that can be used to achieve a variety of different objectives. If you use the same technology to achieve several different objectives, it is much easier to shift people from one objective to another as needed because the skill sets used are the same. Your project plan should foresee and provide for an alternative plan in case of failure or delays in achieving objectives as scheduled. The design of the system you are building should allow you to cut some system features if needed and yet still be able to deliver solid value to the business.

6. *Do Not Try to Build a System Whose Complexity Exceeds the Organization's Capabilities*—The beginning of wisdom is a sense of what is possible, so don't bite off more than you can chew. When defining business goals and the systems to reach those goals, aim for things that are within your reach. Set challenging goals, but not hopeless goals. The people in your organization need to have confidence in themselves in order to rise to a challenge. Avoid exhausting their confidence in vain efforts to reach unrealistic goals.

7. *Do Not Renew a Project Using the Same Project Organization or the Same System Design after It Has Failed Once*—A mere reinforcement of effort or just trying harder is not a sufficient enough change to ensure the success of a project after it has failed once. People are probably demoralized after the first failure and will not rise to the challenge of doing the work again unless there are meaningful changes in the project approach. The new approach must clearly reflect what

was learned from the previous failure and offer a better way to achieve the business goal and performance targets.

TIPS & TECHNIQUES

Strategic System Guidelines

The seven system design guidelines are:

1. Closely align systems with the business goals and performance targets they are intended to accomplish.

2. Use systems to change the competitive landscape.

3. Leverage the strengths of existing systems infrastructure.

4. Use the simplest possible combination of technology and business procedures to achieve the maximum number of performance targets.

5. Structure the design so as to provide flexibility in the development sequence used to create the system.

6. Do not try to build a system whose complexity exceeds the organization's capabilities.

7. Do not renew a project using the same project organization or the same system design after it has failed once.

IN THE REAL WORLD

As Chief Information Officer (CIO) of Network Services Company I applied the strategic guidelines for designing systems to create the design for its supply chain and e-business systems infrastructure. Because of my adherence to these strategic guidelines this system was built in a shorter time and for considerably less money than similar systems built by our competitors. This system continues to be used and enhanced as necessary to meet the evolving business needs of the company.

(Continued)

I created a conceptual design for Network Services' systems infrastructure that would best enable it to meet its performance targets. This design was presented to an audience that ranged from the board of directors to senior management to the people who would build the systems infrastructure and the people who would use the systems. Feedback from all these people helped to finalize the design. The schematic diagram for this conceptual design is shown in Exhibit 8.4.

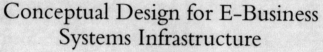

EXHIBIT 8.4

Conceptual Design for E–Business Systems Infrastructure

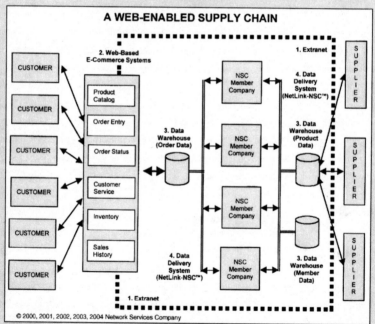

The systems infrastructure is composed of four main components that work together to provide a flexible and cost-effective infrastructure that can change as business conditions evolve and can handle greater and greater volumes of data as business operations grow. The four main components are:

The Extranet—A high-speed, Internet-based network to provide all member companies with a secure environment in which to exchange information and work together to serve national accounts (also known as a virtual private network or VPN).

❷ *Web-Based E-Commerce Systems*—A suite of systems accessed via the Network Services web site. A packaged system from a software-as-a-service (SaaS) provider named Tibersoft was used to provide order entry, inventory, and order status. Network Services developed the sales history reporting system. This suite of e-commerce systems was also made available to member companies to serve their local customers.

❸ *NSC Data Warehouse*—A collection of databases to support the web-based e-commerce operations and internal NSC operations such as proposal development, price file maintenance, account book creation, and sales reporting.

 Data Delivery System (NetLink-NSC)—A two-way, Internet-based data-transfer system to allow each member company's internal systems to read and write data in a common format to support delivery of seamless and consistent national account service. This component incorporated and reused software from an earlier system that provided for receipt and error checking of invoice data from media companies.

The greatest value for the company lay in the construction of the data warehouse to house the databases and in building the data delivery system called "NetLink-NSC." Those components working together best meet the performance criteria defined by the company. In order to meet the financial performance criteria and reduce project risk, we decided to lease the use of an existing web-based product catalog and order-entry system instead of building our own.

Define Project Objectives

When you look at a schematic diagram that illustrates a conceptual design, the system is shown as a set of high-level components. Defining these high-level components is a somewhat subjective process since there is a range of possible ways to design a system—some better than others. The better designs will define high-level components that are highly cohesive in the functions they perform. This means that each component performs a set of tasks that are all closely related to a single and well-defined activity. For instance, a highly cohesive component in a conceptual design could be an order-entry system. This component does all the things that need to be done for a customer to enter an order and that is all it does.

A component that is not cohesive would be a component that did order entry and also managed a database of sales information and also routed orders to different business locations. Showing all those activities as one component in a schematic design does not provide enough definition of the design to enable people to evaluate it effectively. This component should be broken down into three separate components—one for order entry, one for database management, and one for data transmission.

The building of each of these high-level components defines a set of specific, measurable activities or objectives that need to be achieved in order to create the system. There will tend to be somewhere between three and nine high-level components and all other components will resolve into sub-components of these high-level components. Why only three to nine high-level components? Because most of us are just regular folks and we cannot comprehend at a glance or remember more than seven (plus or minus two) things at a time. A clear and simple system design goes a long way toward insuring the success of the project because the people involved with it can understand it.

If a conceptual design is produced that is so complex only a genius can understand it, then the conceptual design is useless. People will not be able to use it to effectively guide their work in the detailed design and building of the system. Without a clear conceptual design, the people involved with building, using, and paying for the system will all have different ideas about what the company is trying to accomplish. People working on the different parts of the system will find it increasingly difficult to coordinate their actions with each other. The level of tension and misunderstanding and arguing will rise higher and higher as the work continues.

The development of each component in the conceptual system design becomes an objective in the project to build the system. Similar to the way that a long-term strategy is broken down into self-sufficient phases that each provide value in their own right, the building of a new system should be broken down into a set of objectives that each provide value in their own right. An objective should not be just an intermediate step along the way that depends on the completion of some future step to be of value. Objectives should each be achievable in three to nine months (or less). Look for objectives that can be achieved quickly. These will begin providing value and repaying the cost of the project before it is even entirely finished. Once achieved, an objective should become a base from which other objectives can be achieved.

Also be careful not to define objectives that lock the project into some rigid sequence of development activities. The world rarely goes according to plan, so the plan must be flexible in order to adapt as reality unfolds. Begin work on as many objectives as possible at the same time (in parallel). As much as possible, make the tasks needed to achieve each objective independent of the tasks needed to achieve the other objectives. This provides maximum flexibility, so that if one objective is delayed, it will not also delay the completion of other objectives being done in parallel. Resources can then be shifted from one objective to another as needed to respond to situations that arise.

Create an Initial Project Plan and Budget

It is always a challenge to create a project plan early in the project when there are so many things that are not entirely known. There will be much agonizing and grumbling about the plan. People will feel that they are being asked to commit to something that they know very little about and that whatever they say will come back to haunt them. In an attempt to give themselves as much wiggle room as possible, some people will create plans that are so high level and vague that they are little more than smoke screens. Other people will plunge into the task with determination and produce a plan showing minute detail about things that can hardly be defined yet. These plans are little more than wishful thinking about a future that will probably be nothing like what is shown.

So what is to be done? Let's start with a definition. Simply stated, a plan is a sequence of non-repetitive tasks that lead to the achievement of one or more predefined objectives that do not yet exist. A plan should not be confused with an operating schedule, which is a repetitive sequence of tasks that perpetuate an already existing state of affairs. This means that the plan should focus on laying out the tasks that need to be performed to achieve each objective that was identified in the conceptual system design. Do not clutter up the project plan with repetitive tasks that are related to ongoing administrative or business operations.

Create a section of the overall project plan for each objective. In the section of the plan for each objective, list the major tasks needed to achieve that objective. There will be tasks related to designing and then building the deliverables necessary for each objective. Show the dependencies between the tasks related to an objective and show the dependencies between the objectives.

When estimating how long each task will take, remember the old saying that "any job will expand to fill the time available." Use a technique called "time boxing" to define the time limits for each task. This technique calls for a trade-off between the work involved in carrying out a task and the time that is available. Realistic and adequate time periods must be assigned to each task but then it is up to the people doing the work to tailor the job to fit the time that is allocated. When setting these time boxes, get input from the people who will be asked to do the work. In a good plan the time boxes for each task are aggressive and they require people to work hard and stay focused, but they should not be so aggressive as to make people feel they have no chance of getting the work done.

A useful way to think about the work on a project and the corresponding time boxes is to divide time spent on a project into three main steps and assign an overall time box to each of the main steps. Then within each step, subdivide the time available to accommodate the tasks that are involved. The three steps and their durations are:

1. Define What Is Going to Be Done—the goal and the objectives (2–6 weeks or can be shortened to 2 days)

2. Design How That Will Be Done—the detailed specifications (1–3 months or can be shortened to 7 days)

3. Build What Is Specified (2–6 months or can be shortened to 13 days)

For each objective set a time box for the design step and the build step. Don't worry about the define step as that is what you are doing right now and showing it on the plan is not necessary. Look at the tasks that are required to achieve each objective. For example, let's say that Objective A has a one-month time box for design and a two-month time box for build. Decide which tasks fall into the design step and which tasks are in the build step. Allocate the time available in design among the tasks involved and do the same for the tasks in the build step. You have now subdivided the larger design and built time boxes for Objective A into smaller time boxes for the tasks that are involved.

Assigning time boxes is an iterative process. It involves adjusting both the time allocations and the scope of the work that will be done. It will probably take several passes through the plan before you have something that seems reasonable—something that is both aggressive and yet still doable. See Exhibit 8.5 for an example of an initial project plan.

EXHIBIT 8.5

How to Create an Initial Project Plan

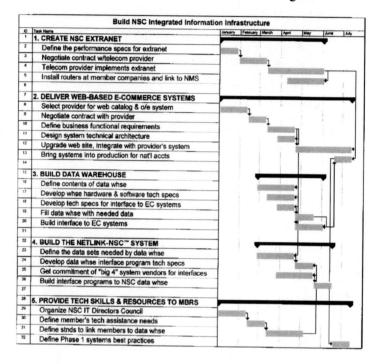

ID	Task Name	January	February	March	April	May	June	July
1	**1. CREATE NSC EXTRANET**							
2	Define the performance specs for extranet							
3	Negotiate contract w/telecom provider							
4	Telecom provider implements extranet							
5	Install routers at member companies and link to NMS							
6								
7	**2. DELIVER WEB-BASED E-COMMERCE SYSTEMS**							
8	Select provider for web catalog & o/e system							
9	Negotiate contract with provider							
10	Define business functional requirements							
11	Design system technical architecture							
12	Upgrade web site, integrate with provider's system							
13	Bring systems into production for nat'l accts							
14								
15	**3. BUILD DATA WAREHOUSE**							
16	Define contents of data whse							
17	Develop whse hardware & software tech specs							
18	Develop tech specs for interface to EC systems							
19	Fill data whse with needed data							
20	Build interface to EC systems							
21								
22	**4. BUILD THE NETLINK-NSC™ SYSTEM**							
23	Define the data sets needed by data whse							
24	Develop data whse interface program tech specs							
25	Get commitment of "big 4" system vendors for interfaces							
26	Build interface programs to NSC data whse							
27								
28	**5. PROVIDE TECH SKILLS & RESOURCES TO MBRS**							
29	Organize NSC IT Directors Council							
30	Define member's tech assistance needs							
31	Define stnds to link members to data whse							
32	Define Phase 1 systems best practices							

Build NSC Integrated Information Infrastructure

The Network Services Co. e-business project objectives were defined by the conceptual system design. The conceptual design had four components:

1. The Extranet
2. Web-Based E-Commerce Systems
3. The Data Warehouse
4. The NetLink-NSC™ Data Delivery System

Thus, the creation of each of these four components became a project objective. There was also a fifth objective to address the strategy of providing technical skills and resources to member companies. This initial project plan laid out the time boxes for the effort needed to achieve each objective. These time boxes defined the amount of time available for each activity. Work was then tailored to fit the times available.

Estimate the Project Budget and ROI

This is the step where you answer one of the most fundamental questions about the project—"Is this project worth doing?" Once a plan has been constructed, the budget can be created. Project plans and budgets are just two sides of the same coin. Plans show the time, people, and material needed to get things done and budgets show the cost of the people and material over the time frames involved. Although, in many cases, the cost and benefits related to a project cannot be defined with absolute certainty, it is still a valuable exercise to get as accurate an estimate as possible.

The value comes in two areas. The first is that this is an opportunity to create a consensus among the people who have to pay for the system. Everyone whose budget will be affected by the project should have an opportunity to review the costs and the benefits of the project. It is often hard to assign specific values to the benefits but it must be done. When in doubt, understate the benefits—just make sure that the benefit numbers are ones that people can understand and support. The sum of these benefit numbers is the value of the project and it is very important to have agreement on the value of a project.

The value of the project is the main reference point to keep in mind when evaluating the rest of the project. The value of the system is what tells you how much can be spent to build the system. If the costs to develop a system add up to more than the benefits that will be produced, then there are two choices. Either find a less expensive way to produce those benefits or simply do not do the project. Businesses exist to make a profit, and that is a discipline that all business people must live with.

Define the Specific Costs and Benefits

From a financial perspective, a system generates a stream of costs and benefits over the length of time in which it is built and used. As a rule, a system should pay for itself and return an appropriate profit within one

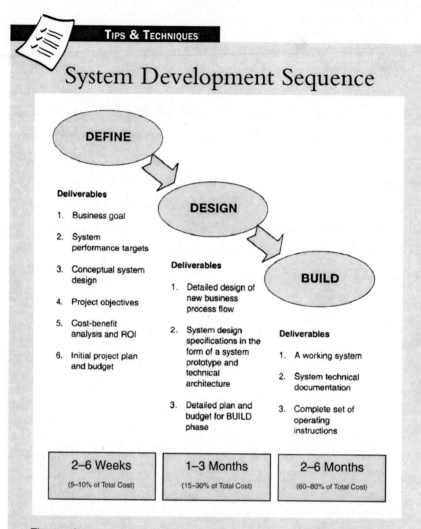

TIPS & TECHNIQUES

System Development Sequence

DEFINE

Deliverables

1. Business goal

2. System performance targets

3. Conceptual system design

4. Project objectives

5. Cost-benefit analysis and ROI

6. Initial project plan and budget

DESIGN

Deliverables

1. Detailed design of new business process flow

2. System design specifications in the form of a system prototype and technical architecture

3. Detailed plan and budget for BUILD phase

BUILD

Deliverables

1. A working system

2. System technical documentation

3. Complete set of operating instructions

2–6 Weeks	1–3 Months	2–6 Months
(5–10% of Total Cost)	(15–30% of Total Cost)	(60–80% of Total Cost)

These three steps provide a useful way to think about the work that has to be done to create a new system. Under each step is shown the deliverables that need to be produced, estimating guidelines for how long each step should take to complete, and how much of the total project budget should be spent on that step.

For those of you who will go on to run projects to develop supply chain systems, you can find a more in-depth discussion of the three step, Define-Design-Build process in my book, *Building the Real-Time Enterprise: An Executive Briefing*. In particular see Chapter 8, "Developing Systems in Real-Time" and Chapter 9, "A Powerful Reinforcing Feedback Loop."

to three years, because after that time the system will usually need major enhancements or a complete reworking. Specific benefits need to be identified and estimates made of their dollar value. Measure system costs and benefits on a quarterly basis. Subtract costs from benefits to arrive at the quarterly cash flow generated by the system. Calculate the value of that cash flow using whatever method the financial decision makers would like (net present value, internal rate of return, etc.). The higher the risk involved in building and operating the system, the higher the profit that the system should generate.

System Costs

In a system development project there are three types of costs:

1. Hardware and Software—Costs for the hardware, software, and communication network components that need to be purchased from vendors for the new system design.

2. Development—Costs as estimated by the time and cost needed to achieve each project objective. Each task that is part of the work plan for an objective will require some number of people with certain skills for some period of time. Each task will also require certain technology and perhaps other expenses, such as travel, hotel rooms, and meals. Set a standard cost for each kind of person and estimate the labor expenses for each kind of person for each step in the system development life cycle: the *define* step; the *design* step; and the *build* step.

3. Operations—Costs have a number of components. Estimate labor expenses for the kinds of people that will be needed for ongoing operation and support of the new system. Estimate the line charges and usage fees for the communication network and technical architecture used by the system.

Obtain yearly licensing and technical support costs from vendors of the hardware and software components used by the new system.

System Benefits

There are four types of benefits provided by a new system:

1. **Direct Benefits**—productivity increases and cost savings due to the capacity increases brought about by a new system. Define the new functions the system provides that the company does not now have. Estimate the productivity increases and labor savings that these new features provide.

2. **Incremental Benefits**—monetary benefits that may not be solely a result of the new system but are measurable and due in some significant degree to the capabilities of the new system. This may be an increased ability to attract and retain new customers and the extra revenue that generates. It may be the new system's ability to help the company avoid bad decisions or manage and plan for certain business expenses and the reduced costs that result.

3. **Cost Avoidance Benefits**—savings related to the increased capacity provided by the new system and the company's ability to grow the business without having to hire new staff or hire as many new staff as would otherwise be the case.

4. **Intangible Benefits**—hard to quantify into a monetary amount, but should be identified and listed. These benefits include such things as maintaining a competitive advantage through better intelligence and adaptability; superior service levels that solidify customer relationships; and leveraging the abilities of talented employees and increasing their job satisfaction.

TIPS & TECHNIQUES

Sample Cost/Benefit Analysis

ITEM PRICING SYSTEM—TOTAL ESTIMATED COSTS AND BENEFITS

Project Description

Build system to assist staff of account development group to more quickly create contract proposals and explore impact of different product costs and pricing structures. Monitor status of existing contracts and provide notice before cost supports expire.

Project Costs and Benefits (Dollars in Thousands)

	Qtr 1	Qtr 2	Qtr 3	Qtr 4	Qtr 5	Totals
Hardware & Software	(7.0)					(7.0)
Development Costs	(68.5)					(68.5)
Operating Costs	0.0	(1.2)	(1.2)	(1.2)	(1.2)	(4.8)
Total Costs	(75.5)	(1.2)	(1.2)	(1.2)	(1.2)	(80.3)
Direct Benefits	0.0	8.4	8.4	8.4	8.4	33.6
Incremental Benefits	0.0	30.0	30.0	30.0	30.0	120.0
Cost Avoidance Benefits	0.0	18.2	18.2	18.2	18.2	72.8
Total Benefits	0.0	56.6	56.6	56.6	56.6	226.4
Net Benefits	($75.5)	$55.4	$55.4	$55.4	$55.4	$146.1
Cumulative Benefits	($75.5)	($20.1)	$35.3	$90.7	$146.1	
Discount Rate	5% (5% per Qtr. = 20% Annual Discount Rate)					
Net Present Value	115.2					

(Continued)

Detailed Schedule of Costs

Cost of Hardware & Software (Dollars in Thousands)

Item	Description	Cost
Application Server	Server to run the system—allocate 1/3 of server cost	3.0
Personal Computers	PCs for use by staff—allocate 1/3 of cost	3.0
Programming Language	Allocated cost of programming language and tools	0.5
SQL Server Database	Allocated cost of SQL Server and tools	0.5
Total		$7.0

Cost of Development (Dollars in Thousands)

Task	Description	Cost
Define Phase	5 days at average cost of $900 per day	4.5
Design Phase	15 days at average cost of $900 per day	13.5
Build Phase—Coding	30 days at average cost of $900 per day	27.0
Build Phase—Test & Train	30 days at average cost of $650 per day	19.5
Build Phase—Roll Out	5 days at average cost of $800 per day	4.0
Total		$68.5

Cost of Operation (Dollars in Thousands)

Activity	Description	Cost
Qtr 1		
Qtr 2	Incremental costs of operating the system	1.2
Qtr 3	Incremental costs of operating the system	1.2
Qtr 4	Incremental costs of operating the system	1.2
Qtr 5	Incremental costs of operating the system	1.2
Total		$4.8

Detailed Schedule of Benefits

DIRECT BENEFITS (revenue and cost savings due to productivity improvements)

Direct Benefit 1	Save staff time on proposal creation: 10 proposals per Qtr.; 20 Hrs. per proposal; $35/Hr.
Direct Benefit 2	Do 2 additional proposals per Qtr.; 20 Hrs. per proposal; $35/Hr.

Value of Incremental Benefit (Dollars in Thousands)

	Qtr 1	Qtr 2	Qtr 3	Qtr 4	Qtr 5
Save time on proposals		7.0	7.0	7.0	7.0
Do 2 additional proposals		1.4	1.4	1.4	1.4
Total Direct Benefit	$0.0	$8.4	$8.4	$8.4	$8.4

INCREMENTAL BENEFITS (benefits due in part to new system, e.g., attract new customers, make better decisions, etc.)

Incremental Benefit 1	Win more proposals due to better pricing decisions: $30,000 per Qtr. in additional profits
Incremental Benefit 2	—

Value of Incremental Benefit (Dollars in Thousands)

	Qtr 1	Qtr 2	Qtr 3	Qtr 4	Qtr 5
Win more proposals		30.0	30.0	30.0	30.0
Incremental Benefit 2		—	—	—	—
Total Incr. Benefit	$0.0	$30.0	$30.0	$30.0	$30.0

COST AVOIDANCE BENEFITS (savings related to growing business without needing to add new staff or incurring other expenses)

Cost Avoidance 1	Avoid hiring more staff as business grows: half a person per year; $35/Hr.
Cost Avoidance 2	—

(Continued)

Value of Cost Avoidance (Dollars in Thousands)

	Qtr 1	Qtr 2	Qtr 3	Qtr 4	Qtr 5
Avoid hiring more staff		18.2	18.2	18.2	18.2
Cost Avoidance 2		—	—	—	—
Total CA Benefit	$0.0	$18.2	$18.2	$18.2	$18.2

INTANGIBLE BENEFITS (benefits that are hard to quantify in dollar amounts but that should be identified and listed)

Maintain Competitive Advantages

- Item Pricing system should be a competitive benefit for next 2 yrs.
- After that, it will simply become a necessary tool to do business

Provide Superior Service Levels

- Provide customers and prospects with timely and accurate proposals

Increase Job Satisfaction

- Release staff from tedious and time consuming pricing calculations
- Allow staff to focus on more valuable and interesting work

Chapter Summary

The work of defining supply chain opportunities will be complete when the following five deliverables are produced:

1. A clear statement of the business goal to be accomplished.

2. The performance criteria required from the system. These criteria fall into four measurement categories: (1) internal

efficiency; (2) customer service; (3) demand flexibility; and (4) product development. These are the conditions of success that the system must meet.

3. A conceptual design for a system to accomplish the business goal and meet the performance criteria. The system design is composed of people, process, and technology. The conceptual design is the embodiment of the strategy being used to attain the goal.

4. A definition of the project objectives that are needed to build the system. The objectives are the things that must be built to create the system outlined in the conceptual design.

5. A cost/benefit analysis that verifies that the project is worth carrying out. The senior business executive or management group who is responsible for accomplishing the business goal that the system will address must confirm that this analysis is valid.

In formulating supply chain improvement projects, it is a far better approach to successfully carry out a sequence of small steps than to attempt to make a great leap forward and risk falling short. In an approach that involves taking a sequence of smaller steps, the stakes at each step are modest and the work is more manageable, so success is easier to achieve. In the approach of taking a great leap forward, the stakes are high—the work is enormous, success is harder to achieve, and the cost of failure is high.

CHAPTER 9

Creating Supply Chains for Competitive Advantage

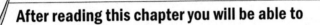

After reading this chapter you will be able to

- Understand how one company created customized supply chains for its customers and in doing so created a strong competitive advantage for itself

- See how to apply concepts and techniques presented in this book to respond to real-world supply chain challenges and opportunities

- Gain some insight into how to leverage supply chain capabilities into longer-term alliances with the customers and suppliers with whom you do business

In many organizations supply chain management has gone from poor cousin to high strategy over the last 25 years. We have seen how companies such as Wal-Mart and Dell have risen to market prominence through their development and use of highly efficient supply chains. What can we learn from their success and the successes of other companies about creating supply chains that become major competitive advantages?

In this chapter we will use a case study of a fictitious company named Charlie Supply, Inc. to present ways in which a company can create supply chains that deliver key competitive advantages. We start with a description of Charlie Supply and its business goal. Then we discuss an initial business situation and a follow-on situation. For each situation there are exercises to work through that explore ways the company can recognize supply chain opportunities and respond effectively to capitalize on them.

I invite your e-mail responses (mhugos@yahoo.com) to the supply chain solutions I offer in this chapter. What do you agree with? What would you do differently? Why?

Charlie Supply Inc.—The Initial Business Situation

Charlie Supply, Inc. is a $2.8 billion company that distributes food-service items, janitorial supplies, and equipment. The company has grown rapidly over the last five years. It has acquired 13 separate companies during that time. Eight of these companies were major regional distributors of janitorial and/or foodservice supplies and five recent acquisitions were smaller distributors who specialized in one or the other of these product lines. Each had good reputations with their local customers and Charlie Supply acquired them in order to round out its geographical coverage in areas where it needed a stronger local presence.

Charlie Supply has followed a policy of decentralized management and left the companies it acquired largely free to run their own operations as they see fit. Each company or "business unit" as they are called, has certain sales targets and profitability levels that they need to meet. They are also required to buy 80 percent of their inventory from an approved list of manufacturers where the company has negotiated special purchasing and support contracts.

The business units serve their own local customers and, increasingly, they work together to win contracts from large national account customers. Local customers often pay a higher price for their products but they also buy smaller amounts. National accounts negotiate lower prices but they buy much more. National account business is growing because more big customers want a single supplier who can service all their facilities across the country and also deliver a range of products and customized supply chain services to help them manage their business and lower their operating costs.

The information technology (IT) infrastructure of each of the business units varies widely. Some of the bigger business units that have multiple branch locations now run a single, full-featured enterprise resource planning (ERP) system provided by a leading software vendor. Other business units still use custom-built suites of systems developed when they were independent companies. The smaller business units run several different ERP packages designed for smaller companies. These systems have been adequate to support operations up to this point. They run on a range of different computer hardware and operating systems. In two cases IT vendors have informed a smaller business unit that they must upgrade or else lose technical support on their hardware and software in the next 24 months.

All of the business units have interfaced their individual ERP systems to a system that Charlie Supply developed to enable the business units to exchange key data files with systems at corporate headquarters. That system is called the Inter-Company Communications Link (ICCL). All of the business units and company headquarters can electronically exchange six documents between their internal ERP systems and the ICCL system. Those documents are: (1) purchase orders; (2) invoices; (3) advance ship notices; (4) customer price books; (5) product masters; and (6) inventory stock status. There is a transaction-processing database built into ICCL that stores these documents and provides for some limited usage reporting.

The ICCL system also has connections to many of the company's customers and with the manufacturers whose products the company sells.

It can send and receive purchase orders and invoices between the business units and these customers and manufacturers. The system does have some drawbacks in the way that it does error checking, so errors in orders, invoices, and product data can take longer to detect and correct than would be the case if every business unit was using the same ERP system.

The Business Goal

Charlie Supply just finished its four-year strategic plan. Among other things, this plan calls for the company to grow its total sales to $5 billion over the next four years. Management has decided that this growth should come from increasing sales to local customers by 50 percent and by growing national account sales by an additional $1 billion. To support this growth the company realizes it will need to review and reengineer selected business processes and the information systems that support those processes.

Senior management spent a lot of time defining the company's mission or goal for the next four years. There were some who felt the goal should be a specific revenue target. Others felt this was too limiting and should instead be more of a statement of the company's intention. It was decided that the goal would be a statement of senior management's intent and that there would be a short list of performance requirements such as the $5 billion sales target and others that would be the tangible measures of success that the company will use. The company's goal is stated as follows:

"Create the low cost and highly responsive supply chain needed to be the distributor of choice in the markets we serve."

Business Strategy

Charlie Supply is a distributor, and distribution is a tough business. Gross margins are under more pressure than ever and national account customers especially are continuously squeezing them. Charlie Supply needs to differentiate itself in some significant way or else engage in a "grim race to the bottom" with its competitors as gross margins get squeezed to small single digit percentages.

Results of some of the analysis done during the strategic planning process are shown in Exhibit 9.1. Based on the markets being served and the strengths of the company, senior management has decided on a strategy it will use to accomplish the company's goal. The strategy is to develop a suite of supply chain service offerings that can be mixed and matched to meet unique customer needs. The company will find customers who need these services in addition to the products themselves and who will pay a few additional percentage points on the item prices in order to get them. It may not be possible to charge individually for specific supply chain services but management believes that the services can be bundled with the company's products and sold as a total package.

The business plan calls for the company to place its main focus on selling to new national accounts. Management feels the need to stabilize company growth and market share by acquiring a portfolio of multi-year contracts with big customers who each generate annual revenues of $10 million or more. Charlie Supply already has a group of national accounts and it is starting to see a good deal of similarity in the requests from these companies.

These big customers are consolidating their procurement activities and looking for single suppliers who can support them nationwide. It is also most likely that these big customers are the ones who value the supply chain services Charlie Supply can offer. This is especially true if these customers are in certain vertical markets where the products that Charlie Supply provides are central to the customer's daily operations. Given Charlie Supply's product offerings, that means customers such as national restaurant and grocery store chains, big property management companies, and building maintenance companies, to name a few.

EXHIBIT 9.1

Results of Business Analysis for Strategic Plan

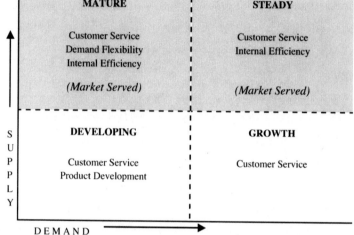

The performance requirements for success in each market quadrant are shown in this table. Charlie Supply currently participates in the supply chains of MATURE and STEADY markets (see page 138, A Framework for Performance Management).

Competitive Analysis	LAG	EQUAL	LEAD	EXCEL
Customer Service			X	
Internal Efficiency	X			
Demand Flexibility		X		
Product Development		X		

Competitive analysis shows Charlie Supply to equal its main competitors in two of the performance areas and to lag in one area and lead in the other. Charlie Supply has long had a reputation for good customer service and it shows in the customer surveys. Because of all its recent acquisitions though there is still some redundancy in its facilities and systems and although its operations are well run, they do not enjoy the economies of scale and thus are not as efficient as those of its main competitors.

One national account in particular is growing fast. This customer is a national restaurant chain named Green Planet. These cozy neighborhood restaurants serve prepared organic foods from brownies and chicken salad sandwiches on whole grain bread to full frozen dinners that can be heated and served to patrons at the restaurants or sold to customers who take them home to eat. In addition to providing great food, Green Planet is committed to promoting sound environmental practices and prides itself on its use of products that are environmentally friendly and recyclable.

Because of its great food and the growing public awareness and demand for organic food, the company's growth has been tremendous and it is opening up more and more restaurants every month. The company is continuously challenging Charlie Supply with new requests and requirements. It needs both products and supply chain services to support its growth and manage its operating costs.

Exercise Number 1: Supply Chain Strategy and Projects

Imagine that you are the Charlie Supply executive in charge of delivering the supply chain capabilities the company's strategy calls for. Take some time to consider how you would go about doing this. What kind of projects would you start? What would you do about the various different ERP systems used by the business units? How would you schedule the work to be done over the next 12 months?

Go back to Chapter 8 and look at the table in Exhibit 8.1. Which of these business operations would you improve and why? Then look at Exhibit 8.5. What would your initial project plans to improve these business operations look like? When you make your plans, follow the time boxes suggested in the Define-Design-Build system development sequence (see Chapter 8). See the sample cost/benefit analysis at end of Chapter 8 and use that template to do a cost/benefit and return on investment (ROI) calculation for your proposed projects.

Take some time now to write up your solution. State the business operations you will improve and why. Sketch out the initial plans for the projects to improve these operations and do quick ROI calculations for these projects. When you are finished, compare your ideas to the solution set I offer in the following section. My solution is not meant to be the definitive answer. It is based on my experience and on discussions with others who have thought about this. Use it as a point of reference to evaluate your own ideas.

Solution to Exercise Number 1

Since Charlie Supply serves steady and mature markets, competitive opportunities lie in improving the capabilities of customer service, demand flexibility, and internal efficiency. Given that the company already has a lead in the customer-service category, the company will get the best results by building on that strength and improving its customer-service capabilities to make them even more valuable to its customers. There is also an opportunity to pull ahead of its competitors in the area of demand flexibility. Improvements in these capabilities can be used to differentiate the company in the eyes of its customers and to provide value that its competitors cannot provide. Exhibit 9.2 shows where the company will make its improvements.

If you elected to make improvements in the company's internal efficiency so that it would equal or even lead its competitors in this area then I believe you have made a mistake. See the seven strategic design guidelines for designing systems presented in the last chapter on pages 252–255. The second guideline says to use systems to change the competitive landscape and the third guideline says to leverage the strengths of existing systems. If you elected to improve internal efficiency by doing something such as putting all the business units on the same ERP system, you are merely making a "me too" move to try to catch up with your competitors. It will be a very expensive move as well.

EXHIBIT 9.2

Charlie Supply Decides to Build on Its Strengths to Differentiate Itself

Competitive Analysis	LAG	EQUAL	LEAD	EXCEL
Customer Service			X– – ➤ X	
Internal Efficiency	X			
Demand Flexibility		X– – ➤ X		
Product Development		X		

The decision was made to undertake improvements in customer service and demand flexibility as the way to achieve its business goal. Improvements in these two areas best leverage the company's existing strengths and they will significantly differentiate Charlie Supply from its competitors. They will change the competitive landscape in the company's favor.

By improving internal efficiency, you are not changing the competitive landscape because it is unlikely that you will actually exceed the internal efficiency of your competitors anytime soon. And by focusing on trying to improve a weakness you are also missing the opportunity to leverage existing systems where you are already strong and could quickly get even stronger. Internal efficiency lags the competition, but it is not so bad as to endanger the company as long as it avoids engaging in a price war with its competitors. And the company has no intention of getting into a price war, anyway.

Charlie Supply defined six performance targets that it would strive to achieve in the areas of customer service and flexibility. These performance targets are:

1. *Take Orders Any Way the Customer Wants (Customer Service)*—as measured by ability to take customer orders through its own

web order entry system, or by electronic data interchange (EDI), by extensible markup language (XML), or by direct, computer-to-computer file transfer protocol (FTP) with customer systems.

2. *Deliver Uniform Quality of Service to All Customer Locations (Customer Service)*—as measured by order-fill rate, on-time delivery rate, and item-return rates.

3. *Support Customer Accounting (Customer Service)*—as measured by ability to submit customized, accurate, and timely invoices and statement bills via whatever medium the customer requests whether it be EDI, XML, FTP, or e-mail attachments.

4. *Support Customer Purchasing and Budgeting (Customer Service)*—by providing them with data for planning and managing their purchasing budgets through online reports showing product purchases by customer location, by item, supplier, and volume over any period from one day to two years.

5. *Be a Valuable Partner in the Supply Chain (Demand Flexibility)*—as measured by order-fill rate and backorder frequency and backorder quantities.

6. *Participate in Markets as They Evolve (Demand Flexibility)*—as measured by ability to anticipate and stock additional products outside of the company's present bundle of products as demand for them emerges.

Twelve-Month Project Objectives

To meet these performance targets I would make improvements in four business operations that support supply chain performance. As shown in Exhibit 9.3 those operations are: (1) demand forecasting; (2) inventory management; (3) order management; and (4) delivery scheduling. The main thrust of these improvements is to deliver improved customer service and demand flexibility. However, since all four of these business operations also affect internal efficiency, improvements here will result in some increase in the company's internal efficiency as well. This is also shown in Exhibit 9.3.

When I look at the four business operations that are to be improved, it is clear that all four of them will benefit from the creation of an enterprise data warehouse. This will be my first project. The data warehouse will provide data to enable better demand forecasting, better inventory management, better order management, and better delivery scheduling.

There is already a transaction-processing database that is part of the ICCL system. This database is the data source that can be tapped to populate the enterprise data warehouse. The daily transaction documents (purchase orders, invoices, advance ship notices, product masters, price books, and inventory status) that ICCL handles form the foundation from which a very clear and detailed supply chain operations picture can emerge. This picture can be updated on a daily or even hourly basis as transactions flow through ICCL.

My second project happens once the first version of the enterprise data warehouse is in place. Software packages can be interfaced to the data warehouse. I would interface two packages and make both packages accessible over the Internet. The first package is demand forecasting and the second one is delivery scheduling. This will enable people in the business to do more frequent 30- to 90-day forecasts as market conditions change from month to month. These more frequent short-term forecasts will tend to be more accurate and will provide the input needed for better inventory management. Using the delivery-scheduling package, people in the individual business units will be able to continuously monitor and optimize their delivery routes as the business grows.

My third project would improve inventory management through the combination of better product demand forecast data and also better

EXHIBIT 9.3

Charlie Supply Strengthens Performance in Customer Service and Demand Flexibility by Improving Four Business Operations

PERFORMANCE CATEGORIES BUSINESS OPERATIONS		CUSTOMER SERVICE As measured by: Fill Rate; On-Time Delivery; Product Returns	INTERNAL EFFICIENCY As measured by: Inventory Turns; Return on Sales; Cash-to-Cash	DEMAND FLEXIBILITY As measured by: Cycle Times; Upside Flex; Outside Flex	PRODUCT DEVELOPMENT As measured by: New Prod. Sales; % Revenue; Cycle Time
P L A N	Demand Forecasts	X	X	X	
	Product Pricing	X	X		
	Inventory Management	X	X	X	
S O U R C E	Procurement		X	X	
	Credit & Collections	X	X		
M A K E	Product Design	X			X
	Production Scheduling		X	X	
	Facility Mgmt.	X	X		
D E L I V E R	Order Management	X	X		X
	Delivery Scheduling	X	X		
	Return Processing	X			X

training in the use of the existing inventory management systems already in place at the business units. The best practices for effective inventory management have been widely understood since the late 1980s. Most inventory-management systems developed since the mid-1990s have incorporated the functionality needed to implement these best practices. No new systems are needed. What is needed is a renewed commitment to rigorous staff training and increased levels of proficiency in using the full functionality provided by existing inventory-management systems.

The increased training and the more accurate forecasting data will enable product managers to do a much better job of inventory management. New product demand can be better anticipated and inventory turns can also be increased. Once people have been trained, they should also have quarterly (not yearly) bonus incentives that keep them focused on delivering high levels of performance month after month.

The fourth project I would do is a project to improve how the ICCL system handles errors and status reporting. This will improve order management because problems and delays that affect customer deliveries, payments, and so on, will be spotted much sooner. This will enable customer-service representatives to be much more proactive problem solvers with their customers. They will be able to coordinate with customers and manufacturers more effectively to resolve issues as they arise.

These error handling improvements can be delivered very cost effectively by using business process management (BPM) software and interfacing it to the ICCL system and its transaction-processing database. The BPM software will provide a user-friendly Web browser-based interface and enable business people in customer service, credit, billing, and so on to define the set of rules they want to apply to each of the company's customers and manufacturers. Then the BPM system will monitor the data flowing through the ICCL system and send e-mail alerts to appropriate people when it detects exceptions to these predefined rules.

The time boxes and the scheduling of these four projects are shown in Exhibit 9.4. Notice how they are run in parallel as much as possible. Only project two depends on the prior completion of an earlier project.

EXHIBIT 9.4

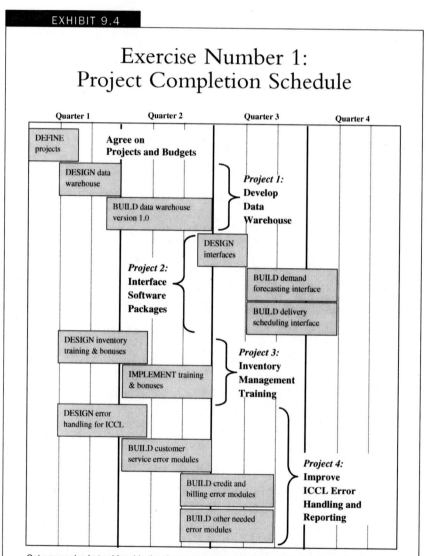

Exercise Number 1:
Project Completion Schedule

Set aggressive but achievable time boxes to accomplish the work involved in each project. Tailor the work to fit the time available. Remember that each project will produce the first version of a system or process. First versions need to have only the most immediately useful features. Get these versions into use as quickly as possible. Further features can be added in following years depending on how business needs unfold.

The other projects all run independently, so a slowdown in one does not impact completion of the others.

It is also important to notice the time boxes allocated to the design and build steps in each project. These time boxes must be strictly adhered to and that means tailoring the work in each step to the time available. Remember, each of these projects will produce just the first version of a system. Every feature does not need to be designed and built in this first version, just the most immediately useful features. Then further features can be added to these systems in following years as needed. This is agile systems development.

The projects are almost all scheduled for completion by the end of the third quarter. It is good to do most project work in the first three quarters of the year. Use the fourth quarter for finishing things up that got delayed earlier in the year and for planning the following year's projects. The fourth quarter also has the year-end holidays and for many businesses this is a very busy period. Development projects in the fourth quarter can hamper a company's ability to handle year-end business.

Integrated Supply Chain Knowledge Manager

Charlie Supply's strategy is to differentiate itself by excelling at customer service and leading in demand flexibility. Both of these capabilities are directly empowered by the data that these projects will enable the company to collect. The company's customers and its manufacturers will come to realize the value of the data Charlie Supply can provide them and this will enhance the company's image and business relationships.

These projects combine to put Charlie Supply in a position to become the organization that knows the most about the supply chains it participates in. This leverages Charlie Supply's position as the distributor (the humble middleman) and enables the company to use its position to collect more information about daily supply chain operations than either its customers or the manufacturers whose products it sells. Supply chain coordination and efficiency will become increasingly important in the markets Charlie Supply serves. And since coordination and efficiency require lots of accurate and timely data, Charlie Supply will be the company people turn to for the data they need. It is important to remember that the success of these projects depends on "having the right people on the bus," as Jim Collins puts it (*Good to Great*, New York, HarperCollins Publishers, 2001). All the visioning and planning is for naught if we can't execute. And execution is a people function, so having the right people is a must.

New Opportunities Emerge—The Follow-On Situation

The successful completion of the projects just discussed has enabled Charlie Supply to grow steadily for several quarters. It is becoming well-known to the customers and the manufacturers in the vertical markets it serves. Its ability to maintain consistently high levels of customer service is indeed making the company the "distributor of choice" as stated in the company's business goal.

Big customers realize that by doing business with Charlie Supply their total cost of use for the products they use is actually lower than would be the case if they merely bought from the supplier with the lowest prices. Charlie Supply's systems allow it to tailor a customized package of products and supply chain services that meet each customer's unique needs. Customers also benefit from getting access to usage reports showing the items purchased every day at every one of their locations. This data is very useful in monitoring and managing current operating expenses. It is also valuable in planning operating budgets for the coming year.

Manufacturers who sell to markets served by Charlie Supply are also coming to realize that Charlie Supply is a very efficient channel to market for their products. Charlie Supply's systems enable it to exchange electronic purchase orders and invoices with suppliers using any format (from ASCII to XML) and any medium (from EDI to FTP) that is most convenient to each supplier. This lowers transaction costs, reduces error rates, and speeds up cash flow. And with select manufacturers, Charlie Supply also shares daily customer usage data. This enables better demand forecasting and production scheduling.

Charlie Supply Identifies a New Growth Market

The markets served by Charlie Supply are mature markets for the most part and they have been so for some time. The products sold to these markets are mostly commodities and supply almost always meets or exceeds customer demand. Under conditions like this you might assume that there is nothing new and exciting going on. That is exactly the assumption that Charlie Supply's competitors made. They continued to focus on improving their internal operating efficiencies. While they were occupied with these activities, Charlie Supply was paying attention to some emerging sales trends and some interesting developments in its markets.

Charlie Supply has just signed up a large new customer that shares a number of similarities with another important customer—Green Planet. These customers are very interested in purchasing environmentally friendly green products. Both customers are willing to pay a higher price for green products as long as they can be shown to work effectively and meet expectations.

The director of marketing at Charlie Supply has done some research and believes the developing market of green products is just about to go into a very strong growth phase. Manufacturers' research and development efforts are starting to yield products from green cleaning chemicals to biodegradable plastics for use in making disposable cups, plates, and eating utensils. Combined with this is the growing trend for certain influential companies and state and city governments to specify the use of green products whenever possible.

Based on this market research and the company's own recent sales experience, the senior management of Charlie Supply has entered into strategic alliances with some manufacturers of green products. To demonstrate its commitment, the company has made major stock purchases of inventory from these manufacturers. The company's entire sales force is now being educated about these products and new bonus plans give big incentives to sell green products to customers.

In return for this early support, the manufacturers of these green products have guaranteed that they will always provide the company with as much product as they can sell. Even if customer demand exceeds supply, these manufacturers will make sure that Charlie Supply will receive as much of their products as it needs. What this means is that if the green market takes off the company will have a secure supply of highly sought after (and thus very profitable) products. While other distributors may not be able to get as much inventory as they need, Charlie Supply will. So customers will come to Charlie Supply when they need a guaranteed source of supply for these products.

Exercise Number 2: Participating in a Growth Market

You have just been promoted to vice president of supply chain operations for Charlie Supply. As a sign of how important this position has become you now report directly to the CEO. The CEO has asked you to prepare a supply chain strategy that you will present to the board of directors.

What will your strategy be and why? What projects will you propose to support this strategy and how will you schedule them over the next 12 months? How will you support the company's new strategic alliances with the manufacturers of green products? Which of the four market capabilities will you improve and what business operations will you use to bring about these improvements? Take some time now to think about these things and draw up your plans. When you are finished compare your plans with the solutions I offer in the following section.

Solution to Exercise Number 2

In a growth market the single most important market capability is customer service. Even though the company already excels in customer service, the company will still get the best results by further improving its customer service capabilities. The company's brand image will be shaped by its abilities in this area. This will make it even more attractive to its important customers.

There is also an opportunity for the company to pull ahead of its competitors in the area of product development. Improvements in this area can be used to support and strengthen strategic alliances with selected manufacturers. In the eyes of these manufacturers the company will be seen as a desirable supply chain partner for identifying market needs and bringing out new products. Exhibit 9.5 shows where the company will make its improvements.

EXHIBIT 9.5

Charlie Supply Continues to Build on Its Strengths for Competitive Advantage

Competitive Analysis	LAG	EQUAL	LEAD	EXCEL
Customer Service				X – →
Internal Efficiency	X			
Demand Flexibility			X	
Product Development		X – – → X		

Continue to invest in improving already strong customer service capabilities because that capability is what defines the company's value and its brand identity in the eyes of its customers. By making improvements in the product development area the company can increase its value as a strategic partner with manufacturers. These improvements will change the competitive landscape in the company's favor.

Once again, if you decided to make investments in improving the company's internal efficiency then you have made a mistake. You got some improvements in internal efficiency from the first round of projects completed earlier but at the same time your competitors continued to focus on improving their internal efficiency. You still lag them in this area. You are not going to change the competitive landscape by improvements there because you cannot be better than your competition.

Internal efficiency is important in mature and steady markets where customers are very price sensitive and companies need to lower their operating costs so they can compete for business by offering lower prices. However it is not a decisive capability in developing or growth markets. Focus instead on reinforcing the strengths the company already has in customer service because they are what you need to succeed in the growth market the company wants to enter.

Improvements in capabilities related to product development will also yield a competitive advantage for the company. As a distributor, Charlie Supply does not actually design or make new products. But it can be very much involved in identifying emerging market demands and introducing customers to new products that meet those demands. To the extent that Charlie Supply is seen by manufacturers to have superior capabilities in this area, it will strengthen the company's ability to attract and provide value to key strategic alliance partners. These decisions are shown in Exhibit 9.6.

The company identified five performance requirements that it would strive to achieve in the areas of customer service and product development. These requirements are:

1. Effectively Employ Collaborative Planning, Forecasting, and Replenishment (CPFR) Procedures with Key Customers and Manufacturers (Customer Service)—as measured by the ability to accurately forecast product demand and manage inventory to cover actual demand.

EXHIBIT 9.6

Charlie Supply Strengthens Customer Service and Improves Product Development Capabilities

PERFORMANCE CATEGORIES BUSINESS OPERATIONS		CUSTOMER SERVICE As measured by: Fill Rate; On-Time Delivery; Product Returns	INTERNAL EFFICIENCY As measured by: Inventory Turns; Return on Sales; Cash-to-Cash	DEMAND FLEXIBILITY As measured by: Cycle Times; Upside Flex; Outside Flex	PRODUCT DEVELOPMENT As measured by: New Prod. Sales; % Revenue; Cycle Time
P L A N	Demand Forecasts	(X)	X	X	
	Product Pricing	X	X		
	Inventory Management	(X)	X	X	
S O U R C E	Procurement		X	X	
	Credit & Collections	X	X		
M A K E	Product Design	X			X
	Production Scheduling		X	X	
	Facility Mgmt.	X	X		
D E L I V E R	Order Management	(X)	X		(X)
	Delivery Scheduling	(X)	X		
	Return Processing	X			(X)

2. Track Product Movement through the Supply Chain from Manufacturers to End Use Customers (Customer Service)—as measured by the ability to provide accurate end-to-end supply chain inventory visibility, which is updated on a near real-time basis.

3. Design Responsive Supply Chain Networks (Customer Service)—as measured by the ability to optimize on-going supply chain performance for high levels of product availability at the lowest operating costs.

4. Track Product Sales and Usage to More Quickly Spot Market Trends (Product Development)—as measured by the ability to plot trends based on near real-time data updates and quickly spot developments of interest.

5. Provide Efficient Pickup and Return Processing of Recyclable Products (Product Development)—as measured by the ability to optimize retrieval of recyclable material from end-use customer locations.

Twelve-Month Project Objectives

To meet these performance targets I would make improvements in five business operations. As shown in Exhibit 9.3 (see page 284), those operations are: (1) demand forecasting; (2) inventory management; (3) order management; (4) delivery scheduling; and (5) return processing. The main thrust of these improvements will be to deliver improved customer service. And to a lesser extent these improvements will also strengthen the company's capabilities in product development. This is illustrated in Exhibit 9.3.

The first project I will start is a project to train selected staff at headquarters and the business units in the techniques and process of CPFR (see Chapter 6, page 199). As people learn how to best use the systems already available to enable better supply chain collaboration they will see improvements in demand forecasting and inventory management.

The second project will be to start a pilot application using passive radio frequency identification (RFID) to better track pallet- and case-level shipments of some of the green cleaning chemicals. These products will be much in demand and thus valuable. That makes it worthwhile to track these products more accurately as they move through the supply chain. RFID tags could be used to track pallets and perhaps cases of these products. Knowing where these products are at all times will improve the company's ability to deliver them to the customer when and where they are needed.

The next project will be to extend the business process management (BPM) system to monitor sales of selected green products. As soon as sales of these products are made to a new customer or if sales increase significantly to any existing customer the BPM system will send alerts to appropriate people.

The fourth project will be to interface a network-modeling software package to the enterprise data warehouse. Once this is done it will enable Charlie Supply to collaborate with its manufacturing partners to design and test the efficiency of different network configurations for making, moving, storing, and delivering inventories of green products. This will work both for delivering products to customers and also for picking up used products that can be recycled. Exhibit 9.7 shows the project schedules.

The last project will be to implement dashboards and performance scorecards that are updated in real-time or at least on a daily basis. These dashboards and scorecards will be displayed and updated by using the BPM software that has already been installed. Different sets of performance targets will be defined for each group involved in supply chain operations and performance toward these targets will be tracked on scorecards designed for use by each of these groups.

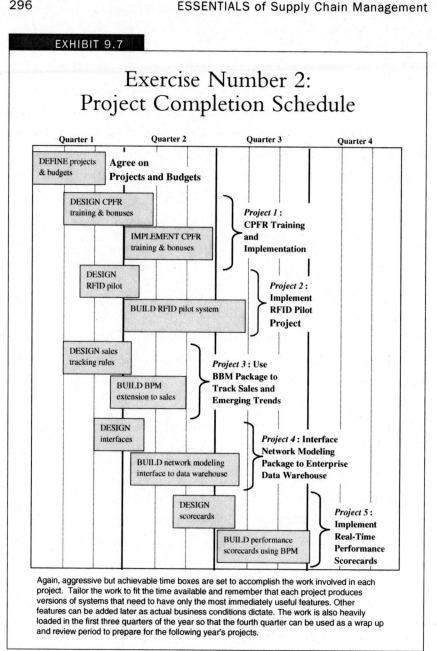

EXHIBIT 9.7

Exercise Number 2: Project Completion Schedule

Again, aggressive but achievable time boxes are set to accomplish the work involved in each project. Tailor the work to fit the time available and remember that each project produces versions of systems that need to have only the most immediately useful features. Other features can be added later as actual business conditions dictate. The work is also heavily loaded in the first three quarters of the year so that the fourth quarter can be used as a wrap up and review period to prepare for the following year's projects.

There will be scorecards to track performance for groups doing business operations such as demand forecasting, inventory management, procurement, credit and collections, delivery scheduling, and return processing. Go back to Chapter 5 and review the metrics for performance

measurement and diagnostics suggested by the supply chain operations reference (SCOR) model. See the sample dashboards shown in
Exhibit 5.2 on page 175.

The operating capabilities provided to people by the first four
projects should all be used to increase performance levels. These performance capabilities are reflected in each group's performance targets. Their
dashboards and scorecards track their actual performance. The point is
to make different business processes visible. Then devise quarterly bonus programs that encourage people to learn to improve and constantly
make the adjustments needed to maintain high levels of performance in
on-going business operations. As this happens, the whole company will
come alive (see Exhibit 9.7).

Respond Effectively to the Opportunities of Growth Markets

In a world where customer demand drives markets, not product supply,
Charlie Supply must be very good at seizing the opportunities presented
to it by a growth market. This kind of market does not come along every
day, so these opportunities cannot be squandered if the company expects
to be successful. The company must develop the skills it needs in its people
to keep up with events as the green products it sells move out of their
development stage and into a major growth market.

Avoid getting bogged down in complicated, time consuming, and
overly expensive projects. Charlie Supply must move fast and light, just
like Alexander the Great! This means creative use of simple tactics and
off-the-shelf technology that empowers and motivates people to work
together (see Chapter 1, page 7). The company's mission is to conquer
as much market share in this green growth market as possible before
product supply catches up with customer demand and market conditions change.

Because of its excellent customer-service capabilities and manufacturer
alliances, Charlie Supply can compete well against any other distributor in

this growth market. But when supply catches up with demand and market conditions shift into steady and then mature, the two main competitors of Charlie Supply will have an advantage because of their greater internal efficiency. They will be able to offer lower prices to lure customers and still earn larger profit margins than Charlie Supply. In steady and mature markets Charlie Supply has to focus on specific customers with unique needs and avoid getting into price wars with its competitors.

One last point to remember is the power of market perceptions. Charlie Supply should maximize use of public relations to strengthen its appeal to customers. The company should be seen as an innovator and leader in the use of green products in its own operations. For instance, the company can convert some of its own delivery vehicles to use biodiesel fuel. Biodiesel is a fuel made from vegetable oil that can be used in a regular diesel engine. It is clean, renewable diesel fuel from waste vegetable oil that can be sourced from restaurants and other foodservice operations (often for free). It makes good business sense and the publicity this generates will be invaluable for building the company's reputation. Customers who value green products will want to do business with Charlie Supply because the company clearly shares their values.

Strategic Alliances for Competitive Advantage

To round out our discussion of creating effective supply chains for competitive advantage, we need to discuss alliances and how to form them. Effective supply chains are first and foremost alliances between cooperating companies. Many people feel that we are entering a time when competition will not just be between individual companies but instead will be between contending supply chains. If this is so then it is clear that some of the most strategic alliances companies make are in regard to their supply chains. This includes both selecting the suppliers they work with as well as selecting the customers they sell to.

Let's start with a working definition of what a "strategic alliance" is. Companies must find ways to outsource activities that are not part of their core value proposition. In this way each company focuses more attention and investments on improving its ability to deliver value to its customers. So a truly strategic alliance is a relationship with another company that enables the first company to better fulfill its core value proposition to its customers. Strategic alliances can be formed with other companies to perform a wide range of support activities that are necessary but not directly connected to producing the core value proposition. This concept of strategic alliances is illustrated in Exhibit 9.8.

Structuring Strategic Alliances

Although the details of every alliance are unique, there is still a common set of characteristics that all strategic alliances have in common. This is true for a supply chain alliance as well as any other alliance. A relationship not exhibiting all of these characteristics is not a strategic relationship. Strategic alliances display four characteristics:

1. Delivery of a customized blend of products and services to meet a specific set of business needs

2. Coordination of inter-company operations so as to achieve predefined performance targets

3. Longer term, three- to five-year contract time frames for the alliance partners to work together

4. Prospects for mutually profitable business growth over the life of the contract

Delivery of a customized blend of products and services to meet a specific set of business needs is the foundation of any strategic alliance. A strategic alliance starts when a company has a set of needs that go beyond short-term cost reduction. This creates the opportunity for

EXHIBIT 9.8

A Company and Its Alliance Partners

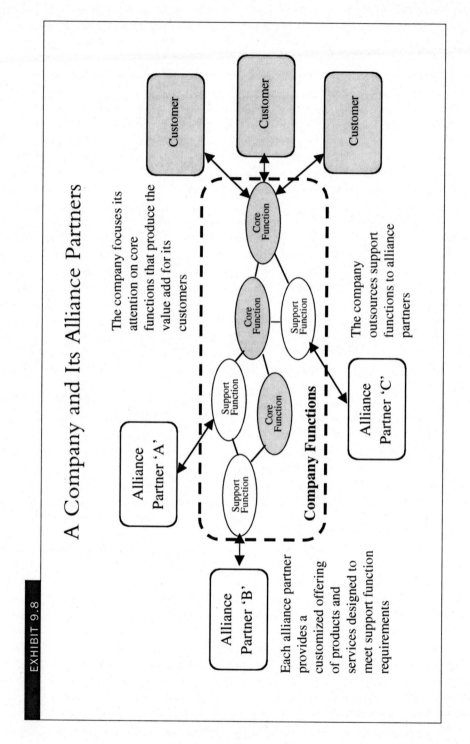

The company focuses its attention on core functions that produce the value add for its customers

The company outsources support functions to alliance partners

Each alliance partner provides a customized offering of products and services designed to meet support function requirements

300

an alliance partner to configure and deliver an offering to meet these needs. It is the customized offering that provides the greatest value to the company receiving it, and also the best profit margins for the company delivering it. If there is no need for a customized offering and simple commodity products or services will suffice, then there is no need for a strategic alliance.

Coordination of inter-company operations so as to achieve predefined performance targets indicates that both companies consider the relationship to be important and not just an arm's length business transaction. It also indicates that the performance targets are challenging and require more effort to achieve than merely negotiating a reduction in the prices that one company charges the other. Once the business requirements of the first company are clearly defined, then key performance indicators (KPIs) should be identified to measure the efficiency of the alliance partner in filling these requirements.

A longer-term, three- to five-year contract means that both companies agree to make a commitment to the alliance that will provide time for learning to work together and for improving the efficiency of the alliance. The extended time commitment allows the alliance partner to invest in staff and technology for delivering the customized offering and meeting the required performance targets. Unless there is a longer-term time frame for the relationship, there will not be much incentive for the two companies to make the effort or the investments that are part of a successful strategic alliance.

Prospects for mutually profitable business growth over the life of the contract are the reasons why two companies go to the trouble of forming an alliance. If there are prospects of profitable business growth for only one company, then whatever the relationship may be, it certainly cannot be called an alliance. In a strategic alliance one company outsources support functions in order to concentrate more on its core value proposition. An alliance partner takes on support functions and delivers a customized package of goods and services that best fits the first company's business requirements. The alliance is motivated by the prospect of growth for each partner. As the first company grows its core business, the alliance partner grows its outsourcing business.

Sustainable Growth and Productivity

If a company merely leverages its buying power to ratchet down the prices it pays to its suppliers, there comes a point where the suppliers will no longer make money in the relationship. They will then either go broke or resign the business because of lack of profits. Then the company has to find new suppliers and it may be hard to find them if the business was so unprofitable to the previous suppliers. Relationships of this sort are common enough in business, but they are not to be confused with what we are calling strategic alliances.

Strategic alliances require sustainable growth and productivity. And that calls for a process that generates rewards in the form of cost savings and/or revenue growth for both parties. In addition to generating rewards, this process must preserve and nurture the underlying source of these rewards. Effective cost management means managing a ratio of costs versus benefits so as to achieve a desired result. Costs can actually rise as long as the result is still a favorable ratio of costs and benefits.

It is this reality—that costs can rise as long as a favorable cost/benefit ratio is achieved—that is the foundation of a sustainable strategic alliance. If the alliance is beneficial it should result in your company being able to reduce operating expenses in noncore areas so as to concentrate on operations that produce your central value proposition. If your company is successful and grows, this results in increased operating costs to support the growth. These increases in operating costs are the increases in revenue and profits that your strategic partners need in order to make the alliance work for them.

The key to sustainable alliances is to define a set of performance targets that, if achieved, will clearly generate measurable benefits such as increased revenue, decreased operating costs, growth of market share, and so on. Make sure that the benefits can be measured and that a monetary value can be assigned to them. The purpose of the alliance then becomes to coordinate activities between companies so as to achieve these benefits. And the alliance is sustained because both your company and the alliance partner share in the benefits that are produced.

The alliance makes money every month from a hundred small adjustments that fine-tune operations so as to achieve performance targets. Since the business environment is constantly changing, constant small adjustments are required to deliver the best possible operating results. In effect, the agreement between two companies to cooperate is the capital in the strategic alliance. The continuous steam of cost savings and revenue enhancements that come from this cooperation is the interest earned on this capital. And to continue the analogy, we can say that the better companies become at cooperating with each other, the higher the rate of interest they earn on their alliances.

In the rush to get as much profit from a situation as quickly as possible, it is common for companies to fall into a pattern of behavior that in effect kills the golden goose. A strategic alliance cannot be a relationship where the only real objective is expense reduction. All strategic alliances provide a mix of benefits. Make sure the mix of benefits is clearly defined and their value is understood. Then make sure the benefits are accurately tracked and the rewards shared between both parties.

Chapter Summary

Charlie Supply maximizes its supply chain opportunities by building on its strengths to differentiate itself from its competitors. Charlie Supply is a distributor that has developed a suite of supply chain services it uses to customize its total offering to meet specific customer needs. By taking this approach, the company has chosen to focus its efforts on doing business with customers who need and will pay the price to get the supply chain services that Charlie Supply has to offer.

This means Charlie Supply will not go after a broad base of customers on the basis of offering the lowest prices on products. It cannot hope to compete this way because its competitors have more efficient internal operations. They will be able to make more money in a purely price–based competition. Charlie Supply chooses instead to focus its resources on developing its capabilities where it is already strong and where it can use these strengths to the best advantage.

Charlie Supply invests in improving its customer service and other capabilities that help it win business from the kind of customers it desires to do business with. Its strategy is to excel in areas valued by its target customers. In order to concentrate the resources to excel in these areas, the company accepts that it will lag its competitors in other areas such as internal efficiency. Its internal efficiency is good enough, as long as the company does not try to compete solely on the basis of product prices.

When Charlie Supply encounters the opportunity to distribute new environmentally friendly green products to a growth market, it moves quickly to capture market share. It makes early alliances with selected manufacturers, takes large inventory positions in green products, and trains and motivates its sales force to find customers for these products.

Charlie Supply maximizes use of its existing IT infrastructure. When systems are stable and work well enough, they are left in place. Performance improvements are gotten through training staff to use these systems more effectively and through selected enhancements to these systems.

New systems development is concentrated in the area of building an enterprise data warehouse and then interfacing several packaged software applications to it. These applications will help the company improve in the areas of demand forecasting, delivery scheduling and routing, and inventory management. Improvements in these capabilities can be used for significant business advantage.

All new development projects are accomplished using the three-step approach called Define-Design-Build. The time frames for each step are strictly adhered to and work is tailored to fit the time available. Development work is concentrated in the first nine months of the year. The last three months of the year are then available for finishing up delayed projects and for planning development projects in the coming year.

Charlie Supply looks for opportunities to enter into strategic alliances with its customers and suppliers. Strategic alliances display these four characteristics:

1. **Need for delivery of a customized blend of products and services to meet a specific set of business needs**

2. **Need for coordination of inter-company operations so as to achieve predefined performance targets**

3. **Longer-term, three- to five-year contract time frames for the alliance partners to work together**

4. **Prospects for mutually profitable business growth over the life of the contract**

CHAPTER 10

The Promise of the Real-Time Supply Chain

After reading this chapter you will be able to

- Appreciate the "always-on" connection and what it means
- Assess the profit potential inherent in the self-adjusting feedback loop and explore how it can be harnessed to drive your supply chain
- Discuss the concept of emergent systems

The pace of business change and innovation is both exciting and relentless. Over the next decade, innovative companies in different market segments will learn to design and deploy their supply chains to improve their competitive positions in the markets they serve. They will create supply chains that enable them to develop and deliver products and provide levels of service at price points that their competitors cannot match.

We all sense that something profound has happened in the last 10 years or so. The Internet is a part of it, but it is not only about the Internet. We learned that in the "dot com" bubble of the late 1990s and early 2000s. It is more about what we can do by using the Internet than it is about any particular technology.

The Start of Something Big

As a historical analogy, consider what happened some 200 years ago at the beginning of an age that came to be known as the Industrial Age. The people of the time sensed that a powerful potential had been released by the invention and spread of the steam engine.

The steam engine for the first time provided a movable source of power that could be generated on demand and efficiently harnessed to perform a wide variety of tasks. The Industrial Age was not so much about the steam engine as it was about the things that could be done and were done with the power that the steam engine made available. Once it was born, the Industrial Age went on to outgrow the steam engine as it evolved more advanced engine technologies such as internal combustion, the jet, the electric motor, and atomic power.

The rise and spread of the Internet has created for the first time a global, multi-directional communications network that is "always-on." The cost of connecting to this network is so cheap that there is no need for companies to save money by staying off-line and only connecting periodically. The normal state for companies is transitioning from being off-line and unconnected to one of being on-line and connected.

As more and more companies use the Internet and other communications networks to create always-on connections with each other, they will find ways to share data that enable them to better coordinate their interactions. They will also learn faster and adapt to changing conditions faster. These capabilities will clearly result in efficiencies that can be turned into business profits.

The always-on connection is a new light that sheds steady illumination on a landscape that had before been seen only in periodic snapshots. We are experiencing something similar to seeing a sequence of still photos turn into a moving picture. As more pictures are taken at shorter intervals, you cease to see a sequence of still photos and instead come to see a continuous, moving image. This continuous, moving image is what we see as we move from the snapshot or batch-time world into the real-time world.

Supply chain management is a process of coordination between companies. Those companies that learn to coordinate in real time will become incrementally more and more efficient. They will become more profitable and quicker to see new opportunities than their competitors who are still working in a batch-time world of snapshot pictures.

The Profit Potential of the Self-Adjusting Feedback Loop

The self-adjusting feedback loop is a very useful phenomena. An example is the cruise control in an automobile. The cruise control constantly reads the vehicle's actual speed and compares that to the speed it was set for. It responds to bring the actual speed in line with the desired speed. It causes the engine to either accelerate or decelerate. The cruise control's goal is to achieve and maintain the desired speed. As the vehicle travels down the highway it continuously monitors speed and operates the engine to achieve its goal.

Other examples of a self-adjusting feedback loop at work are a thermostat that controls the temperature in a room, or a guided missile that zeros in on a heat source or a radar-emission source. Self-adjusting feedback loops use negative feedback to continuously correct their behavior. Negative feedback occurs when a system compares its current state with its desired state (or goal) and takes corrective action to move it in a direction that will minimize the difference between the two states. A continuous stream of negative feedback guides a system through a changing environment toward its goal.

Companies can learn to work together to achieve supply chain performance targets that are profitable to all of them. They can learn to constantly adjust their behavior day after day, hour by hour to respond to events and continue to steer toward their performance targets. The bullwhip effect can be controlled by the introduction of negative feedback to dampen down the wild demand swings that otherwise result.

The opportunity now exists to leverage the power of the self-adjusting feedback loop across entire supply chains. Real-time data sharing and close coordination between companies can be employed to deliver operating efficiencies that result in significant profits over time. The result of these continuous incremental adjustments to supply chain operations is analogous to the growth of capital over time due to the miracle of compound interest.

Harnessing the Feedback Loop to the Supply Chain

How can the power of the self-adjusting feedback loop be brought to bear in a supply chain? The answer is beginning to appear. As companies link up using always-on communication networks to conduct business with each other, they begin to automatically collect useful data as a by-product of their interactions: electronic purchase orders, order status, order receipts, invoices, and payment status. It is no longer a huge administrative chore to regularly track performance in the areas of customer service, internal efficiency, demand flexibility, and product development.

Customers are starting to use supply chain "report cards" to grade the performance of their suppliers. The report cards are more accurate and more frequently produced than was previously possible. The next step is for companies to move beyond the use of these report cards as merely convenient tools for beating up their suppliers. The opportunity exists for customers and suppliers to use this data to work together to meet mutually beneficial performance targets. Companies can select performance targets that will generate quantifiable benefits and profits to reward them for the effort needed to achieve the targets.

Either one dominant company can set the performance targets or groups of companies can negotiate among themselves to set targets. The important thing is that all participating companies in a supply chain believe the targets are achievable and that when they are achieved there will be rewards as a result. The desire to receive these rewards is what brings the self-adjusting feedback loop into being.

The feedback loop happens when peoples' interactions with each other are cast in the form of a game whose object is to achieve the performance targets. If companies and people in a supply chain have real-time access to the data they need then they will steer toward their targets. If they are rewarded when they achieve their targets then they will learn to hit these targets more often than not. The profit potential of negative feedback and the self-adjusting supply chain is now unleashed.

Playing the Game of Supply Chain Management

Human beings are social creatures who love to play games. This is a good thing because through playing games we constantly learn and improve our skills and our performance. Companies such as Wal-Mart and Dell and their supply chain partners have in many ways begun to create an evolving game out of managing their supply chains. They have steadily learned and developed supply chains that are better than those of their competitors and that are clearly business advantages for them.

There are only a few things required to start a game. In his book, *The Great Game of Business*, Jack Stack lays out four conditions that are needed (Stack, Jack, 1992, *The Great Game of Business*, New York, NY: Currency/Doubleday). They are:

1. People must understand the rules of the game and how it is played. They must know what is fair and what is not fair and how to score points.

2. People must be able to pick the roles or positions they want to play in the game. They also need to get the training and

experience necessary to keep developing the skills they need to succeed in their positions.

3. All players must know what the score is at all times. They need to know if they are winning or losing and they need to see the results of their actions.

4. All players must have a personal stake in the outcome of the game. There must be some important reward, either monetary or psychological, that provides a reason for each player to strive to succeed.

Basically, the game of supply chain management is a relatively simple game, as is soccer or basketball. Which is not to say that any of these games can be mastered without years of practice and play. The main techniques and operations of supply chain management are well enough understood to be taught to a wide range of people in different supply chain positions (see Chapters 2 and 3). The Internet is the way for everyone to know the score at all times and see the results of their actions. Profits generated by operating efficiencies provide people with rewards and the reason to strive to succeed.

In supply chain management, everyone can acquire and install technology, so technology alone cannot constitute a significant competitive advantage. The advantage lies in the way the game is played. Let's go back to the example of Alexander the Great (see Chapter 1). His army did not have any technology that was not also possessed by his opponents. In fact Alexander deliberately used less technology. He simplified his army's operations and equipment in order to make it more mobile and more efficient. His army could travel faster and lighter than those of his adversaries.

Advantage goes to those players who learn to use simple technology and simple tactics extremely well. Alexander's soldiers were well trained in how to use their technology and because of the simplicity of their tactics, they could remember and use them effectively in the heat of the moment when it really counted. After all is said and done, success is often just a matter of consistent performance and making fewer errors than your competition.

An example of the kind of system that makes the supply chain game into a reality in the operation of global and regional supply chains is the SCM Globe system described in Chapter 7. This system can be put to several uses. In can train people in supply chain operations; it can be used to design new supply chains and improve existing ones; and it can be used as a collaboration platform between companies to monitor and manage the workings of actual supply chains.

Strengthening Supply Chain Alliances

Strengthen supply chain alliances by making sure three conditions are present. These conditions are interdependent and all three must exist in order for any of them to truly be effective. They are: (1) all parties in the supply chain have easy access to relevant information and performance measures updated on a real-time or near real-time basis so they know what the score is; (2) people know how their actions influence the score and they have the skills and opportunity to act effectively; and (3) people have a stake in the outcome so that they will act to achieve the performance targets and continuously learn to improve. This is illustrated in Exhibit 10.1.

Supply chain alliances depend on close coordination between companies, and effective coordination can only happen when all parties have easy access to the information they need to do their jobs. These alliances are much like a game whose goal is to achieve the predefined performance targets. In order to play this game people need to know what the score is at all times. They need to know if they are moving toward the goal or away from it. They need current information that reflects events as they happen, not batch reports delivered 30 days after the end of the last quarter. This allows them to make good, timely decisions and coordinate effectively.

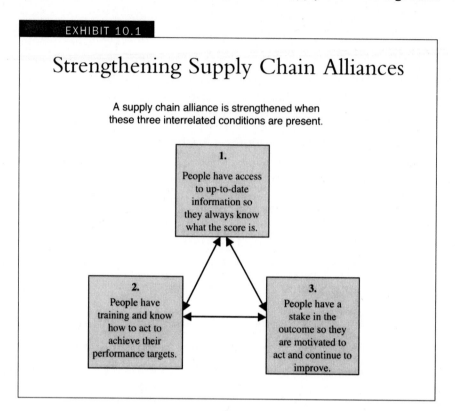

EXHIBIT 10.1

Strengthening Supply Chain Alliances

A supply chain alliance is strengthened when
these three interrelated conditions are present.

1.
People have access to up-to-date information so they always know what the score is.

2.
People have training and know how to act to achieve their performance targets.

3.
People have a stake in the outcome so they are motivated to act and continue to improve.

Once people are able to see the score and track events as they happen, they need to understand how their actions influence the score. If operating results are trending away from performance targets, people need to know what to do to bring operations back on track. If results are on target people need to know how best to sustain them. That means people get the training they need to do their jobs well. It also means that people have the opportunity and authority to act as they see fit when the need arises. If no action can happen until requests and permissions are passed up and down a chain of command, then responses will be too slow and people will become frustrated with the poor results.

When people can see the score at all times and when they know how to act in order to achieve predefined performance targets, there is one more condition that must be present in order for a strong alliance to emerge. That condition is that people have a stake in the outcome.

Often this is in the form of a monetary reward when performance targets are achieved. Without a stake in the outcome, people become bored or indifferent and they will not make the effort to constantly improve and adjust operations to respond as the world changes. And without this constant effort, challenging performance targets cannot be achieved month after month, year after year.

EXECUTIVE INSIGHT

Emergent behavior is what happens when an interconnected system of relatively simple elements begins to self-organize to form a more intelligent and more adaptive higher-level system. Steven Johnson in his book, *Emergence: The Connected Lives of Ants, Brains, Cities, and Software*, explores the conditions that bring about this phenomenon.

In an interview with Steven Johnson I posed six questions and asked him to share his insights on a range of topics. These topics range from what gives a system emergent characteristics to how could companies organize their supply chains so as to encourage and benefit from emergent behavior.

1 What is an "emergent system"? How is an emergent system different from an assembly line?

The catchphrase that I sometimes use is that an emergent system is "smarter" than the sum of its parts. They tend to be systems made up of many interacting agents, each of which is following relatively simple rules governing its encounters with other agents. Somehow, out of all these local interactions, a higher-level, global intelligence "emerges." The extraordinary thing about these systems is that there's no master planner or executive branch—the overall group creates the intelligence and adaptability; it's not something passed down from the leadership. An ant colony is a great example of this:

(Continued)

colonies manage to pull off extraordinary feats of resource management and engineering and task allocation, all by following remarkably simple rules of interaction, using a simple chemical language to communicate. There's a queen ant in the colony, but she's only called that because she's the chief reproductive engine for the colony—she doesn't have any actually command authority. The ordinary ants just do the thinking collectively, without a leader.

A key difference between an emergent system and an assembly line lies in the fluidity of the emergent system: randomness is a key component of the way an ant colony will explore a given environment—take the random element out, and the colony gets much less interesting, much less capable of stumbling across new ideas. Assembly lines are all about setting fixed patterns, and eliminating randomness; emergence is all about stumbling across new patterns that work better than the old ones.

❷ You say that such systems are "bottom up systems, not top-down." These systems solve problems by drawing on masses of simple elements instead of relying on a single, intelligent "executive branch." What does this mean for people who are trying to design and build emergent systems?

One of the central lessons, I think, is that emergent systems are always slightly out of control. Their unpredictability is part of their charm, and their power, but it can be threatening to engineers and planners who have been trained to eliminate unpredictability at every turn. Some of the systems that I've looked at combine emergent properties and evolutionary ones: the emergent system generates lots of new configurations and ideas, and then there's a kind of natural selection that weeds out the bad ideas and encourages the good ones. That's largely what a designer of emergent systems should think about doing: it's closer to growing a garden than it is building a factory.

3 What does it mean when you say that emergent systems display complex adaptive behavior?

The complexity refers to the number of interacting parts, like the thousands of ants in a colony, or the pedestrians on a street in a busy city. Adaptive behavior is what happens when all those component parts create useful higher-level structures or patterns of behavior with their group interactions, when they create something—usually unwittingly—that benefits the members of the group. When an ant colony determines the shortest route to a new source of food and quickly assembles a line of ants to transport the food back to the nest; when thousands of urbanites create a neighborhood with a distinct personality that helps organize and give shape to an otherwise overwhelming city—these are examples of adaptive behavior.

4 What is negative feedback as opposed to positive feedback? What role does negative feedback play in the ability of a system to exhibit adaptive behavior?

Negative feedback is crucial, and it's not at all negative in a value-judgment sense. Positive feedback is what we generally mean when we talk about feedback, as in the guitar effect that we first started to hear as music in the 60s: music is played through a speaker, which is picked up by a microphone, which then broadcasts it out though the speaker, creating a sound that the microphone picks up, and so on until you get a howling noise that sounds nothing like the original music. So positive feedback is a kind of self-perpetuating, additive effect: plug output A into input B which is plugged into input A. Negative feedback is what you use when you need to dampen down a chain like this, when there's a danger of a kind of runaway effect, or when you're trying to home in on a specific target. Think of a thermostat trying to reach a preset temperature: it samples the air, and if the air's too cold, it turns the heat on, then samples it again. Without negative feedback, the room would just keep getting hotter, but the thermostat has been

(Continued)

designed to turn the heat off when the air reaches the target temperature. Ants use a comparable technique to achieve the right balance of task allocation throughout the colony: an individual ant who happens to be on foraging duty will sample the number of ants also on foraging duty that she stumbles across over the course of an hour—if she encounters a certain number, she'll switch over to another task (nest building, say) in order to keep the colony from becoming overrun with foragers.

5 In your book you mention a designer who has proposed building a learning network of traffic lights that will find an optimal solution to continually changing traffic conditions. You observe that, "You can conquer gridlock by making the grid itself smart." What is it that would make the grid smart? Is this grid an example of an emergent system?

The idea proposed in the traffic model is not to take the traditional engineering, top-down approach and say: "let's look at the entire city and figure out where all the problems are, and try to design the roads and the light system to eliminate the problems." The smart grid approach is to give each light a local perspective with a little bit of information, and give it the goal of minimizing delays at its own little corner. So the light would be able to register the number of cars stacked up at the intersection, and it would be able to experiment with different rhythms of red and green, with some feedback from its near neighbors. When it stumbles across a pattern that reduces delays, it sticks to that pattern; if the delays start piling up again, it starts experimenting again. The problem with this sort of approach is that on Day One it's a terrible, terrible system, because it doesn't yet know anything about traffic flows. (You'd have to teach it quite a bit before you could actually implement it.) But it would learn very quickly, and most importantly, it would be capable of responding to changing conditions, in a way that the traditionally engineered approach would not. That's a hallmark of adaptability.

6 Consider a system composed of many different companies whose goal is to provide a market with the highest levels of responsiveness at the lowest cost to themselves. High levels of responsiveness require that these companies work together to design, make, and deliver the right products at the right price at the right time in the right amounts. What are some of the things that these companies could do to organize themselves into an emergent system?

There's a telltale term in supple chain systems, which may well be unavoidable—the term "chain" itself. Almost all emergent systems are networks or grids; they tend to be flatter and more horizontal, with interaction possible between all the various agents. The problem that supply chains have with positive feedback revolves around the distance between the consumer and those suppliers further down the chain—because the information has to pass through so many intermediaries, you get distortion in the message. Most emergent systems that I've looked at have a great diversity of potential routes that information can follow; the more chain-like they become, they less adaptive they are. The other key here is experimentation: letting the system evolve new patterns of interaction on its own, since these can often be more useful and efficient than the pre-planned ones. Of course, you don't want to waste a few economic quarters experimenting with different supply chains, most of which are a disaster. But that's where some of the wonderful new modeling systems for complex behavior can be very handy: you can do the experimenting on the computer, and then pick the best solutions to implement in real life.

Emergent Behavior in Supply Chains

In the workings of a system such as a free market, we witness emergent behavior. This behavior is what the great British economist Adam Smith referred to as the "invisible hand" of the market. This invisible hand emerges to set product prices so as to best allocate available supplies to meet market demands. Local interactions between large numbers of agents, governed by simple rules of mutual feedback, produce a macro effect for the system as a whole that results in what we call emergent behavior.

As we begin to practice supply chain management as a game between companies and people who are motivated to achieve certain performance targets, we will see emergent behavior in supply chains. Good players in the supply chains of particular markets will seek each other out, because by playing together they can create more efficient supply chains and generate better profits.

Supply chains will form like sports teams and these teams will compete with each other for market share. Just as the game of basketball or soccer evolves over time, so too will the game of supply chain management. New tactics, techniques, and technology will come about. Market demands and the desire for competitive advantage will drive companies to collaborate and innovate with each other to win at the game of supply chain management.

Computers are best used to automate the rote, repetitious activities that humans find to be dull and boring. These are all the ongoing and routine activities of recording and monitoring supply chain operations. Computers do these tasks very well. They do not fall asleep, they do not miss details, and they can handle enormous volumes of data without complaint.

People are best used to do the creative and problem-solving activities. These are the activities that do not have clear right or wrong answers. These are the activities that call for people to collaborate with other people and share information and try out different approaches to see which ones work best. People are good at these activities and they like doing them so they learn and keep getting better.

At a macro level, this will give rise to supply chains that, in effect, learn and grow smarter. Computers will listen to the hum and crackle of data flowing through the real-time, always-on supply chain. They will employ pattern recognition algorithms to spot exceptions and events that need to be brought to the attention of human beings. Like good pilots and navigators, people will learn to respond effectively to these developments as they happen. People will learn to keep steering the supply chain on a course toward its desired performance targets.

Adaptive Networks and Economic Cycles

As we learn to recognize and effectively respond to developments in our supply chains, it will tend to lengthen the periods of market growth and stability. Any industry or market where there is a boom-to-bust cycle is an opportunity for us to apply the self-adjusting feedback loop to smooth out the economic ups and downs. The boom-to-bust cycle is caused by the same dynamic that results in the Bullwhip effect in individual supply chains (see Chapter 6).

In industries ranging from manufacturing to real estate development and telecommunications, the boom-to-bust cycle causes economic waste and disruption. It also brings with it all the related human hardships that are caused by the cycle. Examples of this cycle are the "Dot Com" bubble of 1997 to 2001 and the Real-Estate bubble of 2003 to 2008. The ability to recognize and smooth out excessive swings in demand, prices, and productive capacity in different areas of the economy will create greater stability and more sustainable prosperity. Through this stability more wealth will be both generated and preserved. Think of the wealth that was destroyed by the excessive investments that created more dot com companies and more real-estate developments than were really needed. Think of the wealth that disappeared in company closures and job losses that happened when these companies and their suppliers finally had to face the consequences of too much supply and not enough demand.

Adaptive supply chain networks using real-time information and feedback loops can effectively dampen excessive market swings. This ability alone will have a wealth creation effect that is even more powerful than what was created by the effect of the steam engine and the industrial revolution.

Chapter Summary

The "always-on" connection of the Internet and other communication networks allows us to see ourselves in real-time. We can now see the supply chain as a continuous moving picture, whereas in the past we could only see it as a collection of snapshots taken at periodic intervals. This always-on, moving picture makes it possible to constantly adjust supply chain operations week to week and day to day to get significant new efficiencies.

This self-adjusting feedback loop is harnessed to the supply chain through the daily actions of the people who carry out supply chain operations. First motivate people by providing them with monetary or psychological rewards for achieving predefined performance targets. Then provide people with real-time information that shows them whether they are moving toward or away from their targets. People will steer toward their targets and they will learn to hit these targets more often than not.

The effect of this dynamic will be to give rise to supply chains that are both highly responsive and very efficient. Real-time operating adjustments will result in supply chains that can better adapt to business changes and deliver performance and profitability that is of a higher level than anything that has been seen before.

About the Author

Michael H. Hugos is an author, speaker and principle at Center for Systems Innovation. He works with clients to find elegant solutions to complex problems with focus in supply chains, business intelligence and new business ventures. Earlier, he spend six years as chief information officer (CIO) of a national distribution organization in North America where he developed a suite of supply chain and e-business systems that transformed the company's operations and revenue model. For this work he won the CIO 100 Award for resourcefulness, the InformationWeek 500 Award for innovation, and the Computerworld Premier 100 Award for career achievement.

Hugos earned his undergraduate degree in urban planning and design from the University of Cincinnati and his MBA from Northwestern University's Kellogg School of Management. He has spoken at conferences and taught seminars in Asia, Africa, Europe and North America. Hugos is also author of several other books including *Business Agility: Sustainable Prosperity in a Relentlessly Competitive World* and *Business in the Cloud: What Every Business Needs to Know about Cloud Computing*.

He can be reached via his website at www.MichaelHugos.com.

Index

utilization, 47
   rates, 78, 80

V

value–added networks, 112
VAN. *See* value–added networks
vendor selection, 64–65
vertical integration, 21, 23
virtual integration, 21, 23

W

W.W. Grainger, 31
Wal–Mart, 12, 18–20, 45
Wallace, Tom, 207–208
Walton, Sam, 18–20
WAN. *See* wide area network

warehouse management systems, 119
warehouse operations, simulation
   and, 141
web–based e–commerce, 257
Whang, Seungjin, 143
wide area network, 111
work–flow, 193
   coordination, 144
World of Warcraft, 218

X

XML. *See* extensible markup language

Y

Yanasik, Tolga, 136–143
YCH Group, 233–237

CPSIA information can be obtained
at www.ICGtesting.com
Printed in the USA
BVOW02n1149101116

467400BV00005B/17/P